LITERATURE WORKS

A Collection of Readings

COLLECTION 4

Silver Burdett Ginn
A Division of Simon & Schuster
160 Gould Street
Needham Heights, MA 02194

Developed and produced in association with Ligature

ISBN: 0-663-59039-6   1 2 3 4 5 6 7 8 9 10 VHP 01 00 99 98 97 96 95

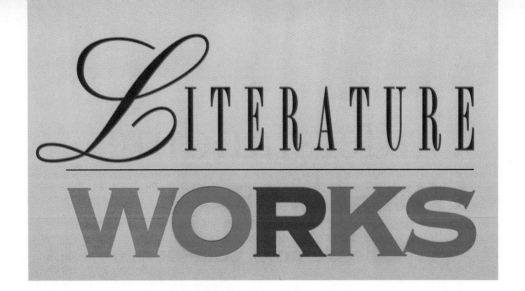

Literature Works

A Collection of Readings

COLLECTION 4

THEMES

Understanding Ourselves

Sharing the Earth

The Stories We Tell

Creative Solutions

Transformations

Discovering Hidden Worlds

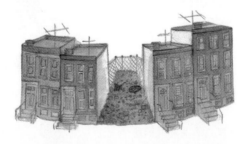

SILVER BURDETT GINN

Needham, MA   Parsippany, NJ
Atlanta, GA   Deerfield, IL   Irving, TX   Santa Clara, CA

Understanding Ourselves

Gaining Confidence

In the Spotlight

Sharing the Earth

Appreciating the Earth

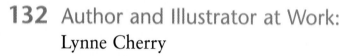

Helping the Earth

The Stories We Tell

The Gift of Storytelling

Good Stories to Tell

Creative Solutions

Real or Imagined?

Imagination at Work!

Transformations

Imaginary Changes

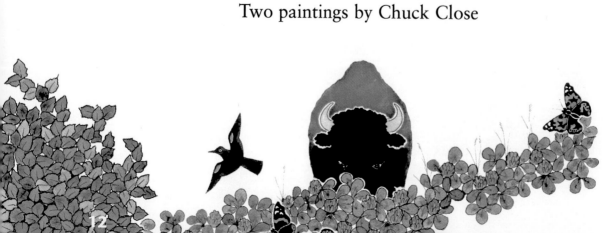

Personal Changes

Discovering Hidden Worlds

Looking Beneath the Surface

Techniques of Discovery

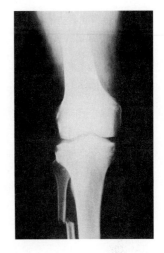

Understanding Ourselves

"What I care to be
Is me"

— Eloise Greenfield
"By Myself"

CONTENTS

Theme Trade Books

Mieko and the Fifth Treasure

by Eleanor Coerr
Five treasures are needed to
paint Japanese word pictures.
Mieko had all five until she lost
the fifth treasure—beauty in the
heart. What must Mieko do to regain
the fifth treasure?

Coming Home

by Floyd Cooper
From his lonely childhood in Lawrence,
Kansas, to his famous life in the Harlem
district of New York City, Langston
Hughes dreams of having a real home.

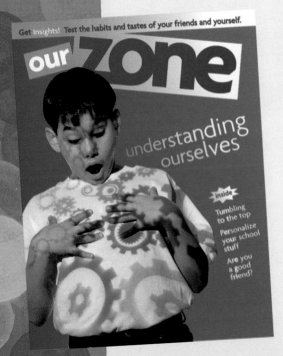

Theme Magazine

How would you rate yourself as
a friend? Does growing up with
brothers and sisters affect who you
are? Explore the possibilities in the
Theme Magazine *Our Zone*.

One hundred years ago in Paris, when theaters and music halls drew traveling players from all over the world, the best place to stay was at the widow Gâteau's, a boardinghouse on English Street.

Acrobats, jugglers, actors, and mimes from as far away as Moscow and New York reclined on the widow's feather mattresses and devoured her kidney stews.

Madame Gâteau[1] worked hard to make her guests comfortable, and so did her daughter, Mirette.[2] The girl was an expert at washing linens, chopping leeks, paring potatoes, and mopping floors. She was a good listener too. Nothing pleased her more than to overhear the vagabond players tell of their adventures in this town and that along the road.

One evening a tall, sad-faced stranger arrived. He told Madame Gâteau he was Bellini, a retired high-wire walker.

"I am here for a rest," he said.

"I have just the room for you, Monsieur Bellini:[3] in the back, where it's quiet," she said. "But it's on the ground floor, with no view."

"Perfect," said the stranger. "I will take my meals alone."

---

1 **Madame Gâteau** (*mah DAHM gah TOH*)
2 **Mirette** (*mee REHT*)
3 **Monsieur Bellini** (*mih SYUR behl LEE nee*)

The next afternoon, when Mirette came for the
sheets, there was the stranger, crossing the courtyard on
air! Mirette was enchanted. Of all the things a person
could do, this must be the most magical. Her feet
tingled, as if they wanted to jump up on the wire
beside Bellini.

Mirette worked up the courage to speak. "Excuse
me, Monsieur Bellini, *I* want to learn to do that!"
she cried.

Bellini sighed. "That would not be a good idea," he
said. "Once you start, your feet are never happy again
on the ground."

"Oh, please teach me!" Mirette begged. "My feet
are already unhappy on the ground." But he shook
his head.

Mirette watched him every day. He would slide his
feet onto the wire, cast his eyes ahead, and cross
without ever looking down, as if in a trance.

Finally she couldn't resist any longer. When Bellini was gone, she jumped up on the wire to try it herself. Her arms flailed like windmills. In a moment she was back on the ground. Bellini made it look so easy. Surely she could do it too if she kept trying.

In ten tries she balanced on one foot for a few seconds. In a day, she managed three steps without wavering. Finally, after a week of many, many falls, she walked the length of the wire. She couldn't wait to show Bellini.

He was silent for a long time. Then he said, "In the beginning everyone falls. Most give up. But you kept trying. Perhaps you have talent as well."

"Oh, thank you," said Mirette.

She got up two hours earlier every day to finish her chores before the sun shone in the courtyard. The rest of the day was for lessons and practice.

Bellini was a strict master. "Never let your eyes stray," he told her day after day. "Think only of the wire, and of crossing to the end."

When she could cross dozens of times without falling, he taught her the wire-walker's salute. Then she learned to run, to lie down, and to turn a somersault.

"I will never ever fall again!" Mirette shouted.

"Do not boast," Bellini said, so sharply that Mirette lost her balance and had to jump down.

One night an agent from Astley's Hippodrome[4] in London rented a room. He noticed Bellini on his way to dinner.

"What a shock to see him here!" he exclaimed.

"See who?" asked a mime.

"Why, the great Bellini! Didn't you know he was in the room at the back?"

---

4 **hippodrome** (*HIHP uh drohm*) an arena or building for horse races, circuses, sporting events

"Bellini . . . the one who crossed Niagara Falls on a thousand-foot wire in ten minutes?" asked the mime.

"And on the way back stopped in the middle to cook an omelette on a stove full of live coals. Then he opened a bottle of champagne and toasted the crowd," the agent recalled.

"My uncle used to talk about that," said a juggler.

"Bellini crossed the Alps with baskets tied to his feet, fired a cannon over the bullring in Barcelona, walked a flaming wire wearing a blindfold in Naples— the man had the nerves of an iceberg," the agent said.

Mirette raced to Bellini's room.

"Is it true?" she cried. "You did all those things? Why didn't you tell me? I want to do them too! I want to go with you!"

"I can't take you," said Bellini.

"But why not?" asked Mirette.

Bellini hesitated a long time. "Because I am afraid," he said at last.

Mirette was astonished. "*Afraid?*" she said. "But *why?*"

"Once you have fear on the wire, it never leaves," Bellini said.

"But you must *make* it leave!" Mirette insisted.

"I cannot," said Bellini.

Mirette turned and ran to the kitchen as tears sprang to her eyes. She had felt such joy on the wire.

Now Bellini's fear was like a cloud casting its black shadow on all she had learned from him.

Bellini paced his room for hours. It was terrible to disappoint Mirette! By dawn he knew that if he didn't face his fear at last, he could not face Mirette. He knew what he must do. The question was, could he succeed?

That night, when the agent returned, Bellini was waiting for him. The agent listened to Bellini's plan with mounting excitement. "I'll take care of it," he promised. To himself he added, "A big crowd will make me a tidy profit. What luck I just happened to be in Paris now."

Bellini went out to find a length of hemp with a steel core. He borrowed a winch and worked until daylight securing the wire.

The next evening, Mirette heard the commotion in the street.

"Go and see what it is," her mother said. "Maybe it will cheer you up."

In the square was a hubbub. The crowd was so thick she couldn't see, at first, that the agent was aiming a spotlight at the sky.

". . . return of the great Bellini!" he was yelling. Could it be? Mirette's heart hammered in her chest.

Bellini stepped out onto the wire and saluted the crowd. He took a step and then froze. The crowd cheered wildly. But something was wrong. Mirette knew at once what it was. For a moment she was as frozen as Bellini was.

Then she threw herself at the door behind her, ran inside, up flight after flight of stairs, and out through a skylight to the roof.

She stretched her hands to Bellini. He smiled and began to walk toward her. She stepped onto the wire, and with the most intense pleasure, as she had always imagined it might be, she started to cross the sky.

"Bravo! Bravo!" roared the crowd.

"Protégée⁵ of the Great Bellini!" shouted the agent. He was beside himself, already planning the world tour of Bellini and Mirette.

As for the master and his pupil, they were thinking only of the wire, and of crossing to the end.

---

5 protégée (*proh tay ZHAY*) a girl or woman, who is instructed and guided, especially in her career, by another person

Extra! Extra!

Think about what happened in the story that led up to Mirette joining the Great Bellini on the high wire. Pretend you are a newspaper reporter who watched them cross the sky that night. Write a headline for a newspaper article describing the event. Follow the headline with a paragraph explaining how Mirette came to be Bellini's protégée.

Announcing . . . the Great Bellini!

Imagine that you are the Great Bellini's agent. Prepare an introduction for Bellini at his next performance. Be sure to mention the amazing tricks from Bellini's past. Then recite your introduction to the class.

A Meaningful Meeting

Both Mirette and Bellini grew from the friendship they shared. With a partner, make a chart showing how they changed from the beginning to the end of the story. Label the columns *Before Meeting* and *After Meeting,* and then fill the chart with your observations. Discuss with a partner what each character learned from the other.

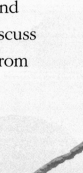

Emily Arnold McCully's illustrations have appeared in more than one hundred books, and many of them have won notable awards.

Although today Ms. McCully divides her time between writing and illustrating, her first love has always been illustration. She began drawing when she was three years old, showing a true gift for art at a very young age. As a child, she wrote her own stories and illustrated them in great detail. Her talents grew in high school, encouraged by praise from an art teacher. Since that time, Ms. McCully has tried many different forms of art, including making collages and poster advertisements, but she has never lost her enthusiasm for book illustration.

Ms. McCully feels a story must be interesting in order to illustrate it. "My first book had to wait until I had a story demanding to be told," she explained. The author-illustrator encourages young writers and artists to follow their instincts and to create from the heart. "Don't worry about what other people are doing," she says. "Work from what is inside you, crying out for expression."

★ **Award-winning Author and Illustrator**

Other Books by . . .

Emily Arnold McCully

The Amazing Felix, written and illustrated by Emily Arnold McCully, Putnam, 1993

Crossing the New Bridge, written and illustrated by Emily Arnold McCully, Putnam, 1994

I Am a Work of **Art**

Artists choose many different ways to show themselves in their work. Some try to record exactly the way they look. Others change the image of themselves, perhaps revealing something that a realistic portrait might not show.

How do you see yourself? What does the sculpture tell you about how the artist was feeling? Does he look sad? peaceful? proud? Why do you think so? How would it feel to look at a sculpture that looks just like you?

Sculpture by André Dimanche (Haitian), *Self-Portrait,* **1947**

What do you see in a self-portrait?

How can you tell this is a painting of a person? How is it different from a photograph? Does the title help you understand the painting? Why or why not?

© Helen Hardin (1976) *Looking Within Myself I Am Many Parts*

Painting by Helen Hardin (United States),
Looking Within Myself I Am Many Parts, 1976

I Can

I can
be anything
I can
do anything
I can
think
anything
big
or tall
OR
high or low
W I D E
or narrow
fast or slow
because I
CAN
and
I
WANT
TO!
— *Mari Evans*

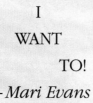

By Myself

When I'm by myself
And I close my eyes
I'm a twin
I'm a dimple in a chin
I'm a room full of toys
I'm a squeaky noise
I'm a gospel song
I'm a gong
I'm a leaf turning red
I'm a loaf of brown bread
I'm a whatever I want to be
An anything I care to be
And when I open my eyes
What I care to be
Is me

— *Eloise Greenfield*

Justin AT THE Ranch

from *Justin and the Best Biscuits in the World*
by Mildred Pitts Walter

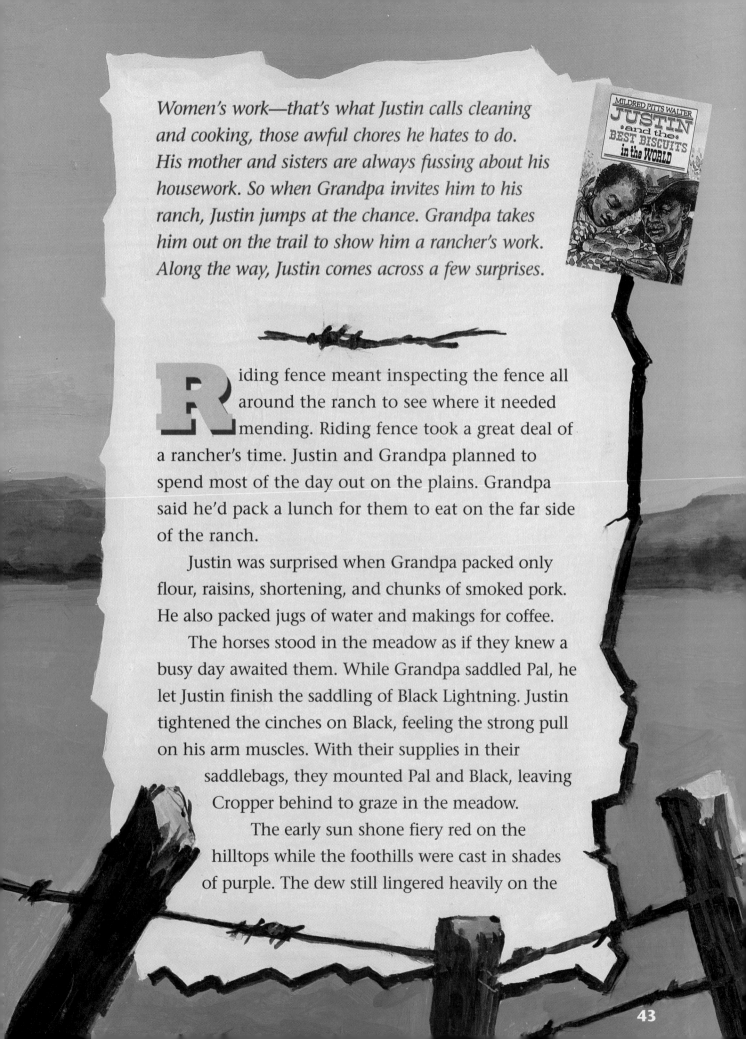

Women's work—that's what Justin calls cleaning and cooking, those awful chores he hates to do. His mother and sisters are always fussing about his housework. So when Grandpa invites him to his ranch, Justin jumps at the chance. Grandpa takes him out on the trail to show him a rancher's work. Along the way, Justin comes across a few surprises.

Riding fence meant inspecting the fence all around the ranch to see where it needed mending. Riding fence took a great deal of a rancher's time. Justin and Grandpa planned to spend most of the day out on the plains. Grandpa said he'd pack a lunch for them to eat on the far side of the ranch.

Justin was surprised when Grandpa packed only flour, raisins, shortening, and chunks of smoked pork. He also packed jugs of water and makings for coffee.

The horses stood in the meadow as if they knew a busy day awaited them. While Grandpa saddled Pal, he let Justin finish the saddling of Black Lightning. Justin tightened the cinches on Black, feeling the strong pull on his arm muscles. With their supplies in their saddlebags, they mounted Pal and Black, leaving Cropper behind to graze in the meadow.

The early sun shone fiery red on the hilltops while the foothills were cast in shades of purple. The dew still lingered heavily on the

morning. They let their horses canter away past the house through the tall green grass. But on the outer edge of the ranch where the fence started, they walked the horses at a steady pace.

The fence had three rows of taut wire. "That's a pretty high fence," Justin said.

"We have to keep the cattle in. But deer sometimes leap that fence and eat hay with the cattle." When it got bitter cold and frosty, Grandpa rode around the ranch dropping bales of hay for the cattle. It took a lot of hay to feed the cattle during the winter months.

"I didn't think a cow could jump very high," Justin said.

"Aw, come on. Surely you know that a cow jumped over the moon." Grandpa had a serious look on his face.

"I guess that's a joke, eh?" Justin laughed.

Justin noticed that Grandpa had a map. When they came to a place in the fence that looked weak,

Grandpa marked it on his map. Later, helpers who came to do the work would know exactly where to mend. That saved time.

Now the sun heated up the morning. The foothills were now varying shades of green. Shadows dotted the plains. Among the blackish green trees on the rolling hills, fog still lingered like lazy clouds. Insects buzzed. A small cloud of mosquitoes swarmed just behind their heads, and beautiful cardinals splashed their redness on the morning air. Justin felt a surge of happiness and hugged Black with his knees and heels.

Suddenly he saw a doe standing close to the fence. "Look, Grandpa!" he said. She seemed alarmed but did not run away. Doe eyes usually look peaceful and sad, Justin remembered. Hers widened with fear. Then Justin saw a fawn caught in the wire of the fence.

Quickly they got off their horses. They hitched them to a post and moved cautiously toward the fawn.

The mother rushed to the fence but stopped just short of the sharp wire. "Stay back and still," Grandpa said to Justin. "She doesn't know we will help her baby. She thinks we might hurt it. She wants to protect it."

The mother pranced restlessly. She pawed the ground, moving as close to the fence as she could. Near the post the fence had been broken. The wire curled there dangerously. The fawn's head, caught in

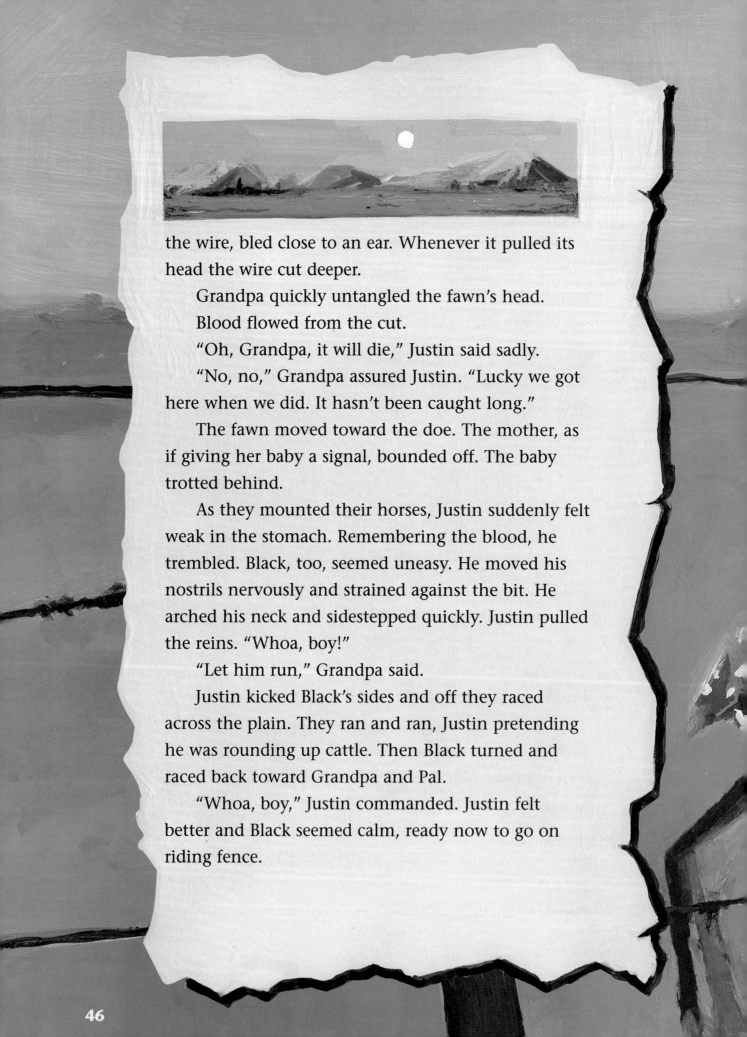

the wire, bled close to an ear. Whenever it pulled its head the wire cut deeper.

Grandpa quickly untangled the fawn's head.

Blood flowed from the cut.

"Oh, Grandpa, it will die," Justin said sadly.

"No, no," Grandpa assured Justin. "Lucky we got here when we did. It hasn't been caught long."

The fawn moved toward the doe. The mother, as if giving her baby a signal, bounded off. The baby trotted behind.

As they mounted their horses, Justin suddenly felt weak in the stomach. Remembering the blood, he trembled. Black, too, seemed uneasy. He moved his nostrils nervously and strained against the bit. He arched his neck and sidestepped quickly. Justin pulled the reins. "Whoa, boy!"

"Let him run," Grandpa said.

Justin kicked Black's sides and off they raced across the plain. They ran and ran, Justin pretending he was rounding up cattle. Then Black turned and raced back toward Grandpa and Pal.

"Whoa, boy," Justin commanded. Justin felt better and Black seemed calm, ready now to go on riding fence.

The sun beamed down and sweat rolled off Justin as he rode on with Grandpa, looking for broken wires in the fence. They were well away from the house, on the far side of the ranch. Flies buzzed around the horses and now gnats swarmed in clouds just above their heads. The prairie resounded with songs of the bluebirds, the bobwhite quails, and the mockingbirds mimicking them all. The cardinal's song, as lovely as any, included a whistle.

Justin thought of Anthony and how Anthony whistled for Pepper, his dog.

It was well past noon and Justin was hungry. Soon they came upon a small, well-built shed, securely locked. Nearby was a small stream. Grandpa reined in his horse. When he and Justin dismounted, they hitched the horses, and unsaddled them.

"We'll have our lunch here," Grandpa said. Justin was surprised when Grandpa took black iron pots, other cooking utensils, and a table from the shed. Justin helped him remove some iron rods that Grandpa carefully placed over a shallow pit. These would hold the pots. Now Justin understood why Grandpa had brought uncooked food. They were going to cook outside.

First they collected twigs and cow dung. Grandpa called it cowchips. "These," Grandpa said, holding up a dried brown pad, "make the best fuel. Gather them up."

There were plenty of chips left from the cattle that had fed there in winter. Soon they had a hot fire.

Justin watched as Grandpa carefully washed his hands and then began to cook their lunch.

"When I was a boy about your age, I used to go with my father on short runs with cattle. We'd bring them down from the high country onto the plains."

"Did you stay out all night?"

"Sometimes. And that was the time I liked most. The cook often made for supper what I am going to make for lunch."

Grandpa put raisins into a pot with a little water and placed them over the fire. Justin was surprised when Grandpa put flour in a separate pan. He used his fist to make a hole right in the middle of the flour. In that hole he placed some shortening. Then he added water. With his long delicate fingers he mixed the flour, water, and shortening until he had a nice round mound of dough.

Soon smooth circles of biscuits sat in an iron skillet with a lid on top. Grandpa put the skillet on the fire with some of the red-hot chips scattered over the lid.

Justin was amazed. How could only those ingredients make good bread? But he said nothing as Grandpa put the chunks of smoked pork in a skillet and started them cooking. Soon the smell was so delicious, Justin could hardly wait.

Finally Grandpa suggested that Justin take the horses to drink at the stream. "Keep your eyes open and don't step on any snakes."

Justin knew that diamondback rattlers sometimes lurked around. They were dangerous. He must be careful. He watered Black first.

While watering Pal, he heard rustling in the grass. His heart pounded. He heard the noise again. He wanted to run, but was too afraid. He looked around carefully. There were two black eyes staring at him. He tried to pull Pal away from the water, but Pal refused to stop drinking. Then Justin saw the animal. It had a long tail like a rat's. But it was as big as a cat. Then he saw something crawling on its back. They were little babies, hanging on as the animal ran.

A mama opossum and her babies, he thought, and was no longer afraid.

By the time the horses were watered, lunch was ready. *"M-mm-m,"* Justin said as he reached for a plate. The biscuits were golden brown, yet fluffy inside. And the sizzling pork was now crisp. Never had he eaten stewed raisins before.

"Grandpa, I didn't know you could cook like this," Justin said when he had tasted the food. "I didn't know men could cook so good."

"Why, Justin, some of the best cooks in the world are men."

Justin remembered the egg on the floor and his rice burning. The look he gave Grandpa revealed his doubts.

"It's true," Grandpa said. "All the cooks on the cattle trail were men. In hotels and restaurants they call them chefs."

"How did you make these biscuits?"

"That's a secret. One day I'll let you make some."

"Were you a cowboy, Grandpa?"

"I'm still a cowboy."

"No, you're not."

"Yes, I am. I work with cattle, so I'm a cowboy."

"You know what I mean. The kind who rides bulls, broncobusters. That kind of cowboy."

"No, I'm not that kind. But I know some."

"Are they famous?"

"No, but I did meet a real famous Black cowboy once. When I was eight years old, my grandpa took me to meet his friend Bill Pickett. Bill Pickett was an old man then. He had a ranch in Oklahoma."

"Were there lots of Black cowboys?"

"Yes. Lots of them. They were hard workers, too. They busted broncos, branded calves, and drove cattle. My grandpa tamed wild mustangs."

"Bet they were famous."

"Oh, no. Some were. Bill Pickett created the sport of bulldogging. You'll see that at the rodeo. One cowboy named Williams taught Rough Rider Teddy Roosevelt how to break horses; and another one named Clay taught Will Rogers, the comedian, the art of roping." Grandpa offered Justin the last biscuit.

When they had finished their lunch they led the horses away from the shed to graze. As they watched the horses, Grandpa went on, "Now, there were some more very famous Black cowboys. Jessie Stahl. They say he was the best rider of wild horses in the West."

"How could he be? Nobody ever heard about him. I didn't."

"Oh, there're lots of famous Blacks you never hear or read about. You ever hear about Deadwood Dick?"

Justin laughed. "No."

"There's another one. His real name was Nate Love. He could outride, outshoot anyone. In Deadwood City in the Dakota Territory, he roped, tied, saddled, mounted, and rode a wild horse faster than  anyone. Then in the shooting match, he hit the bull's-eye every time. The people named him Deadwood Dick right on the spot. Enough about cowboys, now. While the horses graze, let's clean up here and get back to our men's work."

Justin felt that Grandpa was still teasing him, the way he had in Justin's room when he had placed his hand on Justin's shoulder. There was still the sense of shame whenever the outburst about women's work and the tears were remembered.

As they cleaned the utensils and dishes, Justin asked, "Grandpa, you think housework is women's work?"

"Do you?" Grandpa asked quickly.

"I asked you first, Grandpa."

"I guess asking you that before I answer is unfair. No, I don't. Do you?"

"Well, it seems easier for them," Justin said as he splashed water all over, glad he was outside.

"Easier than for me?"

"Well, not for you, I guess, but for me, yeah."

"Could it be because you don't know how?"

"You mean like making the bed and folding the clothes."

"Yes." Grandpa stopped and looked at Justin. "Making the bed is easy now, isn't it? All work is that way. It doesn't matter who does the work, man or woman, when it needs to be done. What matters is that we try to learn how to do it the best we can in the most enjoyable way."

"I don't think I'll ever like housework," Justin said, drying a big iron pot.

"It's like any other kind of work. The better you do it, the easier it becomes, and we seem not to mind doing things that are easy."

With the cooking rods and all the utensils put away, they locked the shed and went for their horses.

"Now, I'm going to let you do the cinches again. You'll like that."

There's that teasing again, Justin thought. "Yeah. That's a man's work," he said, and mounted Black.

"There are some good horsewomen. You'll see them at the rodeo." Grandpa mounted Pal. They went on their way, riding along silently, scanning the fence.

Finally Justin said, "I was just kidding, Grandpa." Then without planning to, he said, "I bet you don't like boys who cry like babies."

"Do I know any boys who cry like babies?"

"Aw, Grandpa, you saw me crying."

"Oh, I didn't think you were crying like a baby. In your room, you mean? We all cry sometime."

"You? Cry, Grandpa?"

"Sure."

They rode on, with Grandpa marking his map. Justin remained quiet, wondering what could make a man like Grandpa cry.

As if knowing Justin's thoughts, Grandpa said, "I remember crying when you were born."

"Why? Didn't you want me?"

"Oh, yes. You were the most beautiful baby. But, you see, your grandma, Beth, had just died. When I held you I was flooded with joy. Then I thought, *Grandma will never see this beautiful boy.* I cried."

The horses wading through the grass made the only sound in the silence. Then Grandpa said, "There's an old saying, son. 'The brave hide their fears, but share their tears.' Tears bathe the soul."

Justin looked at his grandpa. Their eyes caught. A warmth spread over Justin and he lowered his eyes. He wished he could tell his grandpa all he felt, how much he loved him.

IN RESPONSE

What a Day It's Been!

What events do you think Justin would remember most from his day with Grandpa? Write a page that Justin might write in his journal.

Character Connection

Compare how Justin and Mirette ("Mirette on the High Wire") react to new situations. Write a paragraph explaining how they are alike and how they are different. Use examples from each story to explain your answers.

AUTHOR AT WORK

When Mildred Pitts Walter was a teacher in the late 1960's, all of her students were African Americans, yet few books existed that were about African Americans. Ms. Walter decided to write them herself. She invented characters like Justin in hopes that her readers could relate to them and gain a new understanding of themselves.

★ Award-winning Author

Other Books by . . .

Mildred Pitts Walter

Mariah Keeps Cool, by Mildred Pitts Walter, Macmillan Child Group, 1990

Ty's One-man Band, by Mildred Pitts Walter, illustrated by Margot Tomes, Four Winds Press, 1980

Library Link This story was taken from *Justin and the Best Biscuits in the World.* You might enjoy reading the entire book to find out how Justin uses at home what he has learned at the ranch.

Cowboys of the Old West

The early American cowboys were frontiersmen. Nearly half of the cowboys were from minority groups, including African Americans, Native Americans, and Mexicans. Many of the African American cowboys had been slaves. When they became free after the Civil War, some moved out west and became cowboys. For many former slaves, ranching was the only work they were allowed to do. The Native American cowboys came from various tribes throughout the southwest territory of the United States. Many of the Mexican cowboys remained in Texas after it declared its independence from Mexico in 1836.

Nate Love was an African American cowboy who worked on cattle drives for about twenty years. He was well known for his expert horsemanship.

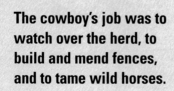

The cowboy's job was to watch over the herd, to build and mend fences, and to tame wild horses.

The spurs helped cow-boys control their horses. Each spur had a spiked wheel called a rowel.

Between Friends

from *Felita* by Nicholasa Mohr

A wonderful thing happened this new school year. Gigi, Consuela, Paquito, and I were all going into the fourth grade, and we were put in the same class. It had never happened before. Once I was in the same class with Consuela, and last year Gigi and Paquito were together. But this—it was too good to be true! Of course knowing Gigi and I were in the same class made me the happiest.

Our teacher, Miss Lovett, was friendly and laughed easily. In early October, after we had all settled into our class and gotten used to the routine of school once more, Miss Lovett told us that this year our class was going to put on a play for Thanksgiving. The play we were going to perform was based on a poem by Henry Wadsworth Longfellow, called "The Courtship of Miles Standish." It was about the Pilgrims and how they lived when they first landed in America.

We were all so excited about the play. Miss Lovett called for volunteers to help with the sets and costumes. Paquito and I agreed to help with the sets. Consuela was going to work on makeup. Gigi had not volunteered for anything. When we asked her what she was going to do, she shrugged and didn't answer.

Miss Lovett said we could all audition for the different parts in the play. I was really interested in being Priscilla. She is the heroine. Both Captain Miles Standish and the handsome, young John Alden are in love with her. She is the most beautiful maiden in Plymouth, Massachusetts. That's where the Pilgrims used to live. I told my friends how much I would like to play that part. Everyone said I would be perfect . . . except Gigi. She said that it was a hard part to do, and maybe I wouldn't be able to play it. I really got annoyed and asked her what she meant.

"I just don't think you are right to play Priscilla. That's all," she said.

"What do you mean by right?" I asked. But Gigi only shrugged and didn't say another word. She was beginning to get on my nerves.

Auditions for the parts were going to start Tuesday. Lots of kids had volunteered to audition. Paquito said he would try out for the brave Captain Miles Standish. Consuela said she was too afraid to get up in front of everybody and make a fool of herself. Gigi didn't show any interest in the play and refused to even talk to us about it. Finally the day came for the girls to read for the part of Priscilla. I was so excited I could hardly wait. Miss Lovett had given us some lines to study.

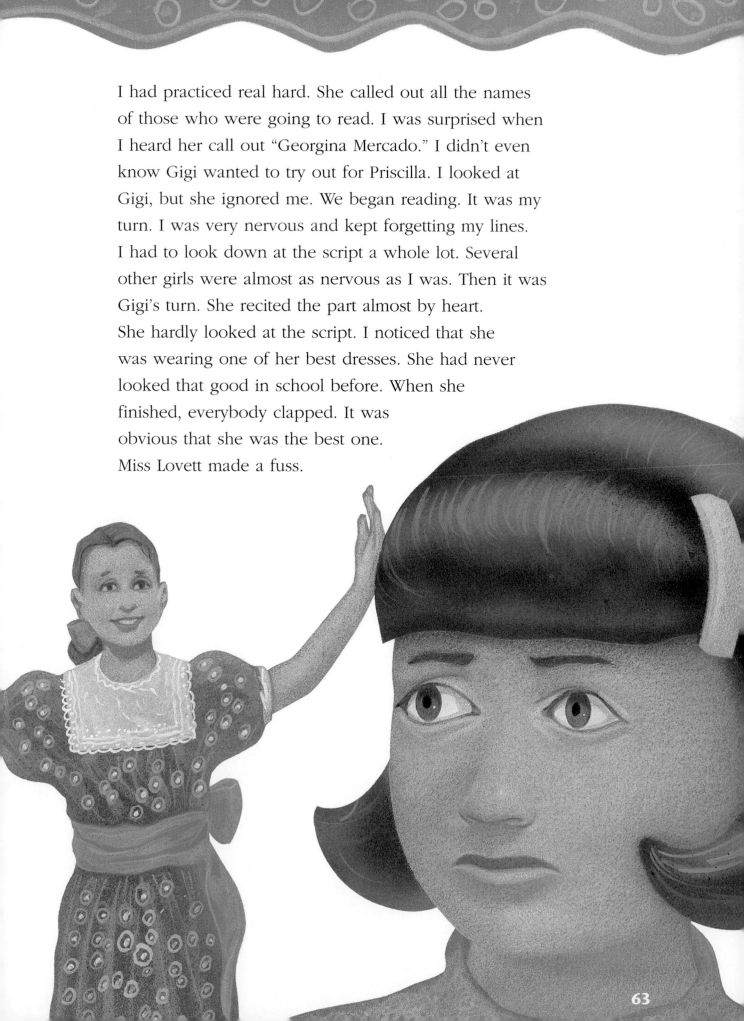

I had practiced real hard. She called out all the names of those who were going to read. I was surprised when I heard her call out "Georgina Mercado." I didn't even know Gigi wanted to try out for Priscilla. I looked at Gigi, but she ignored me. We began reading. It was my turn. I was very nervous and kept forgetting my lines. I had to look down at the script a whole lot. Several other girls were almost as nervous as I was. Then it was Gigi's turn. She recited the part almost by heart. She hardly looked at the script. I noticed that she was wearing one of her best dresses. She had never looked that good in school before. When she finished, everybody clapped. It was obvious that she was the best one. Miss Lovett made a fuss.

"You were just wonderful, Georgina," she said, "made for the part!" Boy, would I have liked another chance. I bet I could have done better than Gigi.

Why hadn't she told me she wanted the part? It's a free country, after all. She could read for the same part as me. I wasn't going to stop her! I was really angry at Gigi.

After school everyone was still making a fuss over her. Even Paquito had to open his stupid mouth.

"Oh, man, Gigi!" he said. "You were really good. I liked the part when John Alden asked you to marry Captain Miles Standish and you said, 'Why don't you speak for yourself, John?' You turned your head like this." Paquito imitated Gigi and closed his eyes. "That was really neat!" Consuela and the others laughed and agreed.

I decided I wasn't walking home with them.

"I have to meet my brothers down by the next street," I said. "I'm splitting. See you." They hardly noticed. Only Consuela said goodbye. The rest just kept on hanging all over Gigi. Big deal, I thought.

Of course walking by myself and watching out for the tough kids was not something I looked forward to. Just last Friday Hilda Gonzales had gotten beat up and had her entire allowance stolen. And at the beginning of the term Paquito had been walking home by himself and gotten mugged. A bunch of big bullies had taken his new schoolbag complete with pencil and pen case, then left him with a swollen lip. No, sir, none of us ever walked home from school alone if we could help it. We knew it wasn't a safe thing to do. Those mean kids never bothered us as long as we stuck together. Carefully I looked around to make sure none of the bullies were in sight. Then I put some speed under my feet, took my chances, and headed for home.

Just before all the casting was completed, Miss Lovett offered me a part as one of the Pilgrim women. All I had to do was stand in the background like a zombie. It wasn't even a speaking part.

"I don't get to say one word," I protested.

"Felicidad Maldonado, you are designing the stage sets and you're assistant stage manager. I think that's quite a bit. Besides, all the speaking parts are taken."

"I'm not interested, thank you," I answered.

"You know"—Miss Lovett shook her head—"you can't be the best in everything."

I turned and left. I didn't need to play any part at all. Who cared?

Gigi came over to me the next day with a great big smile all over her face. I just turned away and made believe she wasn't there.

"Felita, are you taking the part of the Pilgrim woman?" she asked me in her sweetest voice, just like nothing had happened.

"No," I said, still not looking at her. If she thought I was going to fall all over her like those dummies, she was wasting her time.

"Oh," was all she said, and walked away. Good, I thought. I don't need her one bit!

At home Mami noticed something was wrong.

"Felita, what's the matter? You aren't going out at all. And I haven't seen Gigi for quite a while. In fact I haven't seen any of your friends."

"Nothing is the matter, Mami. I just got lots of things to do."

"You're not upset because we couldn't give you a birthday party this year, are you?" Mami asked. "You know how hard the money situation has been for us."

My birthday had been at the beginning of November. We had celebrated with a small cake after dinner, but there had been no party.

"No. It's not that," I said and meant it. Even though I had been a little disappointed, I also knew Mami and Papi had done the best they could.

"We'll make it up to you next year, Felita, you'll see."

"I don't care, Mami. It's not important now."

"You didn't go having a fight with Gigi or something? Did you?"

"Now why would I have a fight with anybody!"

"Don't raise your voice, miss," Mami said. "Sorry I asked. But you just calm down."

The play was going to be performed on the day before Thanksgiving. I made the drawings for most of the scenery. I made a barn, a church, trees and grass,

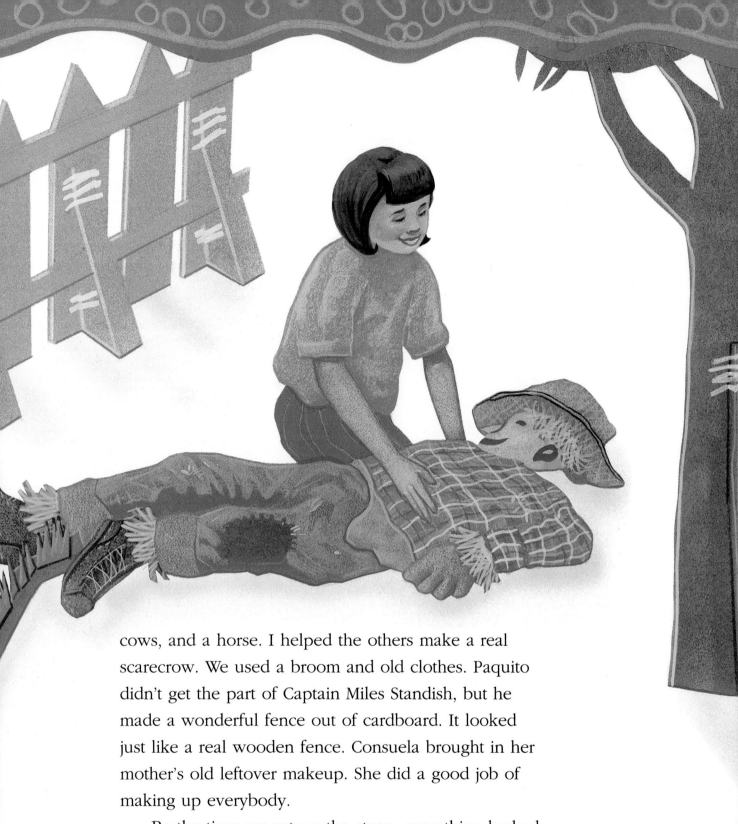

cows, and a horse. I helped the others make a real
scarecrow. We used a broom and old clothes. Paquito
didn't get the part of Captain Miles Standish, but he
made a wonderful fence out of cardboard. It looked
just like a real wooden fence. Consuela brought in her
mother's old leftover makeup. She did a good job of
making up everybody.

By the time we set up the stage, everything looked
beautiful. Gigi had tried to talk to me a few times. But I
just couldn't be nice back to her. She acted like nothing

had happened, like I was supposed to forget she hadn't told me she was going to read for the part! I wasn't going to forget that just because she was now Miss Popularity. She could go and stay with all her newfound friends for all I cared!

The morning of the play, at breakfast, everybody noticed how excited I was.

"Felita," Papi exclaimed, "stop jumping around like a monkey and eat your breakfast."

"She's all excited about the school play today," Mami said.

"That's right. Are you playing a part in the play?" Papi asked.

"No," I replied.

"But she's done most of the sets. Drawing and designing. Isn't that right, Felita?"

"Mami, it was no big deal."

"That's nice," said Papi. "Tell us about it."

"What kind of sets did you do?" Johnny asked.

"I don't know. Look, I don't want to talk about it."

"Boy, are you touchy today," Tito said with a laugh.

"Leave me alone!" I snapped.

"Okay." Mami stood up. "Enough. Felita, are you finished?" I nodded. "Good. Go to school. When you come back, bring home a better mood. Whatever is bothering you, no need to take it out on us." Quickly I left the table.

"Rosa," I heard Papi say, "sometimes you are too hard on her."

"And sometimes you spoil her, Alberto!" Mami snapped. "I'm not raising fresh kids."

I was glad to get out of there. Who needs them, I thought.

The play was a tremendous hit. Everybody looked wonderful and played their parts really well. The stage was brilliant with the color I had used on my drawings. The background of the countryside, the barn, and just about everything stood out clearly. Ernesto Bratter, the stage manager, said I was a good assistant. I was glad to hear that, because a couple of times I'd had to control my temper on account of his ordering me around. But it had all worked out great.

No doubt about it. Gigi was perfect as Priscilla. Even though the kids clapped and cheered for the entire cast, Gigi got more applause than anybody else. She just kept on taking a whole lot of bows.

Afterward Miss Lovett had a party for our class. We had lots of treats. There was even a record player and we all danced. We had a really good time.

Of course Priscilla, alias Gigi, was the big star. She just couldn't get enough attention. But not from me, that was for sure. After the party Gigi spoke to me.

"Your sets were really great. Everybody said the stage looked wonderful."

"Thanks." I looked away.

"Felita, are you mad at me?"

"Why should I be mad at you?"

"Well, I did get the leading part, but . . ."

"Big deal," I said. "I really don't care."

"You don't? But . . . I . . ."

"Look," I said, interrupting her, "I gotta go. I promised my mother I'd get home early. We have to go someplace."

I rushed all the way home. I didn't know why, but I was still furious at Gigi. What was worse was that I was unhappy about having those feelings. Gigi and I had been real close for as far back as I could remember. Not being able to share things with her really bothered me.

We had a great Thanksgiving. The dinner was just delicious. Abuelita[1] brought her flan.[2] Tío[3] Jorge brought lots of ice cream. He always brings us kids a treat when he visits. Sometimes he even brings each one of us a small gift— a nature book or crayons for me and puzzles or sports

---

1 **abuelita** (*ah bway LEE tah*) beloved grandmother

2 **flan** (*flahn*) custard dessert

3 **tío** (*TEE oh*) uncle

magazines for my brothers. He's really very nice to us. One thing about him is that he's sort of quiet and doesn't talk much. Papi says that Tío Jorge has been like that as far back as he can remember.

Abuelita asked me if I wanted to go home with her that evening. Boy, was I happy to get away from Mami. I just couldn't face another day of her asking me questions about Gigi, my friends, and my whole life. It was getting to be too much!

It felt good to be with Abuelita in her apartment. Abuelita never questioned me about anything really personal unless I wanted to talk about it. She just waited, and when she sensed that I was worried or something, then she would ask me. Not like Mami. I love Mami, but she's always trying to find out every little thing that happens to me. With my abuelita sometimes we just sit and stay quiet, not talk at all. That was nice too. We fixed the daybed for me. And then Tío Jorge, Abuelita, and I had more flan as usual.

"Would you like to go to the park with me this Sunday?" Tío Jorge asked me.

"Yes."

"We can go to the zoo and later we can visit the ducks and swans by the lake."

"Great!" I said.

Whenever Tío Jorge took me to the zoo, he would tell me stories about how he, Abuelita, and their brothers and sisters had lived and worked as youngsters taking care of farm animals. These were the only times I ever heard him talk a whole lot.

"It's not just playing, you know," he would say. "Taking care of animals is hard work. Back on our farm in Puerto Rico we worked hard, but we had fun too. Every one of us children had our very own favorite pets. I had a pet goat by the name of Pepe. He used to follow me everywhere." No matter how many times he told me the same stories, I always enjoyed hearing them again.

"Well." Tío Jorge got up. "It's a date then on Sunday, yes?"

"Yes, thank you, Tío Jorge."

"Good night," he said and went off to bed.

Abuelita and I sat quietly for a while, then Abuelita spoke.

"You are getting to be a big girl now, Felita. You just turned nine years old. My goodness! But I still hope you will come to bed with your abuelita for a little while, eh?"

I got into bed and snuggled close to Abuelita. I loved her the best, more than anybody. I hadn't been to stay with her since the summer, and somehow this time things felt different. I noticed how tired Abuelita looked. She wasn't moving as fast as she used to. Also I didn't feel so little next to her anymore.

"Tell me, Felita, how have you been? It seems like a long time since we were together like this." She smiled her wonderful smile at me. Her dark, bright eyes looked deeply into mine. I felt her warmth and happiness.

"I'm okay, Abuelita."

"Tell me about your play at school. Rosa tells me you worked on the stage sets. Was the play a success?"

"It was. It was great. The stage looked beautiful. My drawings stood out really well. I never made such big drawings in my life. There was a farm in the country,

a barn, and animals. I made it the way it used to be in the olden days of the Pilgrims. You know, how it was when they first came to America."

"I'm so proud of you. Tell me about the play. Did you act in it?"

"No." I paused. "I didn't want to."

"I see. Tell me a little about the story."

I told Abuelita all about it.

"Who played the parts? Any of your friends?"

"Some."

"Who?"

"Well, this boy Charlie Martinez played John Alden. Louie Collins played Captain Miles Standish. You don't know them. Mary Jackson played the part of the narrator. That's the person who tells the story. You really don't know any of them."

I was hoping she wouldn't ask, but she did.

"Who played the part of the girl both men love?"

"Oh, her? Gigi."

"Gigi Mercado, your best friend?" I nodded. "Was she good?"

"Yes, she was. Very good."

"You don't sound too happy about that."

"I don't care." I shrugged.

"But if she is your best friend, I should think you would care."

"I . . . I don't know if she is my friend anymore, Abuelita."

"Why do you say that?"

I couldn't answer. I just felt awful.

"Did she do something? Did you two argue?"
I nodded. "Can I ask what happened?"

"Well, it's hard to explain. But what she did
wasn't fair."

"Fair about what, Felita?"

I hadn't spoken about it before. Now with Abuelita
it was easy to talk about it.

"Well, we all tried out for the different parts.
Everybody knew what everybody was trying out for.
But Gigi never told anybody she was going to try out
for Priscilla. She kept it a great big secret. Even after

I told her that I wanted to try for the part, she kept
quiet about it. Do you know what she did say? She
said I wasn't right for it . . . it was a hard part and
all that bunch of baloney. She just wanted the part
for herself, so she was mysterious about the whole
thing. Like . . . it was . . . I don't know." I
stopped for a moment, trying to figure this
whole thing out. "After all, I am supposed to
be her best friend . . . her very best friend.
Why shouldn't she let me know that she wanted
to be Priscilla? I wouldn't care. I let her know my
plans. I didn't go sneaking around."

"Are you angry because Gigi got the part?"

It was hard for me to answer. I thought about it for
a little while. "Abuelita, I don't think so. She was really
good in the part."

"Were you as good when you tried out
for Priscilla?"

"No." I looked at Abuelita. "I stunk." We both
laughed.

"Then maybe you are not angry at Gigi at all."

"What do you mean?"

"Well, maybe you are a little bit . . . hurt?"

"Hurt?" I felt confused.

"Do you know what I think? I think you are hurt
because your best friend didn't trust you. From what
you tell me, you trusted her, but she didn't have faith in
you. What do you think?"

"Yes." I nodded. "Abuelita, yes. I don't know why.
Gigi and I always tell each other everything. Why did
she act like that to me?"

"Have you asked her?"

"No."

"Why not? Aren't you two speaking to each other?"

"We're speaking. Gigi tried to be friendly a few times."

"Don't you want to stay her friend?"

"I do. Only she came over to me acting like . . . like nothing ever happened. And something did happen! What does she think? That she can go around being sneaky and I'm going to fall all over her? Just because she got the best part, she thinks she's special."

"And you think that's why she came over. Because she wants to be special?"

"I don't know."

"You should give her a chance. Perhaps Gigi acted in a strange way for a reason."

"She wasn't nice to me, Abuelita. She wasn't."

"I'm not saying she was. Or even that she was right. Mira,[4] Felita, friendship is one of the best things in this whole world. It's one of the few things you can't go out and buy. It's like love. You can buy clothes, food, even luxuries, but there's no place I know of where you can buy a real friend. Do you?"

I shook my head. Abuelita smiled at me and waited. We were both silent for a long moment. I wondered if maybe I shouldn't have a talk with Gigi. After all, she had tried to talk to me first.

"Abuelita, do you think it's a good idea for me to . . . maybe talk to Gigi?"

"You know, that's a very good idea." Abuelita nodded.

"Well, she did try to talk to me a few times. Only there's just one thing. I won't know what to say to her. I mean, after what's happened and all."

---

4 mira (*MEE rah*) an expression, "Look"

"After so many years of being close, I am sure you could say 'Hello, Gigi. How are you?' That should be easy enough."

"I feel better already, Abuelita."

"Good," Abuelita said. "Now let's you and I get to sleep. Abuelita is tired."

"You don't have to tuck me in. I'll tuck you in instead." I got out of bed and folded the covers carefully over my side. Then I leaned over her and gave her a kiss. Abuelita hugged me real tight.

"My Felita has become a young lady," she whispered.

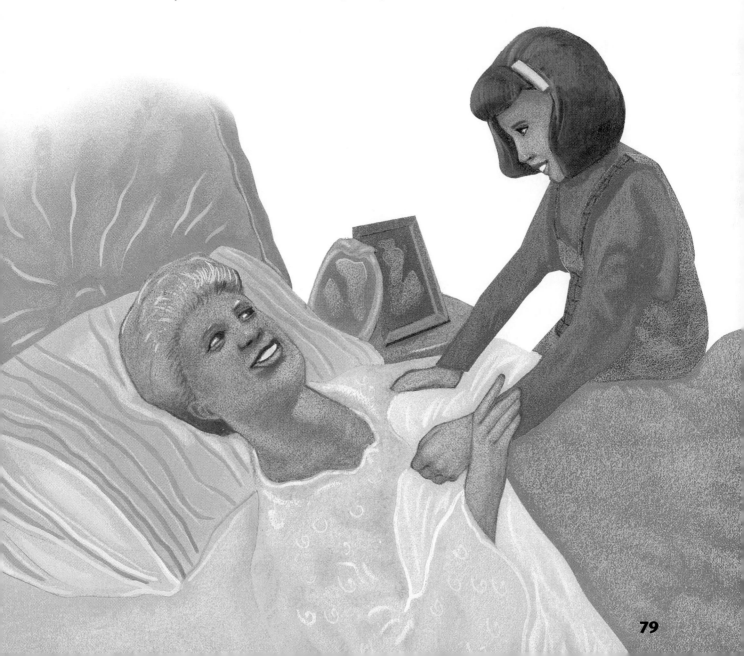

I kept thinking of what Abuelita had said, and on Monday I waited for Gigi after school. It was as if she knew I wanted to talk. She came over to me.

"Hello, Gigi," I said. "How are you?"

"Fine." Gigi smiled. "Wanna walk home together?"

"Let's take the long way so we can be by ourselves," I said.

We walked without saying anything for a couple of blocks. Finally I spoke.

"I wanted to tell you, Gigi, you were really great as Priscilla."

"Did you really like me? Oh, Felita, I'm so glad. I wanted you to like me, more than anybody else. Of course it was nothing compared to the sets you did. They were something special. Everybody liked them so much."

"You were right too," I said. "I wasn't very good for the part of Priscilla."

"Look." Gigi stopped walking and looked at me. "I'm sorry about . . . about the way I acted. Like, I didn't say anything to you or the others. But, well, I was scared you all would think I was silly or something. I mean, you wanted the part too. So, I figured, better not say nothing."

"I wouldn't have cared, Gigi. Honest."

"Felita . . . it's just that you are so good at a lot of things. Like, you draw just fantastic. You beat everybody at hopscotch and kick-the-can. You know about nature and animals, much more than the rest of us. Everything you do is always better than . . . what I do! I just wanted this part for me. I wanted to be better than you this time. For once I didn't wanna worry about you. Felita, I'm sorry."

I was shocked. I didn't know Gigi felt that way. I didn't feel better than anybody about anything I did. She looked so upset, like she was about to cry any minute. I could see she was miserable and I wanted to comfort her. I had never had this kind of feeling before in my whole life.

"Well, you didn't have to worry. 'Cause I stunk!" We both laughed with relief. "I think I was the worst one!"

"Oh, no, you weren't." Gigi laughed. "Jenny Fuentes was the most awful."

"Worse than me?"

"Much worse. Do you know what she sounded like? She sounded like this. 'Wha . . . wha . . . why don't you . . . speeek for your . . . yourself *Johnnnn?*" Gigi and I burst into laughter.

"And how about that dummy, Louie Collins? I didn't think he read better than Paquito."

"Right," Gigi agreed. "I don't know how he got through the play. He was shaking so much that I was scared the sets would fall right on his head." It was so much fun, Gigi and I talking about the play and how we felt about everybody and everything. It was just like before, only better.

IN RESPONSE

What's She Thinking?

Draw pictures of an important scene in the story between Gigi and Felita. Include thought balloons that tell what each girl is thinking about her friend at that moment.

Great Grandparents

Host a talk show with Felita and Justin ("Justin at the Ranch") as guests. The topic is "Grandparents Lend a Hand." In a small group, think of questions the talk show host might ask, such as, "How have your grandparents helped you solve a problem?" Then role-play the dialogue among these two characters and the host.

Nicholasa Mohr began her career as a painter. She felt that her art told a story about her experiences. It wasn't until years later that she discovered the story-telling power of words. She found that words helped her share even more of her feelings and experiences. Ms. Mohr thinks of the switch to writing as learning to "draw a picture with words."

When writing, the author works with her own experiences as a Puerto Rican girl growing up in the United States in the inner city. Her first book, *Nilda,* follows a young girl as she learns about herself, her family, and her neighborhood during hard times. When she began writing the book, Ms. Mohr admits she was a bit nervous. She soon "fell very much in love with writing." Ms. Mohr believes her books can be read and enjoyed by everyone, young and old alike.

★ **Award-winning Author**

Other Books by . . .

Nicholasa Mohr

All for the Better: A Story of El Barrio, by Nicholasa Mohr, illustrated by Rudy Gutierrez, Raintree, 1992

Going Home, by Nicholasa Mohr, Dial Books for Young Readers, 1986

Library Link This story was taken from *Felita.* You might enjoy reading the entire book to find out what else Felita learns about herself in school, at home, and with her friend Gigi.

The Lion
AND
The Mouse

by June Barr

Characters

NARRATOR **THE MOUSE**

THE LION **FIVE HUNTERS**

NARRATOR: The Lion is asleep in the clearing in the forest. The Mouse comes running in. He stops to sniff the air and look for danger. He sees the Lion, and goes close to admire the big animal.

MOUSE: My! What a great and wonderful beast! He must be the King of the Forest, at least.

LION: Arrummph! Mmmph! And who might you be? Don't you know better than to fool with me? You're just the right size for me to eat. And you know, you might taste very sweet!

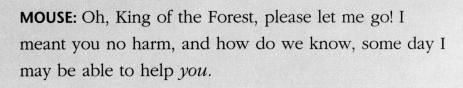

MOUSE: Oh, King of the Forest, please let me go! I meant you no harm, and how do we know, some day I may be able to help *you*.

LION: Ha, ha, ha, ha. *You* help *me?* What could *you* do?

MOUSE: I might do *something,* and I meant you no harm. . . .

LION: All right, I won't eat you . . . feel no alarm.

MOUSE: Thank you, King Lion, I wish you good luck!

LION: I wish you the same, for you've plenty of pluck!

NARRATOR: And so the Lion starts slowly away. Suddenly five hunters appear. They run quietly up behind the Lion and throw a net over him. The Lion struggles and roars. The hunters talk excitedly.

1ST HUNTER: We've got him! We've got him! He's tight in the net!

2ND HUNTER: Don't begin bragging. He isn't safe yet!

3RD HUNTER: Hurry! Be quick now!

4TH HUNTER: He's certainly strong!

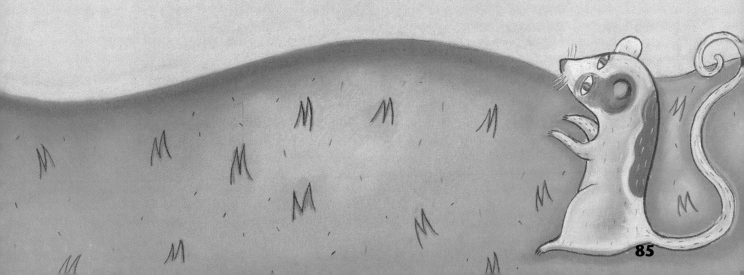

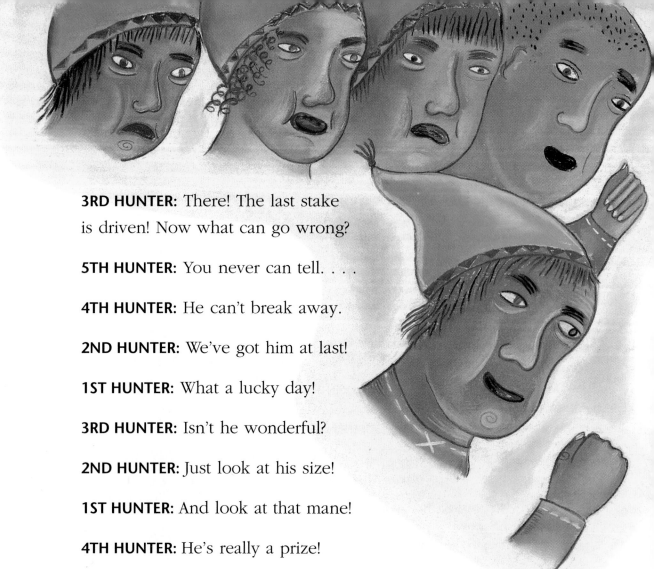

3RD HUNTER: There! The last stake is driven! Now what can go wrong?

5TH HUNTER: You never can tell. . . .

4TH HUNTER: He can't break away.

2ND HUNTER: We've got him at last!

1ST HUNTER: What a lucky day!

3RD HUNTER: Isn't he wonderful?

2ND HUNTER: Just look at his size!

1ST HUNTER: And look at that mane!

4TH HUNTER: He's really a prize!

5TH HUNTER: He's the finest lion I've seen in an age.

3RD HUNTER: Shall we go back to the village and get a cage?

5TH HUNTER: Yes, we'll cage him and take him back to the King.

4TH HUNTER: What a present!

3RD HUNTER: The best any loyal subject could bring.

4TH HUNTER: We're sure to receive a reward for our pains.

1ST HUNTER: And remember, we all share alike in the gains!

2ND HUNTER: Shall I stay and guard him?

1ST HUNTER: Oh, he'll be all right!

3RD HUNTER: He's safe in the net.

4TH HUNTER: And it's fastened down tight!

2ND HUNTER: Let's go get the cage, then.

NARRATOR: The hunters have left. The Mouse has been watching them from his hiding place. He now comes out and approaches the Lion. The Lion speaks to the Mouse.

LION: Oh, little Mouse, did you see what they've done? Alas, this day is an unhappy one! They'll carry me away in a cage and then I shall never see my dear forest again!

MOUSE: Now, wait just a minute. . . .

LION: Oh, woe is me!

MOUSE: Oh, King of the Forest, I can set you free!

LION: What can a mouse do? No, it's too late.

MOUSE: Now, you just be patient, please, and wait. . . . Let me gnaw the rope. . . . There. That rope is free.

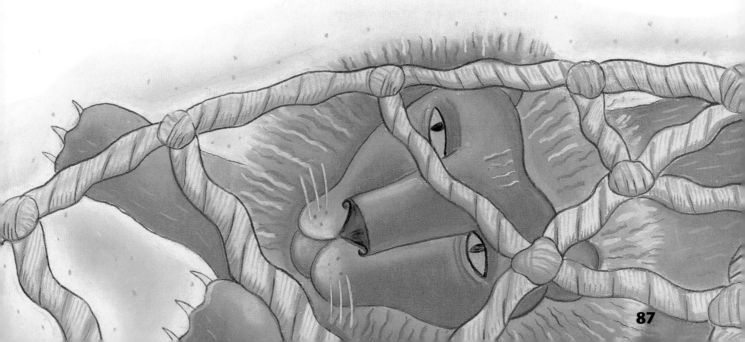

LION: That's nice, but what good can one rope do?

MOUSE: Now just you wait, and I'll gnaw them *all* through!

LION: Oh, hurry, hurry, they'll be back any minute!

MOUSE: They'll find an empty net, with no lion in it!

LION: Oh, I believe you can do it! Oh, hurry, please!

MOUSE: Of course I can do it! . . . I'll gnaw these . . . and these. . . .

LION: I'm free! You've done it! You've set me free! And I thought you were too small to do anything for *me!*

MOUSE: I told you I'd repay. . . .

LION: Yes, I guess in the end a *little* friend is often the *greatest* friend!

MOUSE: Listen! The hunters!

LION: They're close to us, too! Let us hide in the brush and see what they'll do!

NARRATOR: The Lion and the Mouse hide in the brush and watch the hunters come into the clearing with a

large cage on poles. They set it down and look for the Lion. The hunters talk together as they move about.

1ST HUNTER: He's gone!

2ND HUNTER: Oh, he can't be!

3RD HUNTER: We tied him down tight!

4TH HUNTER: He couldn't get loose!

5TH HUNTER: Well, he's vanished, all right!

1ST HUNTER: The stakes are in place.

2ND HUNTER: But these ropes are gnawed through!

3RD HUNTER: A lion can't gnaw rope!

4TH HUNTER: Someone helped him.

5TH HUNTER: That must be true.

1ST HUNTER: Well, he's gone, and that's that.

3RD HUNTER: Who will tell our great King?

4TH HUNTER: You would go and brag of the great beast we'd bring.

1ST HUNTER: And now the King's waiting.

2ND HUNTER: How angry he'll be!

5TH HUNTER: When I wanted to tell him, you were quick to agree!

4TH HUNTER: You made us excited!

3RD HUNTER: And now the lion's escaped!

2ND HUNTER: Well, I'm not to blame, for I offered to stay!

3RD HUNTER: You are in this with us.

1ST HUNTER: You just can't back out!

2ND HUNTER: Oh, yes I can! Goodbye!

5TH HUNTER: And there's surely no doubt that I shall go too, for you are unfair.

4TH HUNTER: Come back!

1ST HUNTER: You'll pay for this!

3RD HUNTER: If you leave us, beware!

4TH HUNTER: They've gone. And now, who'll tell our King?

3RD HUNTER: Yes, who's going to tell him . . . that is the thing.

4TH HUNTER: It ought to be you, for you bragged more than I.

1ST HUNTER: No, it ought to be you!

3RD HUNTER: Me? Why me?

4TH HUNTER: Well, someone must tell him.

3RD HUNTER: That much is true.

1ST HUNTER: It ought to be you!

4TH HUNTER: No, it ought to be you!

NARRATOR: They are still arguing as they go out of the forest. The Lion and the Mouse come from their hiding place. The Mouse looks around.

MOUSE: Are they gone?

LION: Yes, they're gone, full of anger and spite.

MOUSE: They didn't stick together . . . it just doesn't seem right! Now their friendship is broken and never will mend!

LION: Well, we'll stick together! Come along, little friend. There's a part of this forest so deep and so green, a place where the hunters never are seen. We'll go there together. . . .

MOUSE: What good friends we'll be!

LION: Yes, I will help you, and you can help me!

THE END

EL CHINO

ALLEN SAY

My parents came from Canton, China, and had six children in Nogales,[1] Arizona. I was the fourth child. They named me Bong Way Wong, but my brothers and sisters called me Billy.

Our home was a corner grocery store, and we were open for business every day of the year.

"In America, you can be anything you want to be," Dad told us.

That was good news because none of us wanted to be a grocer when we grew up.

Lily, the eldest, was studying to be a librarian. Rose and Florence wanted to be teachers. My older brother, Jack, loved engineering. And Art, my baby brother, said he was going to be a doctor.

All I wanted to do was play basketball.

"Who's ever heard of a Chinese athlete!" They laughed.

El Chino (*ehl CHEE noh*) the Chinese man
1 Nogales (*noh GAH lehs*)

They didn't understand. I wanted to be a
great athlete.

"Why don't you listen to Dad," I told them.

But Dad died suddenly when I was ten. Our days
were dark after that, and we had to be a stronger
family than we were before. We gathered around
Mom and went on with our business.

In high school I finally got to play serious
basketball. I was quick and fast, and I could shoot
from anywhere on the court. "My ace," the coach
used to call me.

But I never got to play in college. I was too short.

"Just think," I said to my brother, Jack. "Four
inches taller and I would've been famous!"

"Who's going to hire a Chinese ballplayer,
anyway?" he asked. "Learn a trade and earn a living
like everybody else."

So, like Jack, I studied engineering.

After college I got a job as a highway engineer. That made everybody happy, especially Mom.

But I kept thinking about shooting the winning basket with the clock running out.

"Give Billy the ball!" they used to yell.

And they always did. I'd spin and shoot all in one motion, and the whole gym would explode with my name.

"Billy! Billy! Billy!"

I never forgot that.

Give me the ball!

But by then I had a trade and earned a living. For my first vacation I went to Europe. I liked Spain best—it was hot there, like it was in Arizona. I saw castles and museums, cathedrals and Gypsy dancers.

Then I saw a bullfight.

It's a sport where the bullfighter fools the bull with a cloth cape and kills it with a sword. Sometimes the bull kills the bullfighter. It wasn't anything like the rodeo shows I'd seen back home.

The first time the bull charged the bullfighter, I closed my eyes.

"Olé!"[2] The crowd screamed, and I paid attention.

It was a spectacle, all right, a very dangerous circus. And the bullfighter was some kind of an athlete. He was graceful, too, like a ballet dancer, and had the steadiest nerves I'd ever seen. The bull kept missing him, and with each miss the audience yelled louder. I shouted with them, until my voice was gone.

When the fight was over, the bull was dead. And now it was the people who charged the bullfighter. Roaring at the top of their voices, they hoisted him onto their shoulders and marched out of the arena. I rushed after them.

I didn't have to chase far. I even managed to stand right next to the amazing daredevil, and I got a shock. He was much shorter than me!

That night I didn't sleep. I couldn't get him to stop dancing inside my head, that short Spaniard in a fancy outfit.

---

2 **olé** (*oh LAY*) hurray

In the morning, I bought myself some Spanish clothes. Then I got a room in a boarding house, where I put away my old clothes and put on the new. In the mirror, I looked like a fine Spanish gentleman.

Using my hands and arms, I asked the landlady, "Where is the bullfighting school?"

"Ah, Señor." She gazed at me with great pity in her eyes. "Only the Spaniards can become true matadors."[3]

She sounded like my mother. And that reminded me to send Mom a telegram, and also one to my boss. Very sorry and please forgive, I am not coming home.

The school was just a clearing in a wood outside the city, but the maestro[4] had been a famous matador

---

3 matadors (*MAH tah dawrz*) bullfighters
4 maestro (*mah AYS troh*) master

when he was young. We took turns playing the bull, and the old master taught us to use the cape and the sword.

"He is a good athlete," I heard one student say about me.

"And he has courage and grace," said another. "But he cannot be a matador. He is not Spanish."

My dad would've said a few things to them, but it was no use. How could they understand? They hadn't grown up in the United States.

Before I knew, it was springtime in Spain. That's when the bull ranchers hired student matadors to test their young cows for courage and spirit. And the students who fought well would go on to become real matadors. Like my classmates, I went looking for work.

Everywhere I went, though, the ranchers took one look at me and shook their heads. My family sent me love and money, and that kept me going, but after two years I still hadn't fought a single cow. Maybe it was time to give up, time to go home and be an engineer again.

But what would Dad have said to me now?

I'd tell him this wasn't Arizona, U.S.A. So I couldn't be a Spanish matador.

But *uno momento,*[5] Señor. A Spanish matador? What had I been thinking all this time?

I'm Chinese!

I searched all over town, and finally found what I was looking for—a Chinese costume. I tried it on and hardly recognized myself in the mirror.

It was as if I were seeing myself for the first time. I looked like a *real* Chinese. And as I stared in the mirror, a strange feeling came over me. I felt powerful. I felt that I could do anything I wished—even become a matador! Could it be that I was wearing a magical costume?

I went outside to see what would happen.

I was a spectacle.

Children followed me everywhere I went. Men greeted me from across the street. Women smiled.

"El Chino!" they shouted. The Chinese!

For the first time, people were taking notice of me, and that was magic.

It was time to go see a bull rancher.

---

5 uno momento (*OO noh moh MEHN toh*) just a minute

Sure enough, the first rancher I saw gave me the nod. Just like that, I was facing my first live bull.

Actually, it was only a heifer, but it looked more like a black rhino, with horns that could gore right through me.

"I will not back off," I said to myself, and waved the cape.

The black hulk stood still, swishing a tail like a lion's.

"*Ojo, toro-o-o!*"[6] I called, giving the cape a good flap.

The charge was sudden and fast.

Like a tumbling boulder, the heifer came straight at me, and I swung the cape. At the last moment she swerved and went for the cape. *Swoosh!* With a hot wind she was past me. I spun around, flapped the cape, and she charged again. Then again.

---

6 **Ojo, toro!** (*OH hoh, TOH roh!*) Look out, bull!

I didn't remember how many passes I'd made before I heard the ranch hands shouting. They wanted to see how I would end the fight.

So I made her charge me one more time, and then I walked away without looking back, as I had seen real matadors do. I prayed the heifer wouldn't gore me in my back. She didn't move.

"Olé, olé!" The crowd applauded me. I'd passed the test.

The next morning a bald-headed man came knocking on my door.

"I hear good things about you, Señor," he said. "I am a manager of bullfighters. Do you want me to help you become a matador?"

"Sí!"[7] I almost shouted. "I would be honored!"

"*Bueno*.[8] But you cannot fight in your strange costume. Come with me," he said, and took me to a tailor's shop.

There, I was fitted for the "suit of lights," which all matadors wear in bullrings. I felt like a prince being groomed for an important ceremony.

And there *was* a ceremony. My manager had made an arrangement for me to fight a real bull in a month's time!

"You are a sensation," he told me. "The plaza is sold out, and it is El Chino everyone wants to see."

Finally it was my day.

---

7 sí (*SEE*) yes
8 bueno (*BWAY noh*) good

In a short while my manager would be arriving with a lot of reporters and photographers. I was big news. And my manager was supposed to help me get into the "suit of lights," but I couldn't wait any longer and got into it on my own.

In the mirror I looked splendid.

"Good thing you weren't four inches taller," I said to myself. "Show them you have grace and courage like the best of them. Don't lose face, for your family's sake . . ."

As I stared in the mirror, I began to feel victorious already. There had never been a Chinese matador before me. I could almost hear the sold-out plaza cheering me on. And if I fought well, maybe a crowd of Spaniards would carry me out of the arena on their shoulders, shouting my name the whole time.

And that's the way it happened. Just as I had dreamed it.

"Olé! El Chino, olé!"

IN RESPONSE

El Chino the Magnificent

El Chino is coming to town. Design a billboard advertising this famous matador. Let people know why they shouldn't miss his show.

Encouraging Words

With a partner, role-play a dialogue between Billy Wong and Justin ("Justin at the Ranch"). What might Justin ask Billy about how it feels to try a new activity? What can Billy tell Justin that he has learned about himself from his experiences?

Allen Say

Allen Say tells a story first in pictures and later in words. He starts out painting ideas about characters and scenes until they "become real" to him. Slowly the pictures form a story, and then he writes words to help carry the story along.

The author-illustrator spends most of his time in the painting phase. It took him eleven months

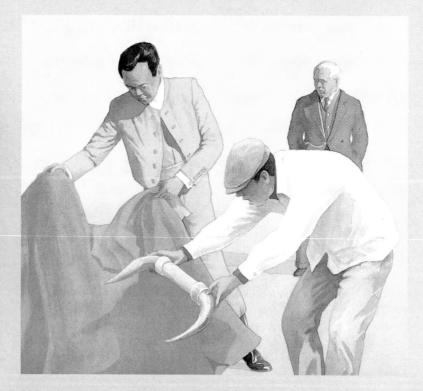

When painting a scene, Mr. Say insists that "everything has to be moving." This sense of movement shows up in his work.

★ Award-winning Author and Illustrator

106

to do the paintings for *El Chino*. After that big task, he sat down and wrote the words to the story in only two days!

Mr. Say grew up in Japan. He didn't learn English until he arrived in the United States at age sixteen. When the right words don't come easily for him in English, he finds that pictures can tell a story in any language.

El Chino is just as much a story about Allen Say as it is a biography of Billy Wong. Both men, for example, left their native country to start life again in a new land. Mr. Say, like Billy, has often faced discouragement from others in his new culture, so Billy's success story became an inspiration to him. "I became him in the process of doing the work," Mr. Say explains.

Author Allen Say at home with a friend

Other Books by . . .

Allen Say

The Lost Lake, written and illustrated by Allen Say, Houghton Mifflin, 1989

Tree of Cranes, written and illustrated by Allen Say, Houghton Mifflin, 1991

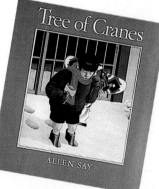

Express Yourself

In Understanding Ourselves, you learned how we can discover who we are by exploring our strengths and desires or by having someone older help us. You also saw that at times it is necessary to take risks in order to gain self-confidence.

Characters With Confidence

Good stories often show characters changing in some way. One way characters in this theme change is by gaining confidence in themselves. For example, Mirette ("Mirette on the High Wire") gains confidence at tightrope walking with practice and help. For each main character in this theme, think about the experiences that helped him or her gain confidence. Which character inspired you the most? Write a letter to that character explaining what his or her story means to you.

Picture Poems

The poems "I Can" and "By Myself" are both about how people picture themselves. Reread the poems, and think how each makes you feel about yourself. Do you feel you can do anything? How do you see yourself? Draw a self-portrait showing how the poems make you feel.

Talent Search

Many characters in this theme search for an activity that they can do well. Compare and contrast what Billy ("El Chino") and Felita ("Between Friends") learned about their talents. What did they want to do originally? What did they succeed at?

Getting to Know Them

Billy ("El Chino") tells his own story using "I," while Mirette's story ("Mirette on the High Wire") is told by a narrator who uses "she." What did you learn about each character's thoughts and feelings? Which character do you feel you know better? Why?

Unforgettable People

Mirette, Justin, Felita, and Billy all learned something about themselves through the help of a parent, a relative, or an older friend. Think back to each character and consider how an older person helped. Is there someone who has taught you something important about yourself? In writing, explain what he or she taught you. How did you change as a result of this lesson?

The Silver Bookcase

Crossing the Starlight Bridge
by Alice Mead, Bradbury Press, 1994

Rayanne's people, the Penobscot, have always lived on an island in Maine. When she has to leave the island, she is sure her new life on the mainland will be miserable. But her mother and grandmother, her drawings, and her new friends at school all help Rayanne realize that change can bring happiness.

Jerry on the Line
by Brenda Seabrooke, Bradbury Press, 1990

The two things Jerry likes most are playing soccer and being a "latchkey" child, responsible for himself after school. When he becomes friends with a second grader named Sherita, he is forced to make some difficult decisions to reach his goal of being a hero.

Dynamite Dinah
by Claudia Mills, Macmillan, 1990

Dinah doesn't mind being in the spotlight. In fact, she prefers it. But when a new baby arrives at home, and her best friend gets the lead in the fifth-grade play, Dinah must find new ways of being dynamite.

Good Luck Gold and Other Poems
by Janet S. Wong, Margaret K. McElderry Books, 1994

An Asian American girl celebrates her heritage through poems that will make you laugh and make you cry. Her poems tell about her family and share some of their special traditions.

A Very Young Musician
written with photographs by Jill Krementz, Simon and Schuster, 1991

In this book you'll meet Josh, who lives in Maine and plays the trumpet. He describes what it's like to be an ordinary boy who happens to be a very skilled musician.

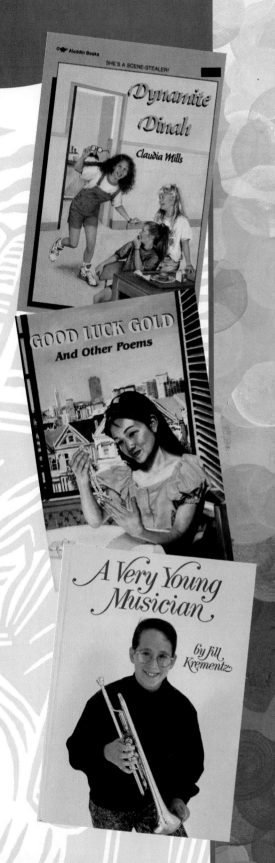

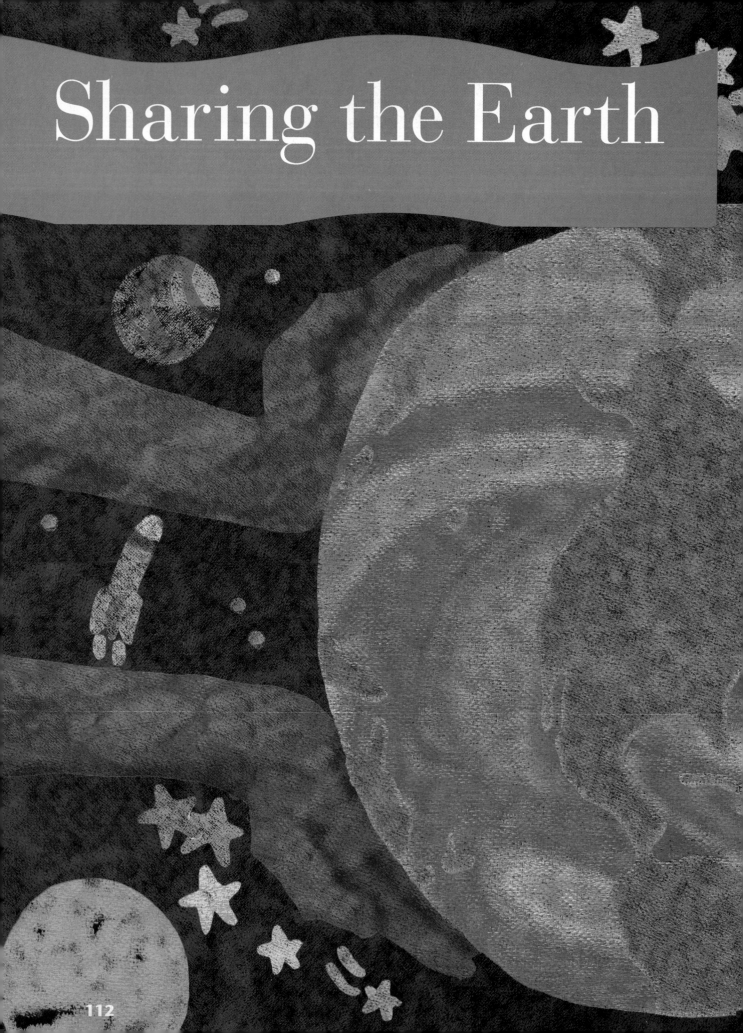

Sharing the Earth

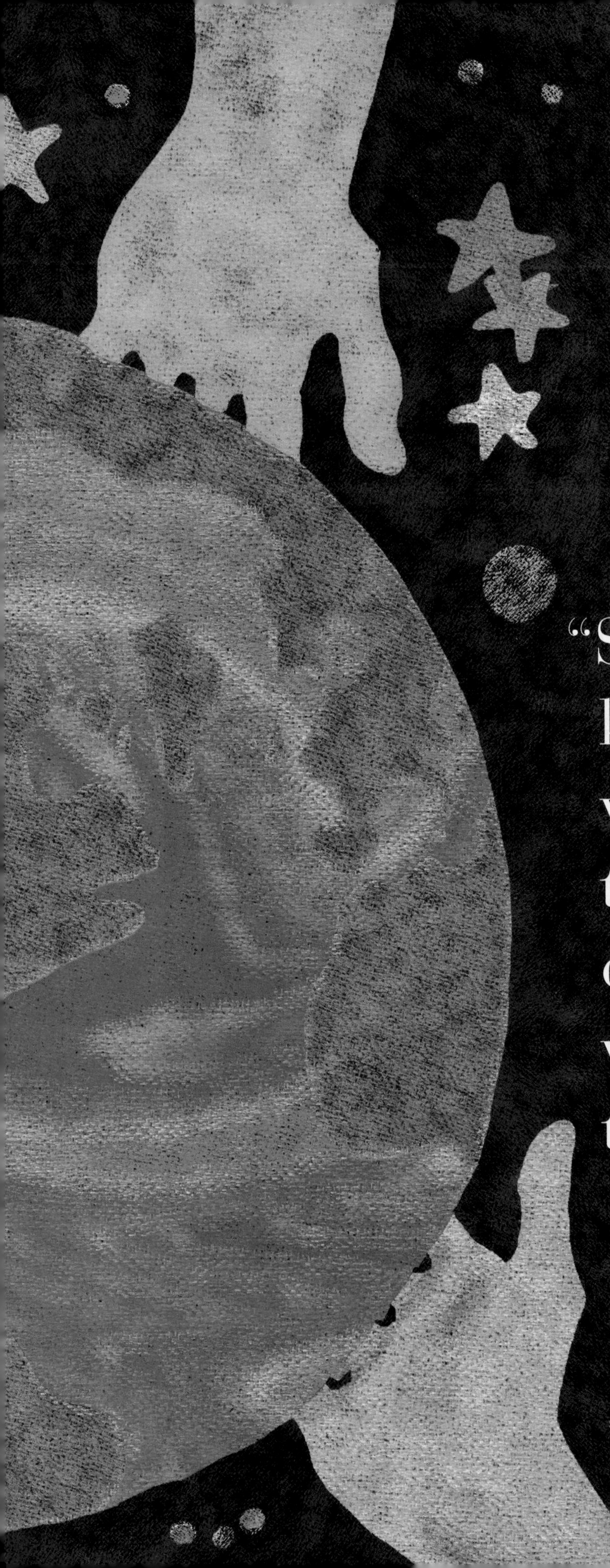

THEME 2

"Surely you know that what happens tomorrow depends upon what you do today."

—Lynne Cherry
"The Great Kapok Tree"

THEME 2

Sharing the Earth

CONTENTS

Appreciating the Earth

Helping the Earth

Theme Trade Books

Come Back, Salmon

by Molly Cone
No salmon had been seen in Pigeon Creek for years. Many people thought the water was hopelessly polluted. Students from Everett, Washington, set out to save the creek anyway.

Alejandro's Gift

by Richard E. Albert
Alejandro lives alone in his small desert home. The desert animals that drink from his watering holes keep him company and give him a valuable gift.

Theme Magazine

Where's the most unusual place you've ever seen a plant growing? How much do you know about otters? Are you eco-hip? Read the Theme Magazine *Eco Zone* to find out.

THE GREAT KAPOK TREE

A TALE OF THE AMAZON RAIN FOREST

by Lynne Cherry

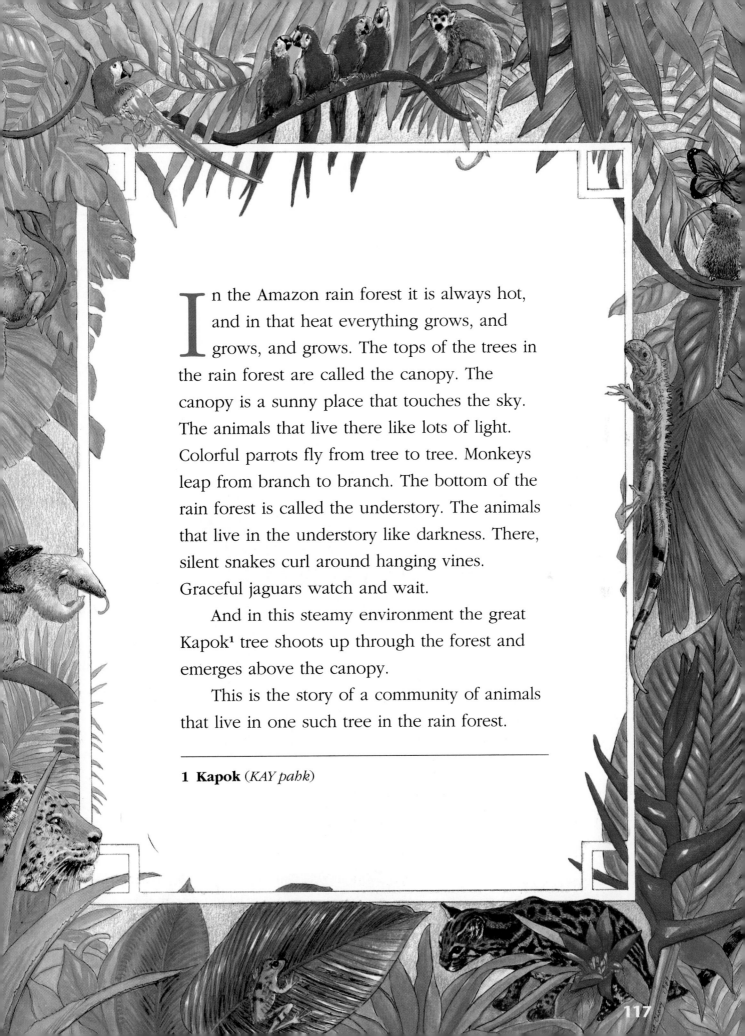

In the Amazon rain forest it is always hot, and in that heat everything grows, and grows, and grows. The tops of the trees in the rain forest are called the canopy. The canopy is a sunny place that touches the sky. The animals that live there like lots of light. Colorful parrots fly from tree to tree. Monkeys leap from branch to branch. The bottom of the rain forest is called the understory. The animals that live in the understory like darkness. There, silent snakes curl around hanging vines. Graceful jaguars watch and wait.

And in this steamy environment the great Kapok[1] tree shoots up through the forest and emerges above the canopy.

This is the story of a community of animals that live in one such tree in the rain forest.

---

1 Kapok (*KAY pahk*)

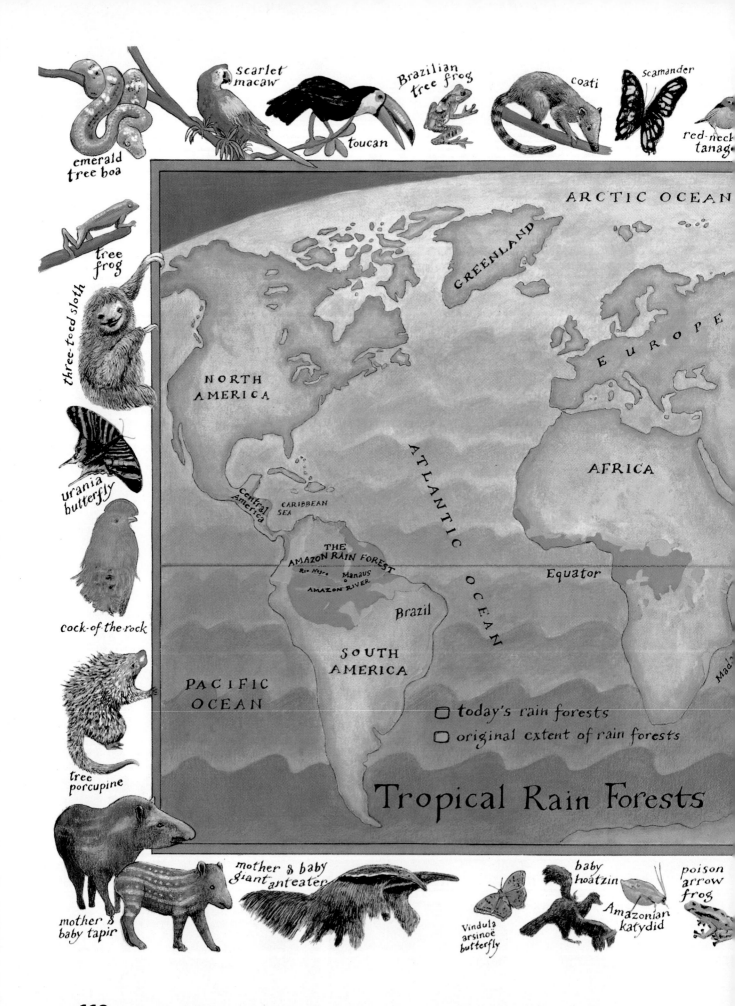

emerald
tree boa

scarlet
macaw

toucan

Brazilian
tree frog

coati

Scamander

red-neck
tanag

tree
frog

three-toed sloth

urania
butterfly

cock-of-the-rock

tree
porcupine

ARCTIC OCEAN

GREENLAND

NORTH
AMERICA

EUROPE

AFRICA

ATLANTIC

Central
America

CARIBBEAN
SEA

THE
AMAZON RAIN FOREST

Rio Negro   Manaus
o
AMAZON RIVER

Brazil

Equator

OCEAN

SOUTH
AMERICA

Mad

PACIFIC
OCEAN

⬭ today's rain forests
⬭ original extent of rain forests

Tropical Rain Forests

mother &
baby tapir

mother & baby
giant anteater

Vindula
arsinoë
butterfly

baby
hoatzin

Amazonian
katydid

poison
arrow
frog

golden
tanager

parrot

squirrel
monkey

jaguar

Anteos
menippe
butterfly

tamandua
-or-
anteater

boa
constrictor

silky anteater

EMERGENTS

Emergents

Emergents

moustached
tamarin

CANOPY

Canopy

woolly
monkey

iguana

ASIA

Japan

PACIFIC
OCEAN

India

Indochina

Philippines

Malaysia

Indonesia

New
Guinea

passion-flower
butterfly

Siproeta
stelenes
butterfly

INDIAN
OCEAN

AUSTRALIA

UNDERSTORY

Middle
Layer

Shrub Layer

kinkajou

Herb
Layer

violet-tailed
sylph

of the World

ANTARCTICA

chestnut-
capped

blue
morpho
butterfly

ocelot

Hamadryas
arinome
butterfly

red-
honey

legged
creeper

papilio
androgeus
butterfly

puffbird

parakeet

119

Two men walked into the rain forest. Moments before, the forest had been alive with the sounds of squawking birds and howling monkeys. Now all was quiet as the creatures watched the two men and wondered why they had come.

The larger man stopped and pointed to a great Kapok tree. Then he left.

The smaller man took the ax he carried and struck the trunk of the tree. Whack! Whack! Whack! The sounds of the blows rang through the forest. The wood of the tree was very hard. Chop! Chop! Chop! The man wiped off the sweat that ran down his face and neck. Whack! Chop! Whack! Chop!

Soon the man grew tired. He sat down to rest at the foot of the great Kapok tree. Before he knew it, the heat and hum of the forest had lulled him to sleep.

A boa constrictor lived in the Kapok tree. He slithered down its trunk to where the man was sleeping. He looked at the gash the ax had made in the tree. Then the huge snake slid very close to the man and hissed in his ear: "Senhor,[2] this tree is a tree of miracles. It is my home, where generations of my ancestors have lived. Do not chop it down."

---

2 senhor (*seen YAWR*) mister

A bee buzzed in the sleeping man's ear: "Senhor, my hive is in this Kapok tree, and I fly from tree to tree and flower to flower collecting pollen. In this way I pollinate the trees and flowers throughout the rain forest. You see, all living things depend on one another."

A troupe of monkeys scampered down from the canopy of the Kapok tree. They chattered to the sleeping man: "Senhor, we have seen the ways of man. You chop down one tree, then come back for another and another. The roots of these great trees will wither and die, and there will be nothing left to hold the earth in place. When the heavy rains come, the soil will be washed away and the forest will become a desert."

A toucan, a macaw, and a cock-of-the-rock flew down from the canopy. "Senhor!" squawked the toucan, "you must not cut down this tree. We have flown over the rain forest and seen what happens once you begin to chop down the trees. Many people settle on the land. They set fires to clear the underbrush, and soon the forest disappears. Where once there was life and beauty only black and smoldering ruins remain."

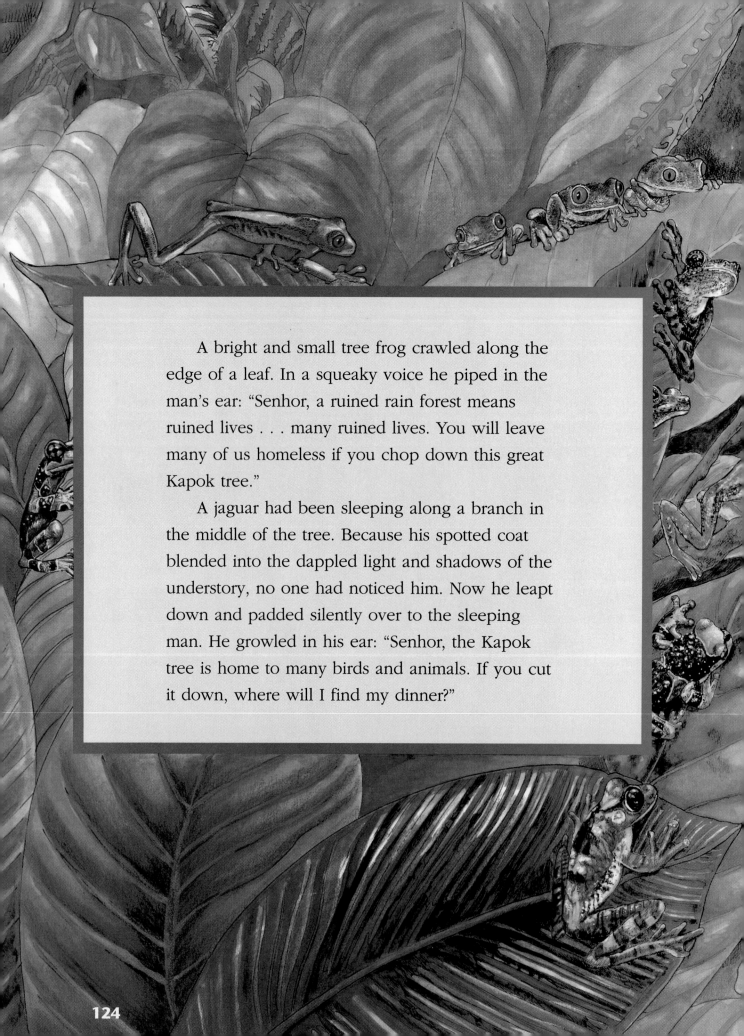

A bright and small tree frog crawled along the edge of a leaf. In a squeaky voice he piped in the man's ear: "Senhor, a ruined rain forest means ruined lives . . . many ruined lives. You will leave many of us homeless if you chop down this great Kapok tree."

A jaguar had been sleeping along a branch in the middle of the tree. Because his spotted coat blended into the dappled light and shadows of the understory, no one had noticed him. Now he leapt down and padded silently over to the sleeping man. He growled in his ear: "Senhor, the Kapok tree is home to many birds and animals. If you cut it down, where will I find my dinner?"

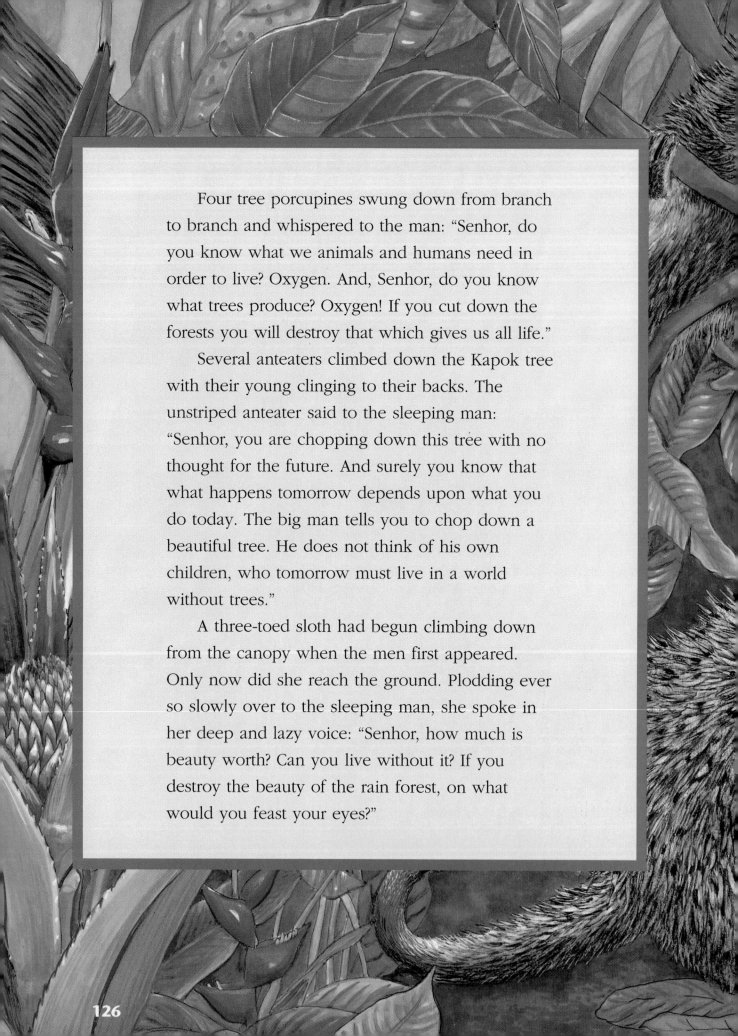

Four tree porcupines swung down from branch to branch and whispered to the man: "Senhor, do you know what we animals and humans need in order to live? Oxygen. And, Senhor, do you know what trees produce? Oxygen! If you cut down the forests you will destroy that which gives us all life."

Several anteaters climbed down the Kapok tree with their young clinging to their backs. The unstriped anteater said to the sleeping man: "Senhor, you are chopping down this tree with no thought for the future. And surely you know that what happens tomorrow depends upon what you do today. The big man tells you to chop down a beautiful tree. He does not think of his own children, who tomorrow must live in a world without trees."

A three-toed sloth had begun climbing down from the canopy when the men first appeared. Only now did she reach the ground. Plodding ever so slowly over to the sleeping man, she spoke in her deep and lazy voice: "Senhor, how much is beauty worth? Can you live without it? If you destroy the beauty of the rain forest, on what would you feast your eyes?"

A child from the Yanomamo[3] tribe who lived in the rain forest knelt over the sleeping man. He murmured in his ear: "Senhor, when you awake, please look upon us all with new eyes."

The man awoke with a start. Before him stood the rain forest child, and all around him, staring, were the creatures who depended upon the great Kapok tree. What wondrous and rare animals they were!

The man looked about and saw the sun streaming through the canopy. Spots of bright light glowed like jewels amidst the dark green forest. Strange and beautiful plants seemed to dangle in the air, suspended from the great Kapok tree.

The man smelled the fragrant perfume of their flowers. He felt the steamy mist rising from the forest floor. But he heard no sound, for the creatures were strangely silent.

---

3 Yanomamo (*yahn oh MAHM oh*) a group of American Indians living in the Amazon rain forest

The man stood and picked up his ax. He
swung back his arm as though to strike
the tree. Suddenly he stopped. He turned and
looked at the animals and the child.

He hesitated. Then he dropped the ax and
walked out of the rain forest.

scarlet
macaw

toucan

parrot

scamander

chestnut-
capped

puffbird

parakeet

blue
morpho
butterfly

Vindula
arsinoë
butterfly

golden
tanager

IN RESPONSE

Dear Diary

Write a diary entry that you think the man who slept in the rain forest might write. Describe his day in the rain forest. Write what you think he learned about himself and the animals that live in the rain forest. Write about the man's new feelings about the forest, the animals, and himself.

Brazilian
tree frog

silky anteater

What Would They Say?

With a partner, role-play a meeting between the two men in "The Great Kapok Tree." How might the man with the ax persuade the other man that cutting down the tree was not right? What reasons will he use to explain why he did not cut down the tree?

red-necked
tanager

poison
arrow
frog

Share the Story

You have been asked to talk about "The Great Kapok Tree" with other people who care about the rain forest. Choose sentences from the story that seem important to you. Write those sentences and explain why you chose them.

Amazonian
katydid

baby
hoatzin

coati

mother & baby
giant anteater

mother &
baby tapir

Lynne Cherry

Before Lynne Cherry wrote "The Great Kapok Tree," she traveled to the Amazon rain forest in Brazil. There she learned about life in the rain forest and gathered ideas for the story. She also sketched rain forest plants and animals. Her trip helped her write and illustrate "The Great Kapok Tree."

Lynne Cherry grew up loving nature. She spent all her free time in the woods. She was so quiet in the woods that animals scampered and fluttered as if she weren't there. She watched and listened to learn about the natural world.

★ **Award-winning Author and Illustrator**

Materials like these helped Ms. Cherry write "The Great Kapok Tree."

Brazil

Lynne Cherry sketches in the Amazon rain forest.

Rain Forest Notes

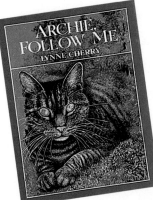

Lynne Cherry relaxes in her plant-filled yard after a long day's work.

Other Books by . . .

Lynne Cherry

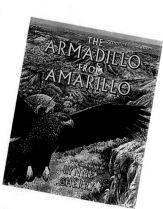

The Armadillo from Amarillo, written and illustrated by Lynne Cherry, Harcourt Brace, 1994

Archie, Follow Me, written and illustrated by Lynne Cherry, Dutton, 1992

El gran capoquero, written and illustrated by Lynne Cherry, Harcourt Brace, 1994

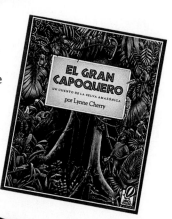

Earthly **Art**

Nature inspires artists in different ways. Some artists create art that looks much like the natural world.

What do you think?

What colors do you see in each painting? Why do you think the artists used these colors? Tell what each painting is about in one sentence.

Painting by Louisa Matthiasdottir (Icelandic), *Sheep in Blue Landscape,* **1991**

Painting by Georgia O'Keeffe (United States), *The Red Hills with Sun* (Red Hills, Lake George), 1927

The Phillips Collection, Washington, D.C.

What do you see?

Some artists create art that shows how they feel when they look at nature. What animals do these art works show? Do these animals look like real animals? Why or why not?

Sculpture by Deborah Butterfield
(United States), *Palma*, 1990

Pastel by Pablo Picasso (Spanish), *Rooster*, 1938

Chi wara headdresses (Bamana culture of Mali), late 1900's

Haiku

by Bashō

A haiku[1] is a three-line poem that has seventeen syllables. Usually the lines of a haiku follow a strict pattern. The first line has five syllables. The second line has seven syllables. The third line has five syllables.

Bashō[2] was a Japanese poet who lived from 1643 to 1694. He made the haiku an important form of poetry. His haiku are among the greatest ever written. The details in these haiku by Bashō create vivid word pictures of nature.

April's air stirs in

Willow-leaves . . . a butterfly

Floats and balances

---

1 **haiku** (*hy KOO*)
2 **Bashō** (*BAH shoh*)

138

The seed of all song
Is the farmer's busy hum
As he plants his rice

An old silent pond . . .
Into the pond a frog jumps,
Splash! silence again

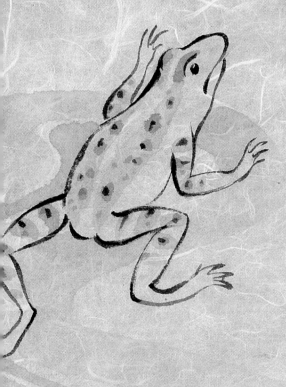

There used to be a building right here on this lot. It was three floors up and down, an empty building nailed up shut for as long as I could remember. My friend Miss Rosa told me Old Man Hammer used to live there—some other neighbors too. But when I asked him about that, he only hollered, "Scram."

Old Man Hammer, hard as nails.

Last year two people from the city came by, dressed in suits and holding papers. They said, "This building is unsafe. It will have to be torn down."

By winter a crane with a wrecking ball was parked outside. Mama gathered everyone to watch from our front window. In three slow blows that building was knocked into a heap of pieces. Then workers took the rubble away in a truck and filled the hole with dirt.

Now this block looks like a big smile with one tooth missing. Old Man Hammer sits on his stoop and shakes his head. "Look at that piece of junk land on a city block," Old Man Hammer says. "Once that building could've been saved. But nobody even tried."

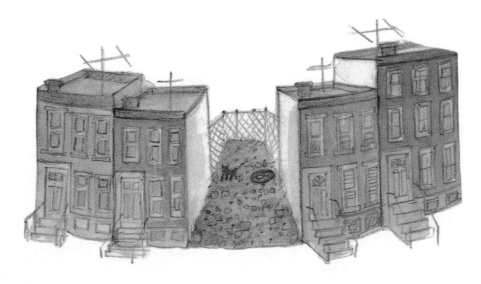

And every day when I pass this lot it makes me sad to see it. Every single day.

Then spring comes, and right on schedule Miss Rosa starts cleaning her coffee cans. Miss Rosa and I keep coffee cans outside our windowsills. Every year we buy two packets of seeds at the hardware store— sometimes marigolds, sometimes zinnias, and one time we tried tomatoes. We go to the park, scoop some dirt, and fill up the cans halfway.

This time Old Man Hammer stops us on the way to the park. "This good for nothin' lot has plenty of dirt right here," he says.

Then all at once I look at Miss Rosa. And she is smiling back at me. "A *lot* of dirt," Miss Rosa says.

"Like one big coffee can," I say.

That's when we decide to do something about this lot.

Quick as a wink I'm digging away, already thinking of gardens and flowers. But Old Man Hammer shakes his finger. "You can't dig more dirt than that. This lot is city property."

Miss Rosa and I go to see Mr. Bennett. He used to work for the city. "I seem to remember a program," he says, "that lets people rent empty lots."

143

That's how Miss Rosa and I form a group of people from our block. We pass around a petition that says: WE WANT TO LEASE THIS LOT. In less than a week we have plenty of names.

"Sign with us?" I ask Old Man Hammer.

"I'm not signin' nothin'," he says. "And nothin' is what's gonna happen."

But something did.

The next week, a bunch of us take a bus to city hall. We walk up the steps to the proper office and hand the woman our list. She checks her files and types some notes and makes some copies. "That will be one dollar, please."

We rent the lot from the city that day. It was just as simple as that.

Saturday morning I'm up with the sun and looking at this lot. My mama looks out too. "Marcy," she says, and hugs me close. "Today I'm helping you and Rosa."

After shopping, Mama empties her grocery bags and folds them flat to carry under her arm. "Come on, Mrs. B.," Mama tells her friend. "We're going to clear this lot."

Then what do you know but my brother comes along. My brother is tall and strong. At first, he scratches his neck and shakes his head just like Old Man Hammer. But Mama smiles and says, "None of that here!" So all day long he piles junk in those bags and carries them to the curb.

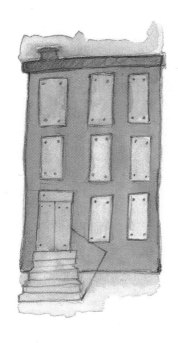

Now, this time of day is early. Neighbors pass by and see what we're doing. Most say, "We want to help too." They have a little time to spare. Then this one calls that one and that one calls another.

"Come on and help," I call to Old Man Hammer.

"I'm not helpin' nobody," he hollers. "You're all wastin' your time."

Sour grapes my mama'd say, and sour grapes is right.

Just before supper, when we are good and hungry, my mama looks around this lot. "Marcy," she says, "you're making something happen here."

Next day the city drops off tools like rakes and brooms, and a Dumpster for trash. Now there's even more neighbors to help. Miss Rosa, my brother, and I say "Good morning" to Old Man Hammer, but Old Man Hammer just waves like he's swatting a fly.

"Why is Old Man Hammer so mean and cranky these days?" my brother asks.

"Maybe he's really sad," I tell him. "Maybe he misses his building."

"That rotten old building?" My brother shrugs. "He should be happy the city tore down that mess."

"Give him time," Miss Rosa says. "Good things take time."

Mr. Bennett brings wood—old slats he's saved— and nails in a cup. "I knew all along I saved them for something," he says. "This wood's good wood."

147

Then Mr. Rocco from two houses down comes, carrying two cans of paint. "I'll never use these," he says. "The color's too bright. But here, this lot could use some brightening up."

Well, anyone can tell with all the excitement that something is going on. And everyone has an idea about what to plant—strawberries, carrots, lettuce, and more. Tulips and daisies, petunias, and more! Sonny turns the dirt over with a snow shovel. Even Leslie's baby tries to dig with a spoon.

For lunch, Miss Rosa brings milk and jelly and bread and spreads a beach towel where the junk is cleared. By the end of the day a fence is built and painted as bright as the sun.

Later, Mama kisses my cheek and closes my bedroom door. By the streetlights I see Old Man Hammer come down his steps to open the gate and walk to the back of this lot. He bends down quick, sprinkling something from his pocket and covering it over with dirt.

In the morning I tell my brother. "Oh, Marcy," he says. "You're dreaming. You're wishing too hard."

But I know what I saw, and I tell my mama, "Old Man Hammer's planted some seeds."

Right after breakfast, I walk to the back of this lot. And there it is—a tiny raised bed of soil. It is neat and tidy, just like the rows we've planted. Now I know for sure that Old Man Hammer planted something. So I pat the soil for good luck and make a little fence to keep the seeds safe.

Every day I go for a look inside our garden lot. Other neighbors stop in too. One day Mrs. Wells comes by. "This is right where my grandmother's bedroom used to be," she says. "That's why I planted my flowers there."

I feel sad when I hear that. With all the digging and planting and weeding and watering, I'd forgotten about the building that had been on this lot. Old Man Hammer had lived there too. I go to the back, where he planted his seeds. I wonder if this was the place where his room used to be.

I look down. Beside my feet, some tiny stems are sprouting. Old Man Hammer's seeds have grown! I run to his stoop. "Come with me!" I beg, tugging at his hand. "You'll want to see."

I walk him past the hollyhocks, the daisies, the peppers, the rows of lettuce. I show him the strawberries that I planted. When Old Man Hammer sees his little garden bed, his sour grapes turn sweet. "Marcy, child." He shakes his head. "This lot was good for nothin'. Now it's nothin' but good," he says.

Soon summertime comes, and this lot really grows. It fills with vegetables, herbs, and flowers. And way in the back, taller than anything else, is a beautiful patch of yellow sunflowers. Old Man Hammer comes every day. He sits in the sun, eats his lunch, and sometimes comes back with supper.

Nobody knows how the sunflowers came—not Leslie, my brother, or Miss Rosa. Not Mr. Bennett, or Sonny, or anyone else. But Old Man Hammer just sits there smiling at me. We know whose flowers they are.

IN RESPONSE

Growing Green

Review what the animals said in "The Great Kapok Tree." Then, think about how hard Marcy and her neighbors worked to create their garden. Why do you think the characters in each story value the forest and the garden so much? Write a list of reasons and share your list with the class.

What's the Plan?

Look through "City Green" to find the steps Marcy and her neighbors took to make their garden. Write a plan for a city garden. List the steps in order and explain how to complete each step.

AUTHOR AND ILLUSTRATOR AT WORK

When DyAnne DiSalvo-Ryan visits New York City, she often sketches  people she sees in the subways. When she lived in New York, Ms. DiSalvo-Ryan used to walk past a neighborhood garden. "City Green" tells the story of that garden.

Ms. DiSalvo-Ryan says, "I make sure to always carry notecards with me. When I have a brilliant idea, I jot it down." She keeps her notecards in a box at home so she can easily find her story ideas.

★ **Award-winning Author and Illustrator**

Another Book by . . .

DyAnne DiSalvo-Ryan

Uncle Willy and the Soup Kitchen, written and illustrated by DyAnne DiSalvo-Ryan, Dutton, 1990

Song

poem and illustration
by Ashley Bryan

Mr. Bryan is best known as a painter and illustrator. This is the first time he has written poems to go with his drawings. He has also published African folk tales and African American spirituals. The poem "Song" comes from a book of Mr. Bryan's poems titled *Sing to the Sun.*

Sing to the sun

It will listen

And warm your words

Your joy will rise

Like the sun

And glow

Within you

Sing to the moon

It will hear

And soothe your cares

Your fears will set

Like the moon

And fade

Within you

I'm Not Afraid to Tell the World How I Feel

from *Tell the World*
by Severn Cullis-Suzuki

A speech given by
twelve-year-old Severn
Cullis-Suzuki at the Earth
Summit in Rio de Janeiro
on June 11, 1992, before
the United Nations
Conference on Environment
and Development

Hello, I'm Severn Suzuki speaking on behalf of ECO, the Environmental Children's Organization. We're a group of twelve- and thirteen-year-olds from Canada trying to make a difference. We raised all the money ourselves to come six thousand miles to tell you adults you *must* change your ways.

Coming up here today, I have no hidden agenda. I am fighting for my future. Losing my future is not like losing an election or a few points on the stock market.

I am here to speak for all future generations. I am here to speak on behalf of the starving children around the world whose cries go unheard. I am here to speak for the countless animals dying across this planet because they have nowhere left to go.

I am afraid to go out in the sun now because of the holes in the ozone. I am afraid to breathe the air because I don't know what chemicals are in it. I used to go fishing in Vancouver with my dad until just a few years ago we found the fish full of cancers. And now we hear about animals and plants becoming extinct every day— vanishing forever.

In my life, I have dreamt of seeing great herds of wild animals, jungles and rainforests full of birds and butterflies, but now I wonder if they will even exist for my children to see. Did you have to worry about these things when you were my age?

All this is happening before our eyes and yet we act as if we have all the time we want and all the solutions. I'm only a child and I don't have all the solutions, but I want you to realize, neither do you!

You don't know how to
fix the holes in our
ozone layer.
You don't know how to
bring salmon back to
a dead stream.
You don't know how to
bring back an animal
now extinct.
And you can't bring back
the forests that once grew
where there is
now a desert.
If you don't know how to
fix it, please stop breaking it!
Here you may be delegates
of your governments,
businesspeople, organizers,
reporters or politicians. But
really you are mothers and
fathers, sisters and brothers,
aunts and uncles. And each
of you is somebody's child.
I'm only a child yet I know
we are all part of a family, five
billion strong—in fact, thirty
million species strong—and
borders and governments will
never change that. I'm only a
child yet I know we are all in
this together and should act as

Young people from around the world attended the Earth Summit. However, Severn was one of only four young people to speak before the official Rio conference.

one single world towards
one single goal. In my
anger I am not blind, and
in my fear I'm not afraid to
tell the world how I feel.

In my country we make
so much waste. We buy and

158

In Canada, we live a privileged life with plenty of food, water and shelter. We have watches, bicycles, computers and television sets—the list could go on for days.

Two days ago here in Brazil, we were shocked when we spent time with some children living on the streets. And this is what one child told us: "I wish I was rich. And if I were, I would give all the street children food, clothes, medicine, shelter and love and affection." If a child on the street who has nothing is willing to share, why are we who have everything still so greedy?

I can't stop thinking that these children are my own age, and that it makes a  tremendous difference where you are born. I could be one of those children living in the *favellas*[1] of Rio, I could be a child starving in Somalia,[2] a victim of war in the Middle East or a beggar in India.

throw away, buy and throw away. And yet northern countries will not share with the needy. Even when we have more than enough, we are afraid to lose some of our wealth, afraid to let go.

---

1 **favellas** (*fah VEHL ahs*) Portuguese for run-down, very poor areas
2 **Somalia** (*soh MAHL yuh*) country in Africa

I'm only a child yet I know how to behave in the world. if all the money spent on *war* You teach us: was spent on ending poverty not to fight with others and finding environmental to work things out answers, what a wonderful to respect others place this Earth would be. to clean up our mess
    At school, even in not to hurt other creatures kindergarten, you teach us to share, not be greedy

Student artists from several different schools contributed to Severn's book, *Tell the World.* This illustration is by Evangelina Maya, age 18.

Then why do you go out and do the things you tell us not to do?

Do not forget why you are attending these conferences, who you are doing this for—we are your own children. You are deciding what kind of world we will grow up in.

Parents should be able to comfort their children by saying, "Everything's going to be all right"; "We're doing the best we can" and "It's not the end of the world." But I don't think you can say that to us anymore. Are we even on your list of priorities?

My dad always says, "You are what you *do,* not what you *say.*"

Severn (*second from left*) with other members of the Environmental Children's Organization who went to the Earth Summit.

Well, what you do makes me cry at night.

You grown ups say you love us. I challenge you, *please,* make your actions reflect your words.

Thank you for listening.

Otter *Emergency*

from *Sea Otter Rescue* text and photographs by Roland Smith

In 1989 a ship named the Exxon Valdez crashed into the rocks in Prince William Sound, Alaska. Millions of gallons of oil leaked from the ship. As the oil moved across the water, fish and animals living in the water were harmed. Rescuers came to the town of Valdez, Alaska, to bring the sea otters back to health.

Sea Otter Rescue
The Aftermath of an Oil Spill
Roland Smith

★ **Award-winning Book**

162

When Sea Otters and Oil Collide

All day long the sea otters had been paying close attention to the rising wind blowing into their isolated, sheltered home in a small bay in Prince William Sound. As the wind grew stronger, their nervousness increased. They knew a storm was coming, but there was no way for them to know what it would bring. By the afternoon many of them had already staked out positions in the kelp bed. Anchoring themselves to the floating tangle with their flippers, they waited patiently as the wind began to howl and the water began to swell and churn. Some of the sea otters sought refuge on land, hauling-out of the icy water onto rocks within a few feet of the shore.

Many sea otters live in a small bay in Prince William Sound.

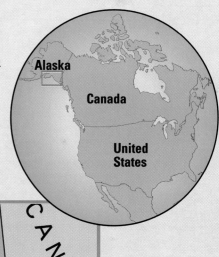

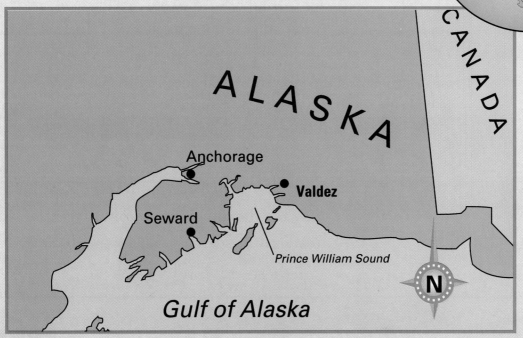

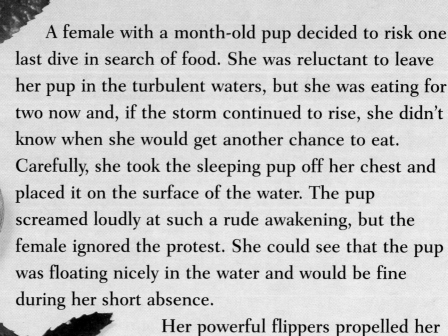

A female with a month-old pup decided to risk one last dive in search of food. She was reluctant to leave her pup in the turbulent waters, but she was eating for two now and, if the storm continued to rise, she didn't know when she would get another chance to eat. Carefully, she took the sleeping pup off her chest and placed it on the surface of the water. The pup screamed loudly at such a rude awakening, but the female ignored the protest. She could see that the pup was floating nicely in the water and would be fine during her short absence.

A mother otter holds a pup on her chest.

Her powerful flippers propelled her deep into the dark silent water in search of food. Nosing her way along the side of a rock outcropping, she found a cluster of large mussels. Using her front paws, she freed two of the mussels, which she then stored in the loose folds of skin under her front legs. Having secured her catch, she pumped her flippers once, then twice, and popped through the surface. In the few seconds that she was under the water the wind seemed to have grown in intensity.

She looked for her pup and, not seeing it right away, she became alarmed. It had started to rain and the bay had become choppy, making it difficult to see very far. In the distance she heard a faint, high-pitched scream.

Quickly, she swam toward the sound. After a few moments she saw her pup bobbing on the rough water.

She picked up her pup and put it on her chest, and immediately began to groom it by licking it all over and blowing air deep into its fur to dry it. When she was satisfied that the pup was dry and comfortable, she allowed the pup to nurse, and only then did she consider her own hunger.

She discovered that in her haste to find her pup, she had dropped one of the mussels. She would have to be satisfied with a partial meal. Cracking the hard shell of the remaining mussel with her teeth, she stripped out the plump orange meat. The storm was now in full force and it was time for her to find a safe spot to ride out the bad weather with her pup.

An otter gets lunch ready by cracking shellfish against a rock.

She swam over to the kelp bed and was lucky to find a reasonably sheltered area that should be safe.

The oil from the *Exxon Valdez*,[1] pushed by the high winds and tides, found its way into the bay.

As the oil made contact with the otters, it immediately stuck to their fur. They tried to get the oil off, but the more they groomed, the deeper the oil worked its way into their fur. In the process of grooming, the sea otters swallowed large quantities of the toxic crude oil and they began to get ill.

As the oil soiled the thick fur, the icy water began to penetrate to the otters' skins. The animals began to get chilled, and lost their ability to stay afloat. The more they groomed, the more energy they burned up, and the colder they became. Some of the otters made their way to shore and hauled-out. Sadly, others, like the mother and her baby, drowned before they were able to reach the shore.

Soon the oil had spread throughout the bay. Some of the otters were badly oiled, others only slightly. But all of them were having a difficult time.

By the next morning several of the sea otters in the group were dead. The others that remained alive were struggling to stay that way.

---

1 **Valdez** (*val DEEZ*)

This otter is covered with oil.

Rescue experts arrive in Valdez twenty-four hours after the oil spill.

The Rescue Begins

Within twenty-four hours after the spill, animal rescue experts from all over the United States began to arrive in Valdez. Valdez is a very small town with only two hotels. Both quickly filled up with people who were trying to clean up the oil and the oiled animals. In order to accommodate the hundreds of people coming to Valdez, Exxon USA (the oil company that owned the supertanker *Exxon Valdez*) paid local residents to open up their homes, so that rescuers and clean-up crews would have places to sleep.

A scientist from Hubb's Sea World Research Laboratory was hired by Exxon to coordinate the sea otter rescue. He recruited veterinarians, zoo biologists, pathologists, toxicologists, plumbers, and carpenters from all over the country to help with the rescue.

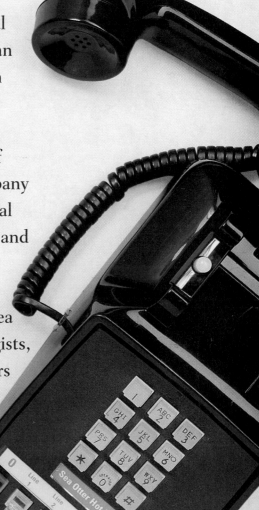

The primary victims of past oil spills had been birds. Because very few sea otters had ever been affected by an oil spill, rescuers did not know exactly how to help the animals. At first they made do with what was available and, as they gained experience, they modified what equipment they had. They built otter washing stations out of plastic barrels cut in half with screens over the tops of them, so that the oil could go down drains as the otters were being washed and rinsed. They constructed holding cages out of "fish totes," which are used by the fishing industry to transport fish to the marketplace. Plumbers piped in hot water so that rescuers could wash the otters in warm water, which helped break down the crude oil and warmed the otters up.

Rescuers pour a sea otter into a fish tote, the pool area where otters are held.

Rescuers from the Otter Rescue Center help an injured sea otter.

The first sea otter rescue center was in a community college building that had been converted into a wildlife rehabilitation center. Most of this building had to be used for the rehabilitation of oiled birds, which left only a couple of rooms available for sea otters. Because of the number of oiled otters coming through the building, it soon became clear that a separate building was needed for the injured sea otters. A large gymnasium in Valdez was rented and converted into an Otter Rescue Center.

Because Valdez was such a small town, and the nearest big city was an eight-hour drive away, getting vital supplies in the quantities that were needed was very difficult. Thousands of pounds of equipment had to be shipped in from large cities in Alaska and the Lower Forty-eight states. Among the equipment were hair driers, combs, crates, handling gloves, nets, medical drugs, rubber boots, rain suits, wire, pipe, wood, towels, veterinary supplies, hoses, nozzles—everything that was needed to set up a facility to save the sea otters.

Many of the rescuers worked twenty-four hours a day and took naps only when they could find chairs to sit in. In order to feed these people, Exxon hired a local restaurant to bring in hot meals.

By the second week of the disaster, the crude oil had spread across 3,000 square miles of Alaska's southern coastal waters. On the surface, the heavy gray goop was weathering into a sticky, tarlike substance the consistency of peanut butter. As the oil spread, pushed by the tides and winds, hundreds of sea otters were being affected.

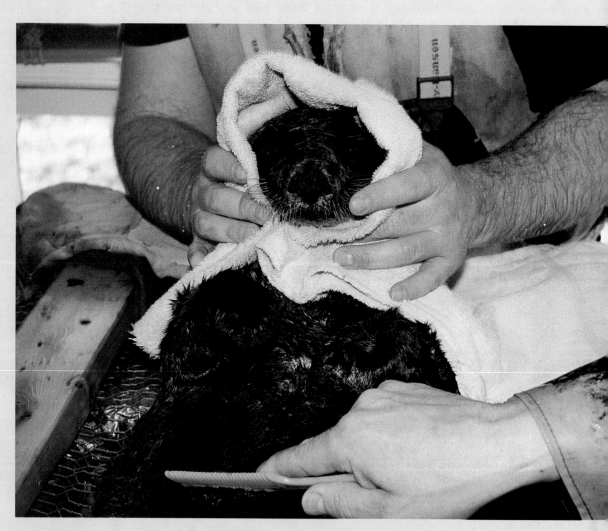

The cleanup crew towel dries an otter, after trying to wash the oil off.

A rescuer at the Seward Otter Rescue Center carries an otter to the next step of recovery.

The Seward Otter Rescue Center

As the oil got farther away from Valdez, it became increasingly more difficult to transport the injured sea otters to the rescue center in time to save them. Because of this, the decision was made to build a second sea otter rescue center in Seward, Alaska, which was closer to where the injured sea otters were being found.

Rescuers used the information they had gained from Valdez to build the Seward facility. Ten buildings were placed near the water. Each building had a separate purpose, and all of the buildings and equipment could be put in storage. If another oil spill occurred in the future, the facility could be moved by barge to the spill and reassembled.

A rescuer prepares a seafood snack for the otters.

It took workers two and a half weeks to build this facility, working twenty-four hours a day. Exxon spent over $2 million to build the Seward Otter Rescue Center, and it cost over a million dollars a month to operate it.

The Seward Otter Rescue Center was staffed with full-time employees who worked twelve-hour shifts. To assist the full-time employees, 200 to 300 volunteers a week were used. Like the Valdez Otter Rescue Center, the Seward facility used professional animal people, veterinarians, pathologists, and toxicologists from all over the United States.

Volunteers arrived daily to work for two or three weeks and, because housing was scarce, some of them had to set up tents along the beach to sleep in.

These volunteers came from all walks of life—housewives, teachers, businessmen, students, lawyers, and artists. Some of the volunteers used their vacations, others simply quit their jobs and came up to Alaska to help save the sea otters.

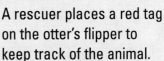

Collecting Sea Otters

The first sea otters to come into the rescue centers were captured by containment crews working the oil booms. Eventually the rescue centers hired local fishermen to help collect the sea otters. These boats were equipped with nets and crates for transporting the injured animals. Sometimes these crews would stay out on the water for several weeks at a time.

A rescuer places a red tag on the otter's flipper to keep track of the animal.

These collection crews had many obstacles to overcome. One problem was working in the oil-infested waters. After a day on the water, many of the crew complained of headaches and nausea. Some of this was caused by the toxic oil fumes rising off the water into the air.

Another problem they encountered was obtaining accurate information about where the oil was. As the oil slick increased in size, strong winds and tides split the slick into hundreds of smaller slicks, which would go into a bay one moment and be gone a few hours later. Therefore, it was difficult for the crews to know where oiled sea otters might be.

There were many ships, planes, and helicopters working on the oil cleanup. As much as possible they tried to stay in touch with the collection boats in order to tell them where the oil might be troubling the sea otters.

Rescuers try to catch an oiled otter.

When an injured sea otter was found by clean-up crews working in the sound, they would radio one of the collection boats. The nearest collection boat would race over and pick the otter up and try to get it to the Otter Rescue Center as quickly as possible.

A sea otter goes ashore.

Many of the otters first affected by the spill were in such bad shape that collectors could literally walk up to them on the beach and put them into crates. But catching the injured otters was not always this easy. It was even sometimes difficult to tell whether an otter was oiled, especially when it was in the water.

A sea otter's security depends on staying in the water where it can maneuver freely. Only as a last resort will it haul-out on land, and, when it does, it stays on the shore so that it can get into the water as soon as it senses danger. Typically, a rescue boat would enter a bay, searching the shore with high-powered binoculars. When a suspected oiled otter was spotted hauled-out on the beach, the collection crew would get into a small inflatable boat and rush the animal, trying to cut off its access to the water. If they succeeded, the crew would jump out of the boat and net the animal. Unfortunately this did not always work. The sea otter would often get into the water before the crew was able to reach it. Since the stress associated with chasing it in the water could be fatal, it had to be let go. Collection crews would note where the "missed" otter was and come back in a day or two to see if they could catch it on the beach again.

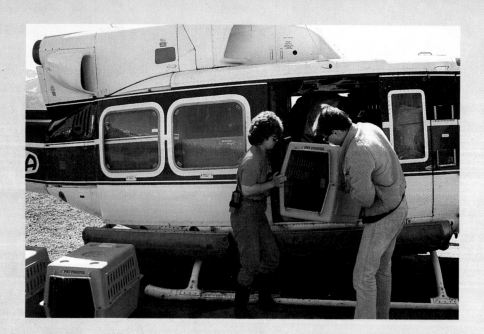

Helicopters are one way the otters were moved to the rescue center.

Collecting sea otters could be very dangerous for the collection crew. Rescuers often fell out of their boats into the frigid waters of the sound. They wore survival suits that helped to keep them floating, but these suits did not keep the cold water out. When someone fell in the water, he or she had to be pulled out right away so as not to get hypothermia like the oiled sea otters.

Sometimes, because of bad weather, collection activities had to be suspended. At times like these, the collection boats would anchor in a sheltered bay and stay there until the storm was over.

Sea otters were sometimes caught as far as a hundred miles away from the Otter Rescue Center. To get the injured otters from the boats to the center, float planes and helicopters would meet the boats at prearranged places and times and fly the otters to the rescue center. But when the weather was bad (as it often was), the aircraft could not fly. When this happened, depending on where the collection boat was, the boat would have to make the long run into the center, which could take all day. This not only wasted valuable time for the injured sea otters, but it also took a badly needed collection boat out of commission until it could drop the otters off and get back to where other otters were being affected by the oil.

Several weeks after the spill, collection crews changed their techniques. Rather than rushing the sea otters when they were hauled-out on the shore, they would set tangle nets in the bays. These are nets that are strung in areas that sea otters are likely to swim through. After setting the nets, collection crews would check them every hour around the clock. When they found an otter in a net, they would untangle it and take it back to the boat. Using this technique they could catch as many as thirty sea otters in a twenty-four-hour period.

Once a sea otter was captured and taken to the center to be treated, it was still a long way from being put back into the wild.

A sea otter wrapped in a bed of kelp sleeps on top of the water.

Rescue Alert

The sea otters needed help. While trying to lick the oil off their fur, the otters swallowed huge amounts of the oil. As the oil seeped through the otter's body, it caused dangerous health problems. Rescue alert!

Rescuers carry an otter to the recovery unit.

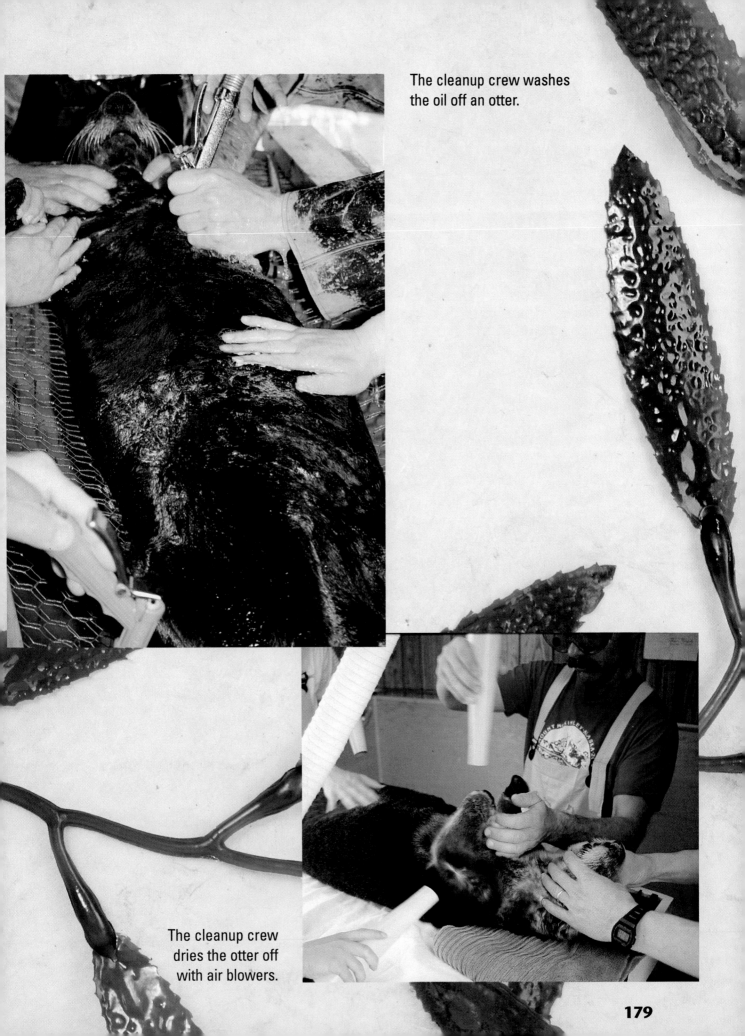

The cleanup crew washes the oil off an otter.

The cleanup crew dries the otter off with air blowers.

179

A rescuer holds and grooms an otter pup until the otter's mom feels better.

Rescuers make the otter's meal of shellfish.

The otters recover as two rescuers watch.

Rescuers release an otter into a big floating pen when the animal feels healthy.

Home Sweet Home

You read about how the animals in the rain forest feel about the kapok tree. Think about the area where "Otter Emergency" took place. How would an otter describe Prince William Sound? Write how the otter would describe its home before and after the oil spill.

How Would You Help?

Imagine that you were in Valdez during the oil spill. Think about the different jobs done by people helping the otters. Pick a job you think you would like to try. Write a few paragraphs describing the job and persuading a partner why you would be good at the job you chose.

Roland Smith was a zookeeper for over twenty years. He joined the otter rescue because he knew so much about caring for animals. He then returned to Alaska alone. On that trip, he took notes and photographs for his book *Sea Otter Rescue*.

Q: Why did you write the book *Sea Otter Rescue*?

A: I was on a boat collecting otters. I realized that our efforts would make an interesting story. I thought people would enjoy reading about the sea otter rescue and would learn important lessons, too.

Q: What effects of the *Exxon Valdez* spill remain today?

A: The water and wildlife have recovered better than people thought they would. There is still oil on some beaches. But most of the oil has sunk into the sand. The oil doesn't actually go away, but it breaks down and changes

★ **Award-winning Author and Photographer**

Another Book by . . .

Roland Smith

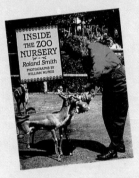

Inside the Zoo Nursery, by Roland Smith, photographs by William Muñoz, Cobblehill Books, 1993

Library Link This story was taken from *Sea Otter Rescue* by Roland Smith. You might enjoy reading the entire book to find out more about the oil spill.

Birdfoot's Grampa

The old man
must have stopped our car
two dozen times to climb out
and gather into his hands
the small toads blinded
by our lights and leaping,
live drops of rain.

The rain was falling,
a mist around his white hair
and I kept saying
you can't save them all
accept it, get back in
we've got places to go.

But, leathery hands full
of wet brown life
knee deep in the summer
roadside grass,
he just smiled and said
they have places to go to
too

    —Joseph Bruchac

Abenaki Traditions

Poet Joseph Bruchac[1] is part Abenaki[2] Indian. Respect for elders and the natural world are Abenaki traditions. In fact, the Abenaki call April "the moon of the frog." In April frogs and toads begin to sing at night, a sure sign of spring.

The poem is based on a real event. One night, Joseph and an older man were driving in the rain. The older man kept stopping the car to move toads off the road. The older man reminded Joseph of how his grandfather used to save animals from the roadside.

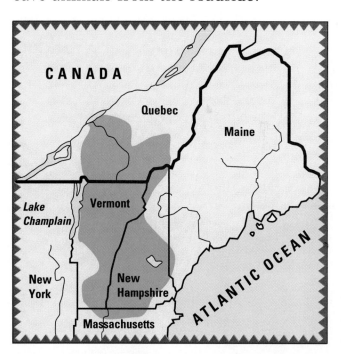

Many Abenaki people live in the northeastern United States and southeastern Canada, in the area shown in green.

---

1 **Joseph Bruchac** (*JOH sehf BROO shac*)
2 **Abenaki** (*ahb uh NAH kee*)

And Now the Good News

from *And Then There Was One*
by Margery Facklam

Alligator

Dolphins

A "doomsday" book lists all the animals in danger of extinction. Its official name is *The Red Data Book*. It's published each year by the International Union for Conservation of Nature and Natural Resources. In a book of so much bad news, can we ever find anything good?

The good news is that some animals get off the list, when they make a comeback. The American alligator was once in danger of extinction because a lot of people thought that alligator skin looked better on shoes and luggage than on the alligator. Then a law was passed in the 1970s to protect the big reptiles from harm. Now there are so many alligators that they are causing problems. They are turning up on golf courses and in private lakes. One huge alligator was found basking in the sun on a runway at the West Palm Beach International Airport. The alligator population is up to a million, and some way must be found for alligators and people to live side by side.

When a large predator like the alligator thrives, dozens of smaller animals thrive with it. Alligators make room for an entire community in their water holes. Fish, turtles, snakes, frogs, and snails settle in. Herons, ibis, egrets, spoonbills, and other birds stay close because they can find food, and so do raccoons, muskrats, wild pigs, and other mammals. As long as the alligator keeps the water hole weeded and open, the whole community lives well.

Elephant

Protecting a large animal is a real bargain because it saves whole ecosystems. When we protect one habitat, we help all the animals that live there. In order to help the African elephant, we must help all the animals of the Serengeti.[1] In that 5,000-square-mile area, there are more than 400 species of birds, 50 kinds of mammals, and tens of thousands of insects and other invertebrates.

Zoos and wildlife sanctuaries are part of the good news. About 90 percent of the mammals and 75 percent of the birds in American zoos were born in captivity. No longer can an expedition go into the jungle and capture a tiger or monkeys. No one is allowed to catch a dolphin in the open ocean for a marine exhibit or research without permission from

---

1 **Serengeti** (*sair ehn GEHT ee*) grasslands in Tanzania, located in Africa

the government. Unfortunately, many dolphins, seals, and sea turtles are trapped illegally in fishing nets that trail for miles behind commercial fishing ships. People are trying to design safer nets that will allow turtles and sea mammals to escape if they are caught. They are also trying out different regulations that would require fishing ships to haul in nets more frequently, which could save large animals caught in them from drowning.

Zoos were once prisons of concrete cages and iron bars. Although some are still prisons, the best zoos display animals in large areas much like the animals' own habitats. Many rare animals have bred and raised their young in zoos, but it's not always easy. Panda babies are rare enough in nature and rarer still in zoos. Only 1,000 pandas live in their native China and Tibet, and only 100 in zoos around the world. Three zoos outside of China—in Mexico, Madrid, and Tokyo[2]— have raised panda cubs. Ling-Ling, a panda at the National Zoo in Washington, D.C., has given birth to several cubs, but none has lived more than a few hours despite careful veterinary care.

Pandas

2 **Tokyo** (*TOH kee yoh*) capital of Japan

For many wildlife experts, the big goal is to breed animals in captivity and return them to their native homes. But that's not as easy as it sounds. You might think that all you'd have to do is open a cage to let an animal know it's free, but that doesn't always work. In Indonesia, workers at one rehabilitation center try to move once-captive orangutans back into the jungle, but many of the animals won't go. The big red apes like to hang around the feeding station, where bananas and other good food are handed out. When workers take them by the hand and lead them into the forests, some orangutans drag their feet like ornery children. A few may stay alone in the forest overnight, but the

Orangutan

Bald eagle

next morning they are back in time for breakfast. Part of the problem is too little forest and too many captured orangutans that need homes in it.

The National Wildlife Refuge System cares for 400 habitats from the Florida Keys to Alaska. They protect green sea turtles and monk seals in Hawaii, whooping cranes in Texas, and trumpeter swans in Montana. They provide safe feeding and resting grounds for the annual migrations of thousands of ducks, geese, and other birds.

Bald eagles have found help in the refuge system, too. When the eagle was chosen as our national symbol in 1782, there were probably 75,000 of the big birds nesting in the U.S. territory. Today there are fewer than 3,000. It wasn't until 1940, when bald eagles were on the edge of extinction, that Congress passed a law to protect them. But even when they were safe from hunters, eagles' eggs were destroyed by DDT because the adult birds had eaten fish contaminated by the pesticide.

Now the wildlife experts take the first clutch of eggs from an eagle's nest and put them in an incubator until they hatch. With her eggs gone, the eagle will lay a second clutch of eggs, which she will raise. When an eagle is found without eggs, or whose chicks have died, the scientists place three-week-old eaglets from an incubator in its nest. The foster parents usually adopt the chicks and raise them as their own.

Sometimes they use a process called *hacking.* Rangers build nests on platforms

Whooping cranes

Rhinoceroses

high atop towers in wilderness areas where there are no eagles. They place eight-week-old eaglets in these nests. At first, humans feed the eaglets, although they are careful to stay out of sight. They use a puppet that looks like an eagle, because they don't want the young eagles to *imprint* on humans. The first moving object a newly hatched baby bird sees is "imprinted" on its brain as its mother. Gradually, the eaglets are fed less and less to encourage them to fly off and hunt their own prey. It's a long, slow process, but it works.

Tiger

The whooping crane is another success story. In 1941, there were only sixteen whooping cranes, but now there are more than 200. They are still on the endangered list, but their numbers are growing.

The Endangered Species Act became law in 1973. It makes it a crime for anyone to sell or transport an endangered species or a product made from the body of an endangered species. That means people can't sell rhinoceros horns or tiger skins. No longer can certain tropical birds be transported or sold or kept as pets. It is illegal for an endangered animal to be "killed, hunted, collected,

Manatee

harassed, harmed, pursued, shot, trapped, wounded, or captured." The law also sets aside some "critical" habitats for some species. That means that no federal government agency can use the habitat of an endangered species. Unfortunately, it does not protect the same area from private projects. For example, where an eagle is nesting, a federal highway or an army base can't be built because it's paid for by our taxes. But someone might be able to build houses or a shopping mall or a factory, unless state or local governments protect the land.

The shy, bashful marine mammal called a manatee is a distant cousin to the elephant, although it looks like a cross between a seal and a baby hippo.

Some grow to be 12 feet long and weigh 3,000 pounds. They used to live a quiet life in Florida's waterways, but there are few left. Now they must compete with hundreds of thousands of small power boats. Someone has said that the manatee is going off the earth for the same reason that television shows go off the air—no sponsor. Who will sponsor the gentle manatee and other animals that cannot speak for themselves?

It's easy to get people interested in saving cuddly animals such as pandas and baby seals, or elegant, dramatic animals such as tigers and snow leopards. But what about a butterfly or a tiny fish called the snail darter? Should those be saved? Does it matter that the last dusky sparrow died in 1989?

We tend to forget that we are the only creatures who can make choices. Instead of adapting to an environment, we can change it. If we're cold, we can put on warm clothes and turn up the heat. Too hot? Just turn on the air conditioner. Want to fly? Just get on an airplane. Run out of food? Buy groceries from anywhere on earth at the supermarket. We can change the rules. We are the animals with imagination and power.

Butterflies

All creatures large and small have the right to live because they share their home planet with us. We can do nothing about the way animals adapt to the changes in the environment, but we *can* do something about how the environment changes. We can keep the earth clean. We can stop polluting and destroying the habitats of other living things. We can learn from the past and begin planning for the future.

IN RESPONSE

Shared Space

Draw a circle and write the word *alligator* in the middle. Around the circle, write the names of animals that share an ecosystem with the alligator. Draw another circle and write *kapok tree* in the middle. What animal names will you write around this circle? Pick one ecosystem. Write how the alligator or the kapok tree is important for the animals around it.

Make a Commercial

Skim "And Now the Good News" to find information about the manatee or another endangered animal. Write a commercial sponsoring the animal you chose. In the commercial, include two ways to help the animal. Perform the commercial for your class.

Margery Facklam has always loved nature and animals. She grew up sharing a bedroom with her older sister and several snakes! In college, Ms. Facklam made money by taking care of a colony of porcupines.

Ms. Facklam says, "Writing is hard work, at least for me, but I can't stay away from it." She wrote her first book, *Whistle for Danger,* when her fifth child was a baby. The book is based on her work at the reptile house of the Buffalo, New York, Zoo.

After writing *Whistle for Danger,* Ms. Facklam was hooked on writing. She worked at a science museum, an aquarium, and a zoo—all to learn more about nature and gather material for new books. Ms. Facklam still writes about what fascinates her most, animals and nature.

★ Award-winning Author

Another Book by . . .

Margery Facklam

What Does the Crow Know? The Mysteries of Animal Intelligence, by Margery Facklam, illustrated by Pamela Johnson, Sierra Club Books, 1994

Library Link "And Now the Good News" was taken from *And Then There Was One* by Margery Facklam. You might enjoy reading the entire book to find out more about endangered species.

Express **Yourself**

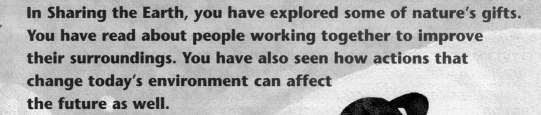

In Sharing the Earth, you have explored some of nature's gifts. You have read about people working together to improve their surroundings. You have also seen how actions that change today's environment can affect the future as well.

Make a Statement

"Surely you know that what happens tomorrow depends upon what you do today," says an anteater in "The Great Kapok Tree." Think about how this statement applies to the actions you have read about in this theme. List some examples of actions that characters took to make the world better tomorrow.

Letter to a Leader

In "Speech at Earth Summit," Severn Cullis-Suzuki tries to persuade world leaders to take better care of the earth. You can also share your opinions through letter writing. Write a letter to your senator or representative to persuade him or her to help protect animals and their habitats. Use information and examples from this theme to support your opinions.

Different Settings

"City Green" takes place in a city, and
"The Great Kapok Tree" takes place in
the rain forest. Write a list of things
you might see, hear, smell, and touch
in each setting. Then write a short
poem that shows how the settings
differ. Use several words from your list
in your poem.

Prove Your Point

Both "The Great Kapok Tree" and "Speech at Earth
Summit" present persuasive arguments for protecting
the environment. Suppose you wanted to persuade a
friend to take care of the earth. Which of the two
works would you give your friend to read? Write a
paragraph explaining your choice.

Make a Booklet

"All creatures large and small have the right to live
because they share their home planet with us."
Margery Facklam wrote this statement in "And Now
the Good News." Draw some of the animals you have
read about in this theme. Under each drawing, write
why you like sharing the earth with this animal. Use
your pictures to make your very own sharing-the-
earth picture book.

The Silver Bookcase

An Adventure in New Zealand
by The Cousteau Society, Simon and Schuster, 1992

Come meet the Maori and explore a land of legends, volcanoes, and amazing plants and animals. This book, filled with stunning color photographs, will guide you through the remarkable world of New Zealand.

One Rainy Night
by Doris Gove, illustrated by Walter Lyon Krudop, Atheneum, 1994

A boy and his mother go looking for snakes, toads, and lizards one rainy night. The creatures are for the nature center where the mother works. Dad doesn't like getting wet, so he drives and takes care of the captured animals.

The Visit of Two Giant Pandas at the San Diego Zoo
by Georgeanne Irvine, Simon and Schuster, 1991

Wonderful photographs help tell the story of Basi and Yuan Yuan, two rare giant pandas from China. Basi and Yuan Yuan visited the United States and helped the two countries work together to save this endangered species.

A Tree Place and Other Poems
by Constance Levy, illustrated by Robert Sabuda, Margaret K. McElderry Books, 1994

This collection of lovely poems about nature reminds us of the little things we don't always take time to notice—an inchworm, the special glow of morning, and the secrets of the forest.

Wetlands
by Downs Matthews, photographs by Dan Guravich, Simon and Schuster, 1994

Filled with colorful photographs, this book takes you on a tour of wetlands and describes the different animals and plants you'll find there.

The Stories We Tell

"Everyone took turns telling tales and listening carefully to one another. . . . And sometimes they invented new stories just for fun."

—Joan Weisman
"The Storyteller"

CONTENTS

The Gift of Storytelling

Good Stories to Tell

Theme Trade Books

Mufaro's Beautiful Daughters
by John Steptoe
Mufaro has two daughters, alike in beauty but not alike in the way they treat others. The king may choose one daughter to be his wife.

A Fairy-tale Life
by Joann Johansen Burch
Hans Christian Andersen is remembered as one of the world's most famous and best-loved storytellers. This is the story of his life.

Turn the story world upside down in *Fractured Fairy Tales.*

Theme Magazine

Pick up a copy of the Theme Magazine Tale Zone. You'll find a story that never ends, letters from your favorite fairy-tale characters, and much, much more.

The Storyteller

written by Joan Weisman
illustrated by David P. Bradley

Why was that lady watching them? Rama looked
up from taking care of her four little brothers and
sisters, who played on the pavement in front of the
apartments. Almost the whole long day—every day—
the old woman sat by her window, watching.

"Oh, Baby Maria, a cigarette butt!" Rama yelled.
"I look away for one minute . . . Let me take that dirty
thing out of your mouth!" Rama wiped
her little sister's mouth. Meanwhile, the
four-year-old twins, Diego and Cody,
tussled and wrestled each other on the
sidewalk. Cody scraped his knee, and
they both began to wail.

Rama called to her other sister for
help, but Reyes was at the corner of
the block, jumping rope with the
neighborhood kids, and didn't hear her.
Reyes was almost eight, only two years
younger than Rama. When they weren't jumping
rope, Reyes and her friends played hopscotch or
raced each other to the corner. Then, every couple of
hours, they sat on the stoop and complained to Rama
that they were bored.

Rama missed Cochiti Pueblo,[1] where there were hundreds of things to do! After school she and her friends played hide-and-seek in the plaza, or they watched the women make pottery and bake bread in the outdoor ovens. Sometimes they acted out the stories that their grandparents told them at night—tales about Coyote the trickster, corn maidens, and the ancestors. "Grandfather," Rama whispered, "when Father is better we will come home again, and you'll tell us stories every night!"

"Rama!" Her mother called from the ground-floor window, interrupting her daydream. "I'll keep an eye on the little ones for a few minutes." She leaned out of the window and stretched out her arms so that Rama could lift Baby Maria up to her.

Rama was surprised her mother found time to watch the children in the middle of the day, in between washing clothes, cooking meals, and cleaning the apartment, and then working nights in the restaurant. Every afternoon she visited Rama's father in the hospital—they now lived in the city so they could be near him while he recovered.

"Rama, I brought a bowl of hot soup to Miss Lottie, the old woman on the third floor. She has been sick." Rama looked up and saw no one at the window. "Miss Lottie wants to talk to you, Rama. Go to her. I'll stay right here."

"Me?" Rama asked. "Why? Did we make too much noise?"

"Why don't you run up there and find out? Remember, I only have a few minutes."

---

1 **Cochiti Pueblo** (*KOH chih tee PWEHB loh*) village in New Mexico

Rama had never been to Miss Lottie's apartment. She stole up the stairs and knocked softly on the old woman's door.

There was no answer.

Rama wondered what she would do if Miss Lottie was very sick. What if she wasn't dressed? What if she was angry? Rama wanted to run for her mother, but she knocked again. Still no answer. Rama turned to run down the stairs. Then a voice stopped her, calling, "Come in, if you want to." Rama wasn't sure she wanted to, but she opened the door and stepped into the doorway.

Miss Lottie was sitting at the kitchen table, staring at a bowl of soup. Her hair was pulled into a loose bun; her blue eyes were watery. She was wrapped in a faded pink robe.

Rama didn't budge from the door.

"What did you want to talk to me about, Miss Lottie?"

"Why, Rama, I just wanted to talk."

Rama tried to think of something to say. She walked a few steps closer to the table. Miss Lottie stared at her with a steady but gentle gaze. Rama's grandfather used to watch her the same way. He would just look and look at her without saying a word, as if he had discovered a new plant on the mesa² and he wanted to learn everything about it. Her grandfather wore his long gray hair in a bun. His eyes were bright and black, but something about Miss Lottie reminded Rama of him.

"I have an idea," Rama said, breaking the silence. "Wait a minute."

---

2 **mesa** (*MAY suh*) high, flat land with steep sides

She rushed out of Miss Lottie's without bothering to shut the door and ran down the steps to her own apartment. Going into the bedroom that she shared with Diego, Cody, and Reyes, Rama sifted through her dresser drawer. She dug under blouses, sweaters, socks, three books, a pencil and tablet, and her blue plastic purse until she found something hard. It was about as big as her mother's shoe, wrapped in layers of white tissue paper.

Rama ran upstairs with the package and into Miss Lottie's kitchen. "I brought you something to keep you company," Rama said.

Miss Lottie carefully unwound the layers of tissue paper to find a pottery doll. It was an old Indian woman who sat with her legs straight out in front of her. Tiny dolls climbed on her arms and chest. Her mouth was wide open.

"Oh, how wonderful. How beautiful!" Miss Lottie exclaimed.

"It's a storyteller doll," Rama said. "In the pueblo we gather around our grandparents just like this. See how the sleepy little ones climb onto her lap?"

"How nice," said Miss Lottie. "How very nice to have all those snugly little children!"

"My grandfather tells us stories about the old days, stories about how Spider-Woman led the first people from the underground world into this one through a hole in the earth called the *sipapu*.[3] He says this is why our worship space, the *kiva*,[4] has a hole in the center of its floor—to remind us of our journey.

---

3 sipapu (*SEE pah poo*) hole where mythical ancestors entered the world
4 kiva (*KEE vuh*) room used for religious purposes

"Some of my favorite stories he tells are about Kokopelli.[5] He plays a flute and brings harmony to the people! Once, Grandfather showed me a picture of Kokopelli that the ancestors made on the rocks. . . ."

Miss Lottie listened to Rama's story. Then she said softly, "Rama, you can't give this away."

"I'd like you to keep it for me, Miss Lottie. The only safe place for it in our apartment is in my dresser drawer." Rama smiled. "If you keep my storyteller doll for me, I'll visit and tell you more of Grandfather's stories."

"That would be a great honor, Rama."

The next day Rama was outside with her sisters and brothers. When she saw Miss Lottie watching from her window, Rama waved to her new friend. And in that split second, Baby Maria grabbed an old candy wrapper from the sidewalk. Rama moaned. She picked up her sister, who howled and wriggled and squirmed to get down. Then Cody pushed Diego down on the sidewalk and sat on his chest. Diego began to cry. Before Rama could scold Cody, he burst out crying even louder than his brother. Just when Rama needed her, Reyes raced down the block with her friends.

Rama was ready to cry, too. Suddenly she looked up to find Miss Lottie standing on the stoop. The little ones hushed for a moment. They all stared at the old woman.

"You were so kind to me, Rama. Now I've come to see if I can help you."

---

5 **Kokopelli** (*koh koh PEHL ee*) mythical figure

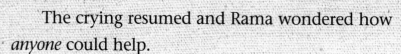

The crying resumed and Rama wondered how *anyone* could help.

"Let me hold Baby Maria, Rama." Miss Lottie sat on the stoop and held out her arms. Baby Maria cried even louder when Rama handed her to Miss Lottie.

"The little mice are creeping, creeping," Miss Lottie said in a soft voice while her fingers crept along Baby Maria's fat arm. "The little mice are eating, eating, eating." And Miss Lottie pretended to eat with her fingers and feed Baby Maria. The crying stopped. "The little mice are sleeping, sleeping." Cody wiped his eyes and nose on his sleeve and climbed up on Miss Lottie's lap. Diego squeezed in next to Cody.

"The big gray cat came walking, walking." Miss Lottie's voice was scary and her fingers were moving slowly in the air. "The little mice go scampering, scampering, scampering." Her hands and fingers moved so wildly the three little children had to hold on tight.

By then Reyes was sitting at Miss Lottie's feet with four of her friends. "Again," they said. "Again!"

Miss Lottie played the finger game three more times, yet the children begged, "Again! Again!"

Rama sat down with them. "Miss Lottie, please tell us about long ago."

"Well, let's see. . . . One day, when I was about as big as Reyes here, I was walking the two miles home from our little one-room schoolhouse when a strong wind came up. It blew me clear across the road and into the ditch. I tried to stand, but that wind blew me right back down. So I crouched there trying to decide what to do, when. . . ."

The little ones snuggled in the old woman's lap and didn't make a sound. Wide-eyed, the older ones sat at

Miss Lottie's feet and listened as she told them how she crawled on her hands and knees along the ditch for half a mile, to her Uncle Ezra's farm. "If Uncle Ezra hadn't been out gathering up the chickens in that ditch, who knows what would have happened."

"What did happen?" asked Reyes.

"Well, I don't remember how I got home. I suppose I stayed with Uncle Ezra and Aunt Belle until the wind calmed down, maybe overnight. Overnights were so much fun there. Uncle Ezra played his fiddle. Aunt Belle and I danced around the room until bedtime. . . ."

On every nice day after that the neighborhood children, Rama, her brothers, sisters, and Miss Lottie spent an hour on the stoop. Everyone took turns telling tales and listening carefully to one another. They shared stories about their favorite vacations, dreams, and memories. They talked about their friends and family, too. And sometimes they invented new stories just for fun.

At the end of summer Miss Lottie invited the children into her apartment to celebrate the recovery of Rama's father, and to say goodbye. Even though Rama and her family would return to Cochiti, the storyteller doll would stay in its place of honor—right in the middle of Miss Lottie's kitchen table.

"She sits where I can always see her," Miss Lottie said. "Thank you, Rama. Thank you very much."

"Now give me Baby Maria. Climb up here Cody, Diego. The rest of you—Rama, Reyes, you others—come close. Did I ever tell you about the time Benny the Bear Cub escaped when the circus came to town? Well, . . ."

Rama smiled because she knew the stories would continue.

IN RESPONSE

Miss Lottie's Diary

Make up a diary for Miss Lottie. Using imaginary dates, write diary entries that tell things Miss Lottie learned about Rama and life at Cochiti Pueblo as they became friends.

Thank-you Card

Design a thank-you card for Miss Lottie. On the inside write what the children in the neighborhood might say they especially liked about telling and listening to stories together.

AUTHOR AT WORK

As a visiting author, Joan Weisman reads her book *The Storyteller* to groups of elementary students. At just

the right moment, she hands a storyteller doll wrapped in tissue to one student for unwrapping. "Even if they've read the book, they're surprised when they unwrap the tissue," she says.

 Award-winning Author

Other Books About . . .

Storytelling

Storm in the Night, Mary Stolz, illustrated by Pat Cummings, Harper & Row, 1988

From Miss Ida's Porch, Sandra Belton, illustrated by Floyd Cooper, Four Winds Press, 1993

Things

by Eloise Greenfield

Award-winning poet Eloise Greenfield has written novels and biographies as well as poetry. Ms. Greenfield has said that her goal in writing is "to give children words to love."

Went to the corner
Walked in the store
Bought me some candy
Ain't got it no more
Ain't got it no more

Went to the beach
Played on the shore
Built me a sandhouse
Ain't got it no more
Ain't got it no more

Went to the kitchen
Lay down on the floor
Made me a poem
Still got it
Still got it

Art Tells

Looking at the same work of art, two people might see different stories.

What do you see?
What stories do you see in the painting and the sculptures on these pages? What is the woman in the painting doing? What was the man doing when he noticed the turtle?

Painting by Romare Bearden (United States), *Early Carolina Morning*, 1978

Sculpture by Francisco Santiago (Mexican), *Old Man*, late 1900's
Sculpture by Martin Santiago (Mexican), *Turtle*, late 1900's
Photograph of sculptures by Vicki Ragan (United States), 1993

Mask used in *Kyōgen* plays (Japanese), 1800's

What do you feel?

This Japanese mask is used in plays to show a character's emotion. What emotion do you think the mask is showing? How can you tell?

Vase by Exekias (Greek), Ajax and Achilles playing a board game, about 540 B.C.

**Painting by Carmen Lomas Garza
(United States), *Sandía/Watermelon*, 1986**

What is happening?

Both the vase and the painting show a scene from
an event. Describe what is happening in the painting
and vase. What details in the picture and the vase
help you tell what is happening?

Sleeping

BY JANE YOLEN

Princess Miserella was a beautiful princess if you counted her eyes and nose and mouth and all the way down to her toes. But inside, where it was hard to see she was the meanest, wickedest, and most worthless princess around.

She liked stepping on dogs. She kicked kittens. She threw pies in the cook's face. And she never—not

Ugly

even once—said thank you or please. And besides, she told lies.

In that very same kingdom, in the middle of the woods, lived a poor orphan named Plain Jane. She certainly was. Her hair was short and turned down. Her nose was long and turned up. And even if they had been the other way 'round, she would not have been a great beauty. But she loved animals, and she was always kind to strange old ladies.

One day Princess Miserella rode out of the palace in a huff. (A huff is not a kind of carriage. It is a kind of temper tantrum. Her usual kind.) She rode and rode and rode, looking beautiful as always, even with her hair in tangles.

She rode right into the middle of the woods and was soon lost. She got off her horse and slapped it sharply for losing the way.

The horse said nothing, but ran right back home. It had known the way back all the time, but it was not about to tell Miserella.

So there was the princess, lost in a dark wood. It made her look even prettier.

Suddenly, Princess Miserella tripped over a little old lady asleep under a tree.

Now little old ladies who sleep under trees deep in a dark wood are almost always fairies in disguise. Miserella guessed who the little old lady was, but she did not care. She kicked the old lady on the bottoms of her feet.

"*Get up and take me home,*" said the princess.

So the old lady got to her feet very slowly—for the bottoms now hurt. She took Miserella by the hand. (She used only her thumb and second finger to hold Miserella's hand. Fairies know quite a bit about *that* kind of princess.)

They walked and walked even deeper into the wood. There they found a little house. It was Plain Jane's house.

It was dreary. The floors sank. The walls stank. The roof leaked even on sunny days. But Jane made the best of it. She planted roses around the door. And little animals and birds made their home with her. (That may be why the floors sank and the walls stank, but no one complained.)

231

"This is not *my* home," said Miserella with a sniff.

"Nor mine," said the fairy.

They walked in without knocking, and there was Jane. "It is mine," she said.

The princess looked at Jane, down and up, up and down. "Take me home," said Miserella, "and as a reward I will make you my maid."

Plain Jane smiled a thin little smile. It did not improve her looks or the princess's mood.

"Some reward," said the fairy to herself. Out loud she said, "If you could take *both* of us home, I could probably squeeze out a wish or two."

"Make it three," said Miserella to the fairy, "and *I'll* get us home."

Plain Jane smiled again. The birds began to sing. "My home is your home," said Jane.

"I like your manners," said the fairy. "And for that good thought, I'll give three wishes to *you*."

Princess Miserella was not pleased. She stamped her foot.

"Do that again," said the fairy, taking a pine wand from her pocket, "and I'll turn your foot to stone."

Just to be mean, Miserella stamped her foot again. It turned to stone.

Plain Jane sighed. "My first wish is that you change her foot back."

The fairy made a face.

"I like your manners, but not your taste," she said to Jane. "Still, a wish is a wish."

The fairy moved the wand. The princess shook her foot. It was no longer made of stone.

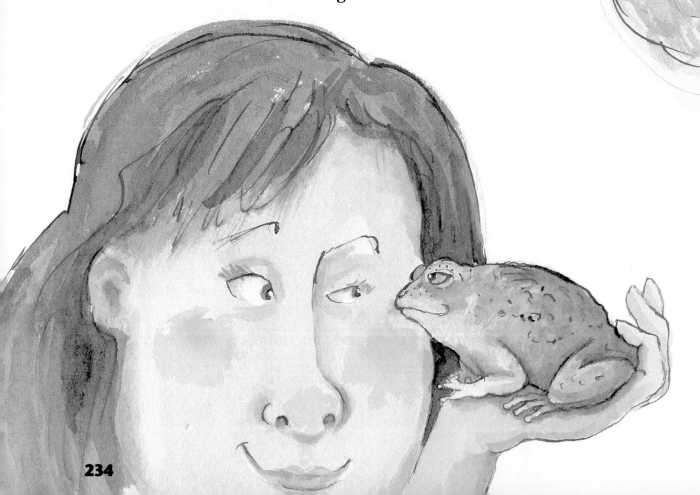

"Guess my foot fell asleep for a moment," said Miserella. She really liked to lie. "Besides," the princess said, "that was a stupid way to waste a wish."

The fairy was angry. "Do not call someone stupid unless you have been properly introduced," she said, "or are a member of the family."

"Stupid, stupid, stupid," said Miserella. She hated to be told what to do.

"Say stupid again," warned the fairy, holding up her wand, "and I will make toads come out of your mouth."

"Stupid!" shouted Miserella. As she said it, a great big toad dropped out of her mouth.

"Cute," said Jane, picking up the toad, "and I *do* like toads, but . . ."

"But?" asked the fairy. Miserella did not open her mouth. Toads were among her least favorite animals.

"But," said Plain Jane, "my second wish is that you get rid of the mouth toads."

"She's lucky it wasn't mouth elephants," mumbled the fairy. She waved the pine wand. Miserella opened her mouth slowly. Nothing came out but her tongue. She pointed it at the fairy. Princess Miserella looked miserable. That made her look beautiful, too.

"I definitely have had enough," she said. "I want to go home." She grabbed Plain Jane's arm.

"Gently, gently," said the old fairy, shaking her head. "If you are not gentle with magic, none of us will go anywhere."

"You can go where you want," said Miserella, "but there is only one place I want to go."

"*To sleep!*" said the fairy, who was now much too mad to remember to be gentle. She waved her wand so hard she hit the wall of Jane's house. The wall broke. The wand broke. The spell broke. And before Jane could make her third wish, all three of them were asleep.

It was one of those famous hundred-year-naps that need a prince and a kiss to end them. So they slept and slept in the cottage in the wood. They slept through three and a half wars, one plague, six new kings, the invention of the sewing machine, and the discovery of a new continent.

The cottage was deep in the woods so very few princes passed by. And none of the ones who did even tried the door.

At the end of one hundred years a prince named Jojo (who was the youngest son of a youngest son and so had no gold or jewels or property to speak of) came into the woods. It began to rain, so he stepped into the cottage over the broken wall.

He saw three women asleep with spiderwebs holding them to the floor. One of them was a beautiful princess. Being the kind of young man who read fairy tales, Jojo knew just what to do. But because he was the youngest son of a youngest son, with no gold or jewels or property to speak of, he had never kissed anyone before, except his mother, which didn't count, and his father, who had a beard.

Jojo thought he should practice before he tried kissing the princess. (He also wondered if she would like marrying a prince with no property or gold or jewels to speak of. Jojo knew with princesses that sort of thing really matters.) So he puckered up his lips and kissed the old fairy on the nose. It was quite pleasant. She smelled slightly of cinnamon.

He moved on to Jane. He puckered up his lips and kissed her on the mouth. It was delightful. She smelled of wild flowers.

He moved on to the beautiful princess.

Just then the fairy and Plain Jane woke up. Prince Jojo's kisses had worked. The fairy picked up the pieces of her wand. Jane looked at the prince and remembered the kiss as if it were a dream.

"I wish he loved me," she said softly to herself.

"Good wish!" said the fairy to herself. She waved the two pieces of wand gently.

The prince looked at Miserella, who was having a bad dream and enjoying it. Even frowning she was beautiful. But Jojo knew that kind of princess. He had three cousins just like her. Pretty on the outside. Ugly within. He remembered the smell of wild flowers and turned back to Jane.

"I love *you*," he said. "What's your name?"

So they lived happily ever after in Jane's cottage. The prince fixed the roof and the wall and built a house next door for the old fairy.

They used the sleeping princess as a conversation piece when friends came to visit. Or sometimes they stood her up (still fast asleep) in the hallway and let her hold coats and hats. But they never let anyone kiss her awake, not even their children, who numbered three.

Moral: Let sleeping princesses
lie or lying princesses sleep,
whichever seems wisest.

IN RESPONSE

Make a Wish

Imagine that you are Plain Jane and the fairy has
given you one more wish. In writing, describe what
you would wish for and explain why. How would this
wish change the story?

Drawing Different Impressions

At first Rama ("The Storyteller") is afraid of Miss Lottie
but soon realizes her first impression was wrong. What if
you were to meet Miserella or Jane? Choose one of
these characters. Draw a picture of how she might seem
at first and how she might seem after you got to know
her. In writing, explain how your impression changed.

Jane Yolen

Jane Yolen prefers to be called a storyteller, not a writer. When asked what makes her a good storyteller, she said, "I have stories in my head all the time. I love stories." "Sleeping Ugly" is Ms. Yolen's favorite story to tell.

Ms. Yolen writes stories just as she reads them—she does not know the ending until she gets there. Discovering what the ending will be is her favorite part of writing. How does she know when she finds the right ending? "When everything comes together, you know it inside. Your whole body knows. Everything just goes 'yes!'"

Ms. Yolen offers three pieces of advice for young writers: read a lot, write everyday, and always believe in yourself.

★ Award-winning Author

Like Plain Jane, Jane Yolen feels at home among the flowers.

Storyteller Jane Yolen has often read her stories for children at schools and museums.

Other Books by . . .

Jane Yolen

Encounter, by Jane Yolen, illustrated by David Shannon, Harcourt Brace Jovanovich, 1992

The Emperor and the Kite, by Jane Yolen, illustrated by Ed Young, World Publishing, 1967

The Emperor and the Kite

by JANE YOLEN   illustrated by ED YOUNG

Ms. Yolen keeps all her ideas for stories in a "big, fat and messy file" until she decides to use them for a story.

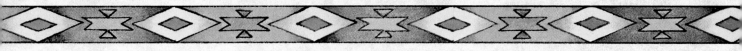

IF YOU SAY SO, CLAUDE

written by Joan Lowery Nixon
illustrated by Lorinda Bryan Cauley

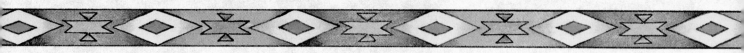

In the spring, after the last of the big snows, Shirley and Claude drove down from the silver-mining towns of the Rocky Mountains. They headed for that great state called Texas.

Claude was as short as he was broad, with a curly gray beard that waggled when he talked. Shirley was as tall as a doorpost, and almost as thin, with hair and skin the color of prairie dust with the sun on it. They drove in a covered wagon pulled by two sway-backed, but good-natured, horses.

"I can't abide those minin' towns any longer, Shirley," Claude said. "All that shootin' and yellin' is too rough a life for me. I've heard there's plenty of peace and quiet to be found in that great state called Texas."

"If you say so, Claude," Shirley said. But she missed the mountains and the forests and the plumb good looks of the Colorado Territory.

They followed a trail that cut south and turned east into upper West Texas, where long canyons dug deep into the hard rock.

"Will you look at that!" Claude cried. He eased the horses and wagon down a trail to the bottom of a narrow, rocky canyon. The purple shadows lay over them, and the silence lay around them.

"Shirley, I do believe this is the peaceful place we've been lookin' for," Claude said.

"I hope not," Shirley said. "I don't really take to this place, Claude. I feel like I'm in a four-sided box."

"Never mind. This land will grow on you, Shirley," Claude said. "For now, why don't you take the rifle and see if you can hunt up some meat for the table. I'll get our sleepin' pallets out of the wagon and tend to the horses."

So Shirley unfolded her long legs and stuck her feet in her boots, hiked up her skirts, and climbed down from the wagon. She took the rifle and edged past the back of the wagon. Right off she spied a fat, lop-eared rabbit sitting on a rock ledge just across the narrow canyon; so she raised the rifle and fired.

Shirley's aim never was very good, so she missed the rabbit; and that old bullet bounced off the rock and back and forth across the canyon, whanging and banging, zinging and zanging, making a terrible racket. Shirley and the rabbit just froze, staring wide-eyed at each other.

Well, Claude took that moment to stick his head out the back of the wagon to see what that awful noise was, and the bullet tore right through the top of his hat, dropping it in the dust at Shirley's feet.

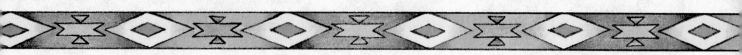

Claude looked across the canyon just in time to
see the rabbit hightail it behind the ledge. He thought
on it for a moment. Then he said, "Shirley, get back in
the wagon. I don't think we want to live in a place
where we can't go out to get meat for the table
without the rabbits shootin' back. We're gonna have to
move on."

Shirley picked up Claude's hat, climbed back into
the wagon, and gave a happy sigh of relief.

"If you say so, Claude," she said.

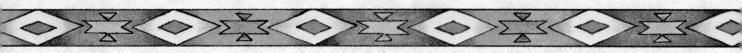

For two days Shirley and Claude headed south, farther down into that great state called Texas. The sun was mean enough to sizzle lizards and curl up the cracks in the dried-out earth, when Claude pulled the sweating, but good-natured, horses to a stop.

He said, "Shirley, I do believe this is the peaceful place we've been lookin' for."

Shirley gazed at the flat landscape that stretched before her gray and bleak, broken only by clumps of scrubby mesquite.[1] And she said, "I hope not, Claude. This land has got the worst case of the uglies I've ever seen."

"Never mind. It'll grow on you, Shirley," Claude said. "For now, why don't you go see what you can find in the way of firewood. I'll get our sleepin' pallets out of the wagon and tend to the horses."

So Shirley unfolded her long legs, stuck her feet in her boots, hiked up her skirts, and climbed down from the wagon. She walked back aways, among the clumps of mesquite. Suddenly she heard an angry rattle. She looked down, and her right boot was planted square on the neck of a mad five-foot diamondback rattler that had stretched out in the shade to take a nap.

Before she could think what to do, she heard another noise. She looked over to her left to see a mean little wild hog. Its beady eyes glared, its sharp

---

1 **mesquite** (*mehs KEET*) thorny bush

tusks quivered, and its small hooves pawed the
ground, getting ready to charge.

Quick as she could, Shirley stooped down,
grabbed the snake careful like around the neck, and,
using it as a whip, flipped its tail at the wild hog. That
tail, rattle and all, wrapped itself tight about the neck
of the hog.

But the hog was coming fast, and all Shirley could
do was hang onto the snake and use all her strength to
twirl the hog clear off his feet and round and around
her head. With a zap she let go. The snake fell to the
ground, done for. But the hog flew off, squealing and
snorting and carrying on something awful.

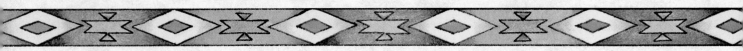

Shirley's aim never was very good, so it happened that just as Claude climbed down from the wagon to see what was making the terrible racket, that hog sailed right past his face, nearly brushing the end of his nose.

Claude watched the hog until he was out of sight, way yonder past a far clump of mesquite, and he thought on it for a moment.

"Shirley," he called, "get back in the wagon. It seems to me a man has a right to set foot outside his wagon without gettin' bad-mouthed by a wild hog who wants the right of way. Especially," he added, "when that hog's in a place no hog ever ought to be. We're gonna have to move on."

Shirley climbed back into the wagon and gave a happy sigh of relief.

"If you say so, Claude," she said.

For the next few days Shirley and Claude headed east in that great state called Texas. The dusty trail rose and took them into land that was strewn with rocks and boulders of all sizes.

Claude pulled the stumbling, but good-natured, horses to a stop and said, "Shirley, I do believe this is the peaceful place we've been lookin' for."

Shirley gazed out at the ridges and rocks and the stubby trees whose roots clung to the patches of soil. And she said, "I hope not, Claude. This land is nothin' but bumpy-lumpy and makes me feel dry enough to spit cotton."

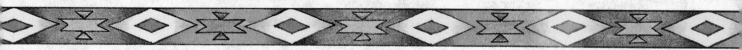

"Never mind. This place will grow on you, Shirley,"
Claude said. "For now, why don't you set things to
right around here. I'll get our sleepin' pallets out of
the wagon and tend to the horses."

So Shirley unfolded her long legs, stuck her feet in
her boots, hiked up her skirts, and climbed down from
the wagon. She strung a line between the rim of the
wagon and a branch of a nearby tree, and on it she
hung out to air Claude's long johns and his other shirt,
and her petticoats and second-best, store-bought dress.

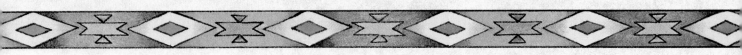

She was just finishing this chore when she heard a crackle of a broken twig. She turned around to see a large, mangy wolf creeping closer and closer. His eyes were narrow slits, his ears were laid back, and he was up to no good.

Shirley grabbed the nearest thing at hand, the frying pan that was hanging on the back of the wagon, and she let fly at the wolf.

Shirley's aim never was very good, so the frying pan hit the clothesline instead, sweeping it down, just as the wolf leaped forward.

Unfortunately for the wolf, he dove right inside the skirt and on up through the bodice of Shirley's second-best, store-bought dress. His head poked out of the sweetheart neckline, and his front paws were pinned so he couldn't use them.

Well, he set up a snarling and a yelping, meanwhile bouncing around on his back legs and making a terrible racket.

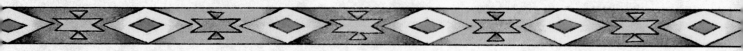

Just as Claude came around the front of the
wagon to see what was going on, that old wolf
bounced and leaped right on past him, carrying on
something awful.

Claude watched the wolf until he disappeared
around a far boulder, then he thought on it for a
moment.

"Shirley," he said, "get back in the wagon. I don't
know why that pointy-nose lady has got her dander up,
but I sure don't want any near neighbors that mean
and noisy. We're gonna have to move on."

Shirley gathered up their things, put them into the
back of the wagon, and climbed up on the seat next to
Claude. She gave a happy sigh of relief and said, "If
you say so, Claude."

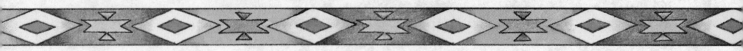

The trail into that great state called Texas curled east and southeast into its heartland. And as it rose it softened into rolling hills, with meadows cupped between. Splashes of blue and gold and red wildflowers dotted the grassy hillsides, and great oaks spread their branches to make deep pools of shade.

Upward they went, until they crested a gentle hill.

Shirley put a hand on Claude's arm and said, "Stop the wagon, Claude."

He pulled the tired, but good-natured, horses to a stop under a stand of oaks, and she said, "Take a look around us. Breathe in that pure air. How's this for a place of peace and quiet?"

"I don't know," Claude said. "Any place that looks this good is bound to get filled up with people afore long. And then we wouldn't remember what peace and quiet were all about."

"Down at the foot of the hill is a stream, probably just jumpin' with fish," Shirley said. "And you can look far enough in both directions goin' and comin' so you could spot a traveler and think on him two days afore he got here."

"I don't know," Claude said again. "Get down from the wagon, Shirley, and see what you can put together

for supper. I'll get our sleeping pallets out of the
wagon and tend to the horses."

Shirley unfolded her long legs, stuck her feet in
her boots, hiked up her skirts, and climbed down from
the wagon. She took out the stew pot and set it on the
ground under an old and gnarled oak tree. Then she
took down the rifle. She was going into the woods to
find some fresh meat for the table.

Suddenly she heard the rustle of small leaves, and
she looked up to see a big bobcat on a branch near
her head. His narrow eyes were gleaming, his lips were
pulled back in a snarl, and his tail was twitching.
Shirley knew he was getting his mind set to spring.

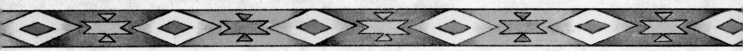

Well, Shirley stared that bobcat square in the eyes and said to him, "I've found my peaceful place, and you're not goin' to spoil it for me." She raised her rifle, aimed it dead center at the bobcat, and pulled the trigger.

Shirley's aim never was very good. The shot hit that old tree branch, snapping it with a crack that flipped the bobcat in an arc right over the wagon. He came down so hard against a boulder that the force knocked it loose, and it rolled down the hill, tearing up the turf.

Behind it came the screeching bobcat, all spraddle-legged, with every pointy claw digging furrows in the soil as he slid down the hill.

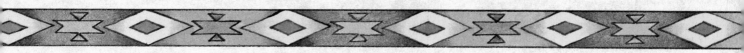

Splat! went the boulder into the stream, knocking two good-sized, unsuspecting trout up on the bank and damming up a nice little pond. The bobcat flew over the stream and ran off so fast that Shirley knew she'd seen the last of him.

Claude came running and said, "Shirley, what was makin' all that racket?"

"Nothin' much," Shirley said. "Just a few things gettin' done around here after a branch fell off that tree."

Claude peered at the tree. "Seems there's something oozin' out of that tree into our stew pot," he said.

"What pure good luck!" Shirley said. "Looks like when that branch broke, it opened a honey cache, Claude. You'll have somethin' good on your biscuits tonight."

She took his arm and pointed him toward the sloping hillside. "Take notice that my vegetable garden's already plowed, and there's two good-sized trout down by the stream that are goin' to be pan-fried for supper."

Claude thought on this a moment. Then he said, "Shirley, get back in the wagon and start pullin' out the stuff we'll need. If you can just learn to do your chores without makin' so much noise, then I think we've found us our place of peace and quiet."

Shirley leaned against the wagon and gave a happy sigh of relief. She looked down at the stream that was sparking with pieces of afternoon sunlight, and she

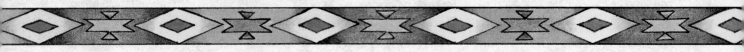

gazed out over the hills and the meadows that were soft and pleasing to the eyes.

She gave Claude the biggest smile he'd ever seen anyone come up with, and she said, "If you say so, Claude."

IN RESPONSE

On the Spot

Draw a picture of each place Shirley and Claude picked for a home. Write a sentence or two beneath each picture, describing the place. Which place would you pick? On the back of the picture showing the place you prefer, explain your choice.

Peaceful Persuasion

Think about how Shirley and Claude acted toward the wild animals they met on their trip. How do they need to change if they are to live at their new home in peace with them? Write a letter to Shirley and Claude, giving reasons why they need to treat the wild animals living around them with respect.

AUTHOR AT WORK

Joan Lowery Nixon gathers materials for her books by jotting down ideas as they occur to her. The ideas may be about places  where she has lived, people she has known, or interesting things she has seen or done. She keeps her ideas in an "idea bank," a pocket file folder. She looks in her file folder to find one idea that is just right for her next book.

★ Award-winning Author

ILLUSTRATOR AT WORK

Lorinda Bryan Cauley uses bright colors to make her pictures inviting. When drawing animals, she gives them bodies that look like those of real animals. Her animals feel and act like human beings.

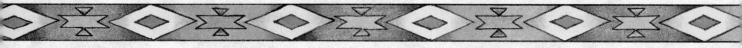

TALL-TALE MAN

by Barbara Winther

Characters

STORYTELLER   **ANTELOPE**

TALL-TALE MAN   **ANANSI,**[1] *the Spiderman*

LEOPARD

BEFORE RISE: **STORYTELLER** *is sitting onstage.*
     STORYTELLER *rises.*

SETTING: *Forest of equatorial Africa. Kola nut tree is*
     near center.

AT RISE: **TALL-TALE MAN** *is sitting under tree, staring up.*

---

1 Anansi (*ahn AHN see*)

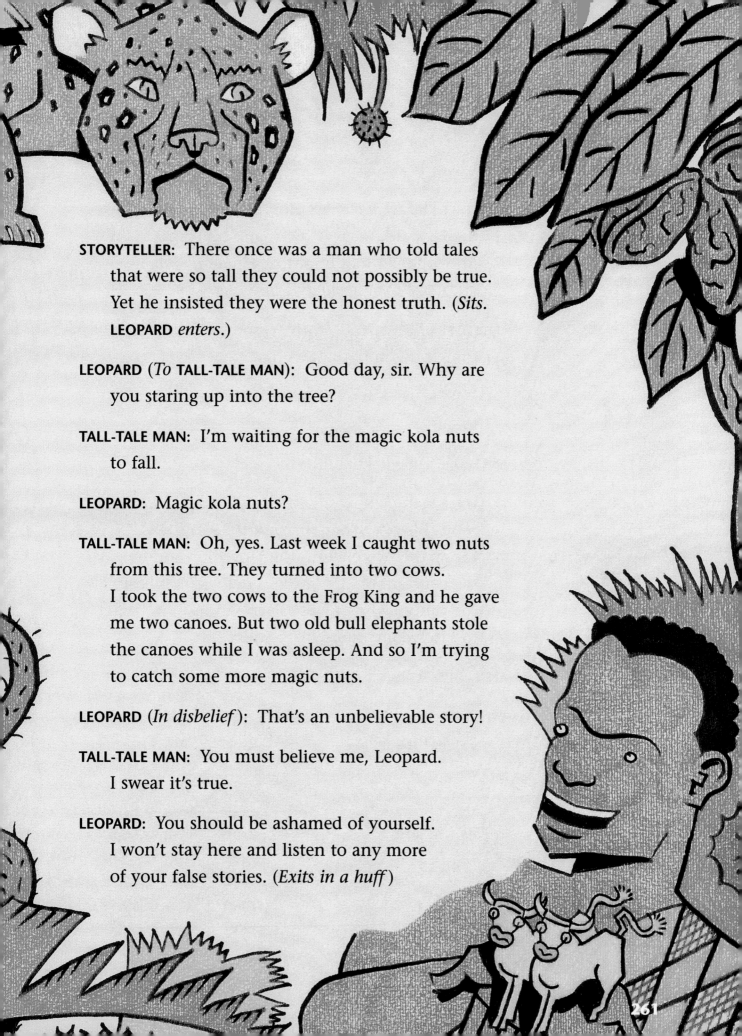

STORYTELLER: There once was a man who told tales that were so tall they could not possibly be true. Yet he insisted they were the honest truth. (*Sits.* **LEOPARD** *enters.*)

LEOPARD (*To* **TALL-TALE MAN**): Good day, sir. Why are you staring up into the tree?

TALL-TALE MAN: I'm waiting for the magic kola nuts to fall.

LEOPARD: Magic kola nuts?

TALL-TALE MAN: Oh, yes. Last week I caught two nuts from this tree. They turned into two cows. I took the two cows to the Frog King and he gave me two canoes. But two old bull elephants stole the canoes while I was asleep. And so I'm trying to catch some more magic nuts.

LEOPARD (*In disbelief*): That's an unbelievable story!

TALL-TALE MAN: You must believe me, Leopard. I swear it's true.

LEOPARD: You should be ashamed of yourself. I won't stay here and listen to any more of your false stories. (*Exits in a huff*)

TALL-TALE MAN (*Laughing*): Ho, ho, ho! I really fooled the Leopard. (*Looks off*) Aha! Here comes Antelope. I'll fool him, too. (*Stares up into tree;* **ANTELOPE** *comes bounding in*)

ANTELOPE (*To* **TALL-TALE MAN**): Good day, sir. Is there something important in that tree?

TALL-TALE MAN: I'm waiting for the magic kola nuts to fall.

ANTELOPE: Magic kola nuts?

TALL-TALE MAN: Oh, yes. Last week I caught two nuts from this tree. They turned into two cows. I took the two cows to the Frog King and he gave me two canoes. But two old bull elephants stole the canoes while I was asleep. And so I'm trying to catch some more magic nuts.

ANTELOPE: What a ridiculous story!

TALL-TALE MAN: You must believe me, Antelope. I swear it's true.

ANTELOPE: Sir, it is bad of you to tell such tall tales and call them true. Someone should teach you a lesson. (*Exits in a huff*)

TALL-TALE MAN (*Laughing*): Ho, ho, ho! I really fooled the Antelope. (*Looks off*) Aha! Here comes Anansi, the Spiderman. I'll fool him, too. (*Stares up into tree*)

ANANSI (*Entering*): Good day, sir. What's so important in the tree?

TALL-TALE MAN: I'm waiting for the magic kola nuts to fall.

ANANSI: Magic kola nuts?

TALL-TALE MAN: Oh, yes. Last week I caught two nuts from this tree. They turned into two cows. I took the two cows to the Frog King and he gave me two canoes. But two old bull elephants stole the canoes while I was asleep. And so I'm trying to catch some more magic nuts.

ANANSI: My, my! Next time hide your canoes so the two bull elephants won't find them.

TALL-TALE MAN (*Startled*): You mean you believe me?

ANANSI: Why, of course. And I'll tell you why. Last week I planted a field of okra. It grew so tall it touched the sky. I made seven hundred pots of soup and fed five villages. But two bull elephants came along and squashed the field with two enormous canoes. Then the Frog King stole the canoes and left two magic kola nuts in their place. I planted the magic kola nuts. And that's how *that* tree got here.

TALL-TALE MAN (*Stunned*): That's an impossible story!

ANANSI: You must believe me, sir. I swear it's true.

TALL-TALE MAN: I won't stay here and listen to any more of your silly tall tales. (*Exits in disgust*)

ANANSI (*To audience*): I have a moral to this tale. He who dishes it out should be able to eat it! Goodbye. (*Starts to exit as curtain closes.* **STORYTELLER** *rises and starts to exit, shaking his rattle, keeping step to beat.*)

STORYTELLER (*Chanting*):
Anansi, the Spiderman,
Clever and sly.
Though nobody fools him,
Many still try.
(*Last two lines of chant are repeated until* **STORYTELLER** *is offstage.*)

THE END

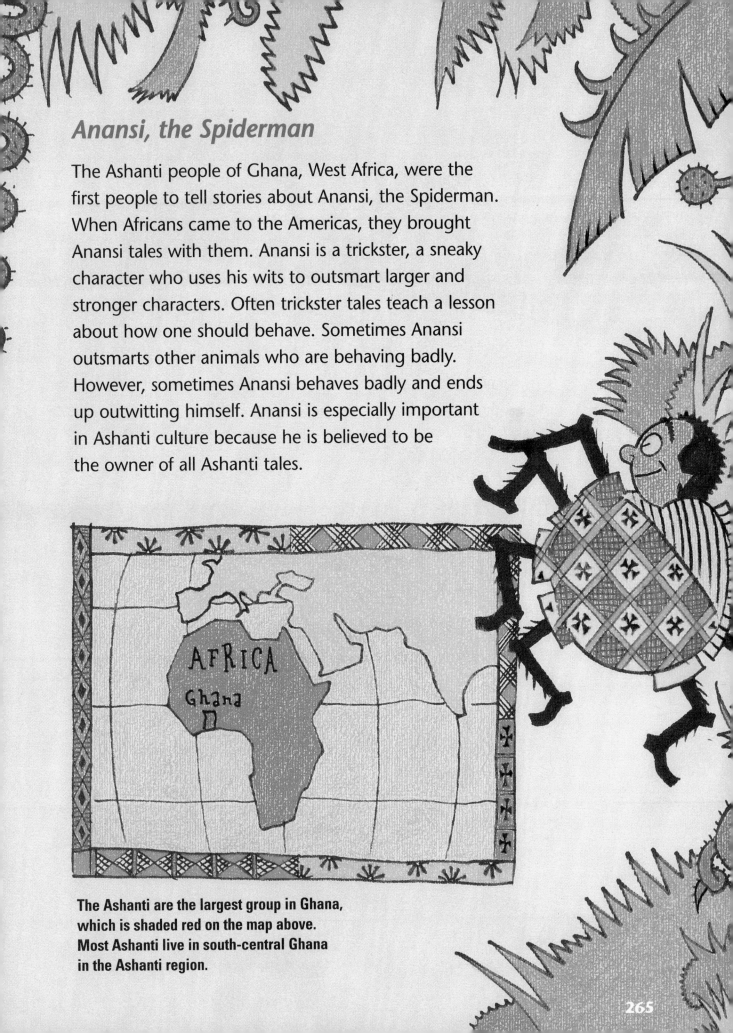

Anansi, the Spiderman

The Ashanti people of Ghana, West Africa, were the first people to tell stories about Anansi, the Spiderman. When Africans came to the Americas, they brought Anansi tales with them. Anansi is a trickster, a sneaky character who uses his wits to outsmart larger and stronger characters. Often trickster tales teach a lesson about how one should behave. Sometimes Anansi outsmarts other animals who are behaving badly. However, sometimes Anansi behaves badly and ends up outwitting himself. Anansi is especially important in Ashanti culture because he is believed to be the owner of all Ashanti tales.

The Ashanti are the largest group in Ghana, which is shaded red on the map above. Most Ashanti live in south-central Ghana in the Ashanti region.

Why Mosquitoes Buzz in People's Ears

Verna Aardema | pictures by
Leo and Diane Dillon

One morning a mosquito saw an iguana drinking at a waterhole. The mosquito said, "Iguana, you will never believe what I saw yesterday."

"Try me," said the iguana.

The mosquito said, "I saw a farmer digging yams that were almost as big as I am."

"What's a mosquito compared to a yam?" snapped the iguana grumpily. "I would rather be deaf than listen to such nonsense!" Then he stuck two sticks in his ears and went off, mek, mek, mek, mek, through the reeds.

The iguana was still grumbling to himself when he happened to pass by a python.

The big snake raised his head and said, "Good morning, Iguana."

The iguana did not answer but lumbered on, bobbing his head, badamin, badamin.

"Now, why won't he speak to me?" said the python to himself. "Iguana must be angry about something. I'm afraid he is plotting some mischief against me!" He began looking for somewhere to hide. The first likely place he found was a rabbit hole, and in it he went, wasawusu, wasawusu, wasawusu.

When the rabbit saw the big snake coming into her burrow, she was terrified. She scurried out through her back way and bounded, krik, krik, krik, across a clearing.

A crow saw the rabbit running for her life. He flew into the forest crying kaa, kaa, kaa! It was his duty to spread the alarm in case of danger.

A monkey heard the crow. He was sure that some dangerous beast was prowling near. He began screeching and leaping kili wili through the trees to help warn the other animals.

As the monkey was crashing through the treetops, he happened to land on a dead limb. It broke and fell on an owl's nest, killing one of the owlets.

Mother Owl was not at home. For though she usually hunted only in the night, this morning she was still out searching for one more tidbit to satisfy her hungry babies. When she returned to the nest, she found one of them dead. Her other children told her that the monkey had killed it. All that day and all that night, she sat in her tree—so sad, so sad, so sad!

Now it was Mother Owl who woke the sun each day so that the dawn could come. But this time, when she should have hooted for the sun, she did not do it.

The night grew longer and longer. The animals of the forest knew it was lasting much too long. They feared that the sun would never come back.

At last King Lion called a meeting of the animals. They came and sat down, pem, pem, pem, around a council fire. Mother Owl did not come, so the antelope was sent to fetch her.

When she arrived, King Lion asked, "Mother Owl, why have you not called the sun? The night has lasted long, long, long, and everyone is worried."

Mother Owl said, "Monkey killed one of my owlets. Because of that, I cannot bear to wake the sun."

The king said to the gathered animals:

"Did you hear?
It was the monkey
who killed the owlet—
and now Mother Owl won't wake the sun
so that the day can come."

Then King Lion called the monkey. He came before him nervously glancing from side to side, rim, rim, rim, rim.

"Monkey," said the king, "why did you kill one of Mother Owl's babies?"

"Oh, King," said the monkey, "it was the crow's fault. He was calling and calling to warn us of danger. And I went leaping through the trees to help. A limb broke under me, and it fell taaa on the owl's nest."

The king said to the council:

"So, it was the crow
  who alarmed the monkey,
  who killed the owlet—
  and now Mother Owl won't wake the sun
  so that the day can come."

Then the king called for the crow. That big bird came flapping up. He said, "King Lion, it was the rabbit's fault! I saw her running for her life in the daytime. Wasn't that reason enough to spread an alarm?"

The king nodded his head and said to the council:
"So, it was the rabbit
who startled the crow,
who alarmed the monkey,
who killed the owlet—
and now Mother Owl won't wake the sun
so that the day can come."

Then King Lion called the rabbit. The timid little creature stood before him, one trembling paw drawn up uncertainly.

"Rabbit," cried the king, "why did you break a law of nature and go running, running, running, in the daytime?"

"Oh, King," said the rabbit, "it was the python's fault. I was in my house minding my own business when that big snake came in and chased me out."

The king said to the council:
"So, it was the python
who scared the rabbit,
who startled the crow,
who alarmed the monkey,
who killed the owlet—
and now Mother Owl won't wake the sun
so that the day can come."

King Lion called the python, who came slithering, wasawusu, wasawusu, past the other animals. "But, King," he cried, "it was the iguana's fault! He wouldn't speak to me. And I thought he was plotting some mischief against me. When I crawled into the rabbit's hole, I was only trying to hide."

The king said to the council:

"So, it was the iguana

who frightened the python,

who scared the rabbit,

who startled the crow,

who alarmed the monkey,

who killed the owlet—

and now Mother Owl won't wake the sun

so that the day can come."

Now the iguana was not at the meeting. For he had not heard the summons.

The antelope was sent to fetch him.

All the animals laughed when they saw the iguana coming, badamin, badamin, with the sticks still stuck in his ears!

King Lion pulled out the sticks, purup, purup. Then he asked, "Iguana, what evil have you been plotting against the python?"

"None! None at all!" cried the iguana. "Python is my friend!"

"Then why wouldn't you say good morning to me?" demanded the snake.

"I didn't hear you, or even see you!" said the iguana. "Mosquito told me such a big lie, I couldn't bear to listen to it. So I put sticks in my ears."

"Nge, nge, nge," laughed the lion. "So that's why you had sticks in your ears!"

"Yes," said the iguana. "It was the mosquito's fault."

King Lion said to the council:

"So, it was the mosquito,

who annoyed the iguana,

who frightened the python,

who scared the rabbit,

who startled the crow,

who alarmed the monkey,

who killed the owlet—

and now Mother Owl won't wake the sun

so that the day can come."

"Punish the mosquito! Punish the mosquito!" cried all the animals.

When Mother Owl heard that, she was satisfied. She turned her head toward the east and hooted: "Hoo! Hooooo! Hooooooo!"

And the sun came up.

Meanwhile the mosquito had listened to it all from a nearby bush. She crept under a curly leaf, semm, and was never found and brought before the council.

But because of this the mosquito has a guilty conscience. To this day she goes about whining in people's ears: "Zeee! Is everyone still angry at me?" When she does that, she gets an honest answer.

KPAO!

AUTHOR AT WORK

As a girl, Verna Aardema was often in trouble for reading instead of doing her chores. She decided to

become a writer after receiving an A on a poem in sixth grade. "That was the first time I can recall being noticed for any good reason," she says.

Now, Ms. Aardema reads books about Africa and often writes stories set on that continent. In one book she found words Africans use to describe animal sounds, like *wasa-wusu* and *kaa, kaa*. She used these sound-words to retell *Why Mosquitoes Buzz in People's Ears*.

★ Award-winning Author

Another Book by . . .

Verna Aardema

Misoso: Once Upon a Time Tales from Africa, retold by Verna Aardema, illustrated by Reynold Ruffins, Alfred A. Knopf, 1994

ILLUSTRATORS AT WORK

Leo and Diane Dillon, a husband-and-wife team, both grew up loving to paint and draw. "I was forever scrawling something," Mr. Dillon remembers, "people, furniture, animals, drums, horns, and flags." Ms. Dillon dreamed of becoming an artist but learned in school that art is only for "fun" or "playtime." Later she found out how many kinds of serious art jobs there are. "It's not always easy or fun," she says, "but it's a rewarding career."

★ Award-winning Illustrators

THE TIGER, the PERSIMMON and the RABBIT'S TAIL

RETOLD BY SUZANNE CROWDER HAN

A long, long time ago, a huge tiger lived deep in the mountains. His roar was so loud that all the other animals would hide when they heard him coming. He was so confident of himself that as he roamed through the forest he would roar out a challenge for any creature to match his strength.

Then one cold winter day, hunger forced him to leave the snow-covered forest in search of food. Stealthily he crept into the yard of a house at the edge of a village and looked around.

He saw a large fat ox in a stall near the gate. The sleeping animal made his mouth water. He crept closer to the stall. Then, just as he was ready to pounce, he heard a baby crying.

"Human babies certainly have an odd way of crying," said the tiger and, being very curious, he crept closer to the house. "He's really loud. How can his mother stand the noise?" he wondered.

"Stop crying! Do you want the tiger to get you?" shouted the mother.

"How did that woman know I was here?" the tiger asked himself and he crept closer to the house.

"Hush! If you don't stop crying, the tiger will get you," said the mother.

But the baby cried even louder, which angered the proud tiger. "That baby isn't afraid of me? I'll show him!" said the tiger, creeping closer to the room.

"Oh! Here's a dried persimmon!" said the mother and the baby stopped crying at once.

"What in the world is a dried persimmon? That bratty baby stopped crying immediately. A dried persimmon must be really scary and strong. Even stronger than me," said the tiger and a chill ran up and down his spine. "I better forget the baby and go eat that ox before that dried persimmon gets me. I should have known better than to come to a house on a day like this. I surely don't want to run into that dried persimmon."

The tiger slinked into the stall and, since he was shaking all over, sat down to calm his nerves. At that moment, however, something touched his back and felt up and down his spine. "Oh, no!" he said to himself. "It's the dried persimmon. It's got me. I'm going to die for sure."

"What a nice, thick coat. And so soft," said the man who had sneaked into the stall to steal the ox. "I'll get a lot of money for this calf!" The thief put a rope around the tiger's neck and led him out of the stall.

"Oh my. What can I do? This is without a doubt that dried persimmon," moaned the tiger to himself. "Oh what can I do? I can't roar. I can't run. I can only follow it. Oh this is the end of me."

The thief was very happy to have in tow what he thought was a very fine calf that he could sell for a lot

of money. Thinking he should get away from the area as fast as possible, he decided to ride the calf and thus jumped onto the tiger's back.

"That's strange," said the thief, "this doesn't feel like any calf I've been on before." He began to feel the tiger's body with his hands. "Oh my god. This isn't a calf. It's a huge tiger," he cried. "What can I do? What can I do?"

The thief was so frightened to discover he was riding a tiger, he nearly fell off. "Oh, I have to hold on," he said, grasping the tiger tighter. "If I fall off, that will be the end of me for sure. He'll gobble me up before I even hit the ground," he said, squeezing the tiger with his legs. "Just calm down," he told himself, "and try to think of how to get away."

"I'm going to die. I'm going to die," moaned the tiger as the thief tightened his hold on him. "What rotten luck to die at the hands of a dried persimmon!

I must try to get him off my back. That's the only thing
I can do," he said and he began to shake his body.
Then he tried jumping and bucking. Over and over he
shook and jumped and bucked as he ran but the thief
held on tight.

After a while they came to a grove of trees. When
the tiger ran under a large one, the thief grabbed hold
of a branch, letting the tiger run out from under him,
and quickly climbed through a hole in the tree trunk
and hid inside.

The tiger knew immediately that the dried
persimmon was off his back but he didn't even think
about trying to eat it. He just kept running as fast as
he could deeper into the mountain. Finally he stopped
and let out a sigh of relief. "Oh, I can't believe I'm
alive. I just knew that dried persimmon was going to

kill me." He was so happy to be alive, he rolled over and over on the ground, smiling all the while.

"Oh Mr. Tiger," called a rabbit which had been awakened by the tiger rolling around on the ground, "why are you so happy? How can you be so happy in the middle of the night?"

"I almost died today," replied the tiger, "so I'm happy to be alive."

"What's that?" asked the rabbit, hopping closer to the tiger. "You almost died?"

"That's right," explained the tiger. A horrible dried persimmon caught me. I've just this moment escaped from it."

"What in the world is a dried persimmon?" asked the rabbit.

"You fool! You don't know what a dried persimmon is?" laughed the tiger. "Why it is the scariest, strongest thing in the world. Just thinking about it gives me chills."

"Well what in the world does it look like?" asked the rabbit.

"I don't know," said the tiger, "I was so scared I really didn't get a good look at it."

"Well where is it now?" asked the rabbit.

"I think it must be up in a tree," said the tiger.

"Where is the tree?" asked the rabbit. "I think I'll go have a look at that dried persimmon."

"What? Are you crazy? As weak as you are, it will devour you right away," said the tiger.

"If it looks like it is going to grab me, I'll run away. After all, there's no one faster than me," laughed the rabbit.

The tiger told the rabbit the directions to the tree. "I'm warning you," he said as the rabbit hopped away, "that dried persimmon is a scary, horrible thing. Be careful."

At last the rabbit came to the tree. He looked all around the tree and up in the branches but he did not see any thing that looked scary. He looked again. Then he looked in the hole in the trunk and saw a man who was pale and shaking all over.

The rabbit laughed all the way back to where the tiger was waiting. He explained what he found, but the tiger wouldn't believe him.

"I'll go back to the tree and prevent him from leaving and you come see for yourself," said the rabbit and he left.

The rabbit went back to the tree and stuck his rump in the hole in the tree trunk to wait for the tiger to come.

"Come on, Tiger," called the rabbit when he saw the tiger slowly approaching. "There's nothing to worry about. I have the hole plugged up."

When he heard this, the thief decided he must do something to keep the tiger from coming in the hole. He took some strong string from his pocket and tied it to the rabbit's tail. Then he pulled it hard to keep the rabbit from running away.

The rabbit shrieked because of the pain and the tiger took off running. "See I told you not to mess with that dried persimmon. Now the horrible thing has you," yelled the tiger.

The rabbit struggled with all his strength to get away. The harder he tried to run, the harder the thief pulled on the string. The rabbit finally got away but not with his tail—that was left dangling from the thief's string. And that is why to this day the rabbit has a stumpy tail.

Fearing the Worst

Many characters in these two "why tales" act out of fear.
Pick one character who is afraid of something. Draw
what the character imagines might happen. On the
picture, write what the character does to escape what is
frightening. Then write what you would do.

Why Tell Tales?

Miss Lottie in "The Storyteller" tells stories to help
Rama with the children. The monkey in "Why
Mosquitoes Buzz in People's Ears" tells a story to the
lion. Who has a better reason for telling a story, Miss
Lottie or the monkey? Write why you think so.

A U T H O R   A T   W O R K

Suzanne Crowder
Han was introduced
to Korean folk tales
when she worked
as a member of the
United States Peace
Corps in Korea.
She was a volunteer trying to help
the people of a developing nation.
When Han arrived in Korea, she
could not speak the country's
language and knew little of its
culture. A friend at work helped
make learning the language fun by
telling her Korean folk tales during
coffee breaks. The author enjoyed
these tales so much she developed
a deep interest in Korean culture,
including its literature and art.

Another Book by . . .

Suzanne Crowder Han

The Rabbit's Judgment,
by Suzanne Crowder Han,
illustrated by Yumi Heo,
Henry Holt, 1994

Express **Yourself**

In The Stories We Tell, you've met storytellers and learned the kinds of stories people tell. Stories can make us laugh, teach us a lesson, or give us information about our heritage. Good stories help us learn about ourselves, other people, and the ways of the world around us.

Sketch and Tell

The events of a story make up its plot. With a partner, select four important events from "If You Say So, Claude" or "Sleeping Ugly." Draw a picture to illustrate each event. Then, with your partner, use your drawings to retell the story to another pair of students. Why did you choose these events? How would the plot change if the stories were missing one of these events?

The Story Behind Stories

People tell stories for many reasons—to entertain others, to teach lessons, to pass on heritage, or to answer difficult questions. For instance, "The Storyteller" teaches the reader about Pueblo Indian storytelling traditions. Choose another story from this theme and give three reasons why the writer may have written the story. In writing, explain your reasons, using examples from the stories. Then share your ideas with a classmate.

Story Award Ceremony

Good stories have interesting characters, settings, and plots. With a group of classmates, make up a list of Students' Choice Awards, such as Best Character, Best Setting, and Most Humorous Story, or Best Story. Then decide which story or character from the theme should receive each award. Read aloud from the stories to justify your choices.

Remember Real People

In "The Storyteller," Miss Lottie reminds Rama of her grandfather. Make a list of characters from the stories in this theme who remind you of people you know. Choose one character and write a paragraph describing him or her. Then explain whom the character reminds you of and why.

Making Masks

Stories can make you smile, cry, or think. For instance, "Sleeping Ugly" may have made you laugh or feel sorry for the mean princess. Select another story from this theme. Make a paper mask, like the Kȳogen mask (Fine Art Portfolio), that portrays the emotion you feel when you think about that story.

The Silver Bookcase

The Tales of Olga da Polga
by Michael Bond, illustrated by Hans Helweg, Macmillan, 1971

Olga da Polga is no ordinary guinea pig. Olga tells tall tales and dreams of having adventures. Her dreams begin to come true when she is purchased from the pet shop by the Sawdust People.

Doctor Coyote: A Native American Aesop's Fables
retold by John Bierhorst, illustrated by Wendy Watson, Macmillan, 1987

When the mischievous Coyote travels the world trying to trick others, he learns many things along the way. This collection of stories is an Aztec version of Aesop's famous fables.

Where the Flame Trees Bloom
by Alma Flor Ada, illustrated by Antonio Martorell, Atheneum, 1994

Alma Flor Ada grew up on a hacienda in Cuba surrounded by a large, loving family and beloved friends. You will enjoy reading these moving stories about her childhood.

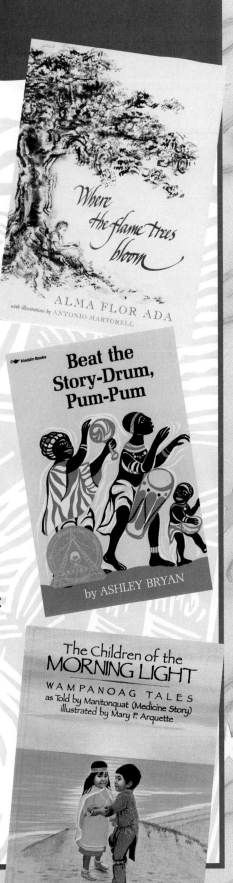

Beat the Story-Drum, Pum-Pum
retold and illustrated by Ashley Bryan, Atheneum, 1980

These five stories, based on traditional African folk tales, feature clever and foolish people and animals. The stories are as fun to read as they are to tell.

The Children of the Morning Light
retold by Manitonquat, illustrated by Mary F. Arquette, Macmillan, 1994

The Native American tales in this delightful collection are told by an elder of the Wampanoag tribe. The collection includes stories about how the world came to be, the meaning of porpoises and dolphins, and a special story about children.

Creative Solutions

"There must be a
way, but how?"

—Wayne Grover
"Underwater Rescue"

Creative Solutions

CONTENTS

Real or Imagined?

Imagination at Work!

Theme Trade Books

Looking for Atlantis
by Colin Thompson

A young boy searches through his grandfather's wooden chest and finds many treasures. The one treasure he cannot find is Atlantis. His grandfather promises that if the boy learns how to look, he will find Atlantis.

Jackson Jones and the Puddle of Thorns
by Mary Quattlebaum

Jackson Jones decides he can make money by growing flowers in his new garden plot. He quickly realizes that this business is harder than he expected.

Theme Magazine

How did earmuffs come to be? How might you use painting to express things you are unable to say? Read about these and other creative solutions in the Theme Magazine *Aha! Zone.*

The Chicken-Coop Monster

by Patricia C. McKissack

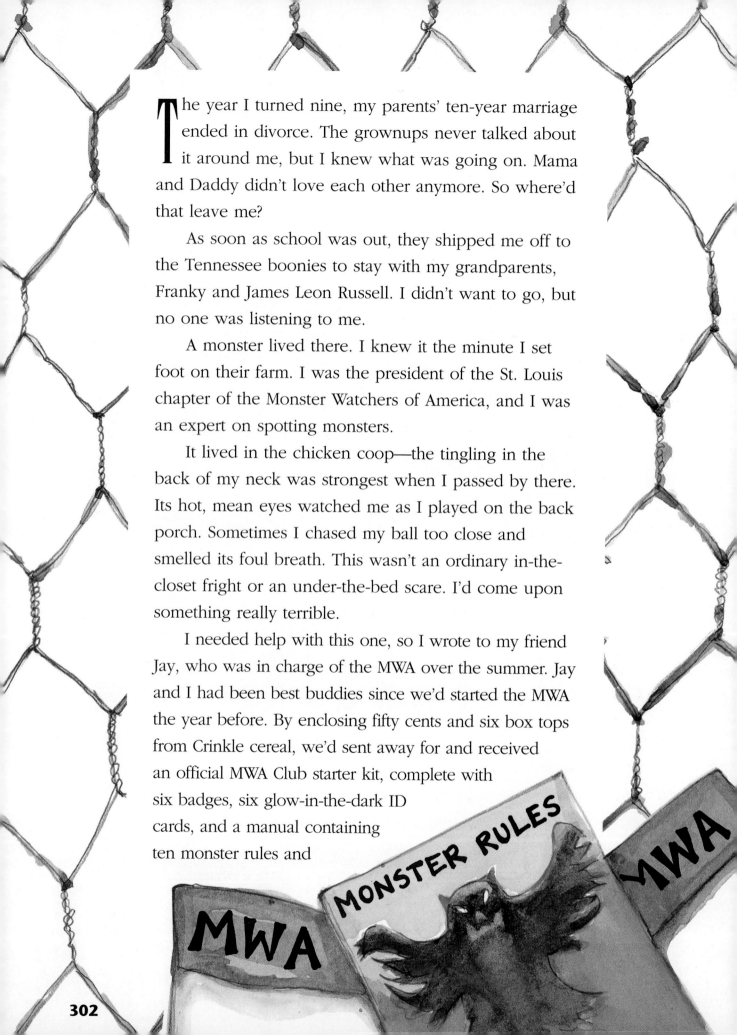

The year I turned nine, my parents' ten-year marriage ended in divorce. The grownups never talked about it around me, but I knew what was going on. Mama and Daddy didn't love each other anymore. So where'd that leave me?

As soon as school was out, they shipped me off to the Tennessee boonies to stay with my grandparents, Franky and James Leon Russell. I didn't want to go, but no one was listening to me.

A monster lived there. I knew it the minute I set foot on their farm. I was the president of the St. Louis chapter of the Monster Watchers of America, and I was an expert on spotting monsters.

It lived in the chicken coop—the tingling in the back of my neck was strongest when I passed by there. Its hot, mean eyes watched me as I played on the back porch. Sometimes I chased my ball too close and smelled its foul breath. This wasn't an ordinary in-the-closet fright or an under-the-bed scare. I'd come upon something really terrible.

I needed help with this one, so I wrote to my friend Jay, who was in charge of the MWA over the summer. Jay and I had been best buddies since we'd started the MWA the year before. By enclosing fifty cents and six box tops from Crinkle cereal, we'd sent away for and received an official MWA Club starter kit, complete with six badges, six glow-in-the-dark ID cards, and a manual containing ten monster rules and

MONSTER RULES

MWA

MWA

everything else we needed to know about creepy stuff.
We'd invited Nora, Jeff, Latisha, and Alandro to join us.

Writing to Jay made me feel better. Meanwhile, I
had to be careful not to break any monster rules,
because that would make the thing stronger and bolder.

One evening Ma Franky called me to the kitchen.
"Missy, I forgot to throw the latch on the chicken coop.
Go lock it for me, please."

The sun had set, but there was a little light left in
the sky. The backyard was already engulfed by a
blanket of darkness, but I could see the silhouette of
the old chicken shack against the sky.

I stood on the back porch, a statue of fear. This is
what the monster had been waiting for. I heard the
whisper of its tail swishing in the straw.

"Melissa?" My own name startled me. "Why haven't you done what I asked you to do?" Ma Franky's voice quavered with impatience.

She was asking me to break monster rule number five: *Get in the house before dark and don't go out by yourself.*

"There's a monster in your chicken coop," I blurted out. "So I'm not going out there."

Of course Ma Franky had other ideas. "Girl," she said, "if you don't stop this foolishness!" She gave me a little push. "Go on, now. Go close the door, or something will get in the coop and scare my setting hens."

Her hens? What about me? "I hate to tell you this, Ma Franky, but something's in the chicken coop already. That's why I'm not going out there."

"Yes you are, this very minute."

Obviously this monster had fourth-level power, because it'd put a spell on Ma Franky. Why else would she fall for the oldest trick in the book? *Monsters make helpers out of unsuspecting victims.*

"But—" I started to say.

"No buts!" And the next thing I knew, my own grandmother had me by the hand and was pulling me toward the chicken coop. "I want to show you there's nothing out here."

I looked into her eyes. "No!" I screamed. "Don't you see? It's made you a helper." I jerked away from Ma Franky and ran into the house. Even though I was

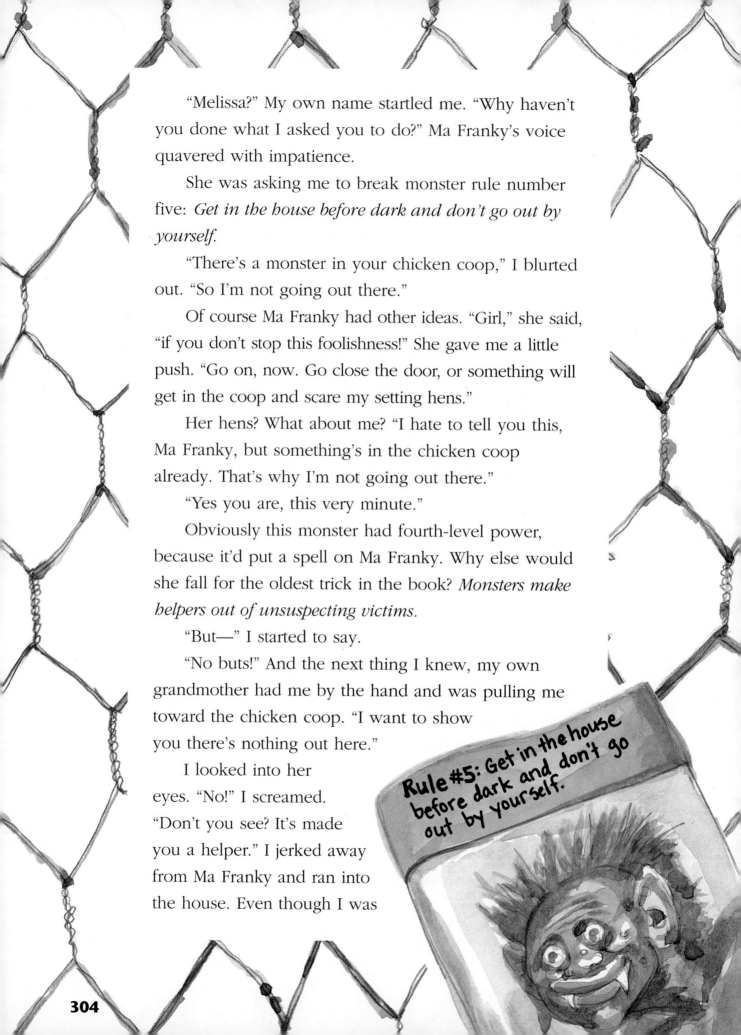

Rule #5: Get in the house before dark and don't go out by yourself.

breaking monster rule three—*Never let a monster see you crying*—I couldn't stop the tears.

Then I felt big, strong hands wiping my face with a cool washcloth. "Oh, sweets," Daddy James whispered softly. "There's nothing round here to fear." His eyes smiled. The monster spell hadn't gotten to him. "No need to fret. I closed the door for you."

Dark thoughts flee in morning light. But the old wooden coop was surrounded by permanent shadows, a sure sign that it was occupied by a hateful thing. I had to be very careful. It would do anything to lure me into its evil hole.

"Bring me my clothespins off the porch," Ma Franky called.

Just as I passed the coop the door creaked open slowly. Sunlight pushed away the darkness just long enough for me to see something large and shapeless. But the monster leaped back into the shadows before I got a really good look at it. I must have screamed, 'cause Ma Franky came running.

"What is it? What is it?"

"I saw the monster. It pushed open the door."

Ma Franky said nothing but walked purposefully into the coop. I wouldn't look, *couldn't* look as she disappeared behind the darkness. I never expected to see her again. But within a few seconds out she came holding a tiny little chick.

She gently transferred it from her hands to mine. "But that isn't the monster," I cried.

"I know. There isn't one. Period!"

Poor Ma Franky. She really believed that, I'm sure. "Won't you come in and look around?" she asked. "Come see where the chickens set on their eggs and hatch little chicks like this one."

It was another monster trick, and I wasn't going for it. "No! I'll never go inside!"

Ma Franky sighed and shook her head. "Whenever you're ready," she said, and went back to hanging out her wash. My back was turned, but I could feel the creature laughing at me.

During the week, separate letters came from Mama and Daddy. I wrote them back right away—Mama's went to our old house, Daddy's to a new address. Mama wanted to know all about my new friends. Daddy was happy I could swim in deep water and had caught a fish. But I still hadn't heard from Jay, so I wrote to him again.

First I told him about my new pet chick, Tissy, and how she followed me everywhere, answering my voice and eating the feed I threw out to her. Then I told him about the creature. "I feel it's stronger now, because I've broken a couple of monster rules. It's a tricky one, but I'm watching out for myself. Write soon. Missy."

Following rule nine, I didn't go near the thing's lair. In fact I didn't even play in the backyard. But late one afternoon I missed Tissy. I felt she was in danger. Sure enough, the chick was out back, heading straight for the coop. And the door was open!

Tissy belonged to me. The monster knew it. Monster rule six clearly stated: *Watch out for those*

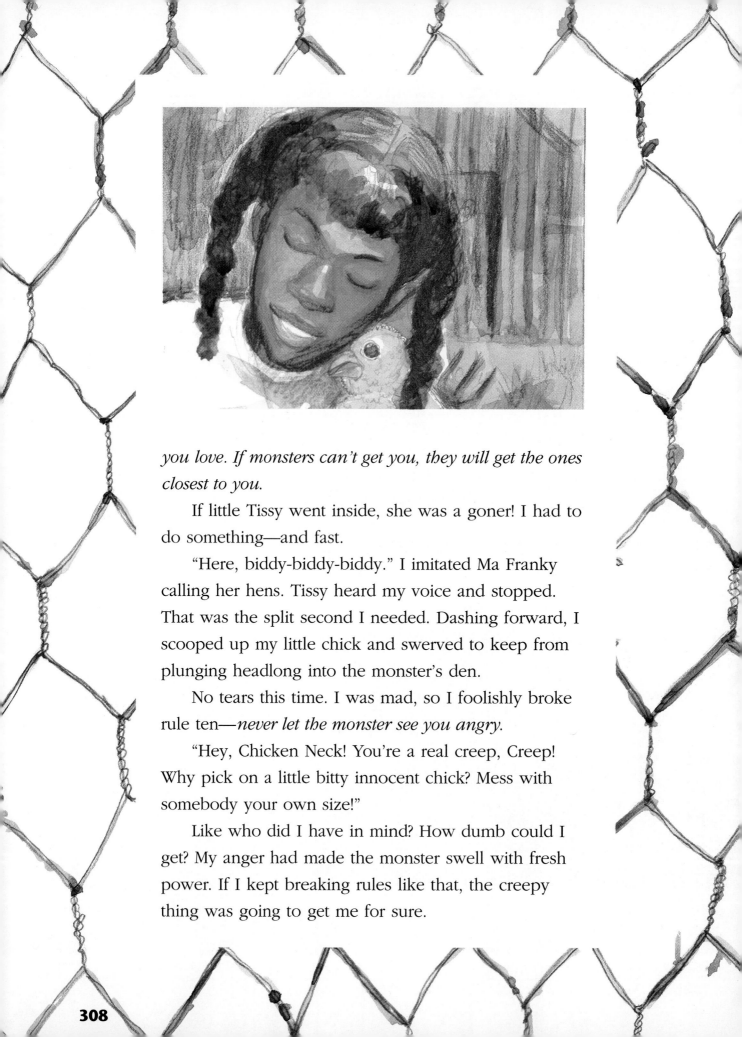

*you love. If monsters can't get you, they will get the ones
closest to you.*

If little Tissy went inside, she was a goner! I had to
do something—and fast.

"Here, biddy-biddy-biddy." I imitated Ma Franky
calling her hens. Tissy heard my voice and stopped.
That was the split second I needed. Dashing forward, I
scooped up my little chick and swerved to keep from
plunging headlong into the monster's den.

No tears this time. I was mad, so I foolishly broke
rule ten—*never let the monster see you angry.*

"Hey, Chicken Neck! You're a real creep, Creep!
Why pick on a little bitty innocent chick? Mess with
somebody your own size!"

Like who did I have in mind? How dumb could I
get? My anger had made the monster swell with fresh
power. If I kept breaking rules like that, the creepy
thing was going to get me for sure.

At last a letter came from Jay.

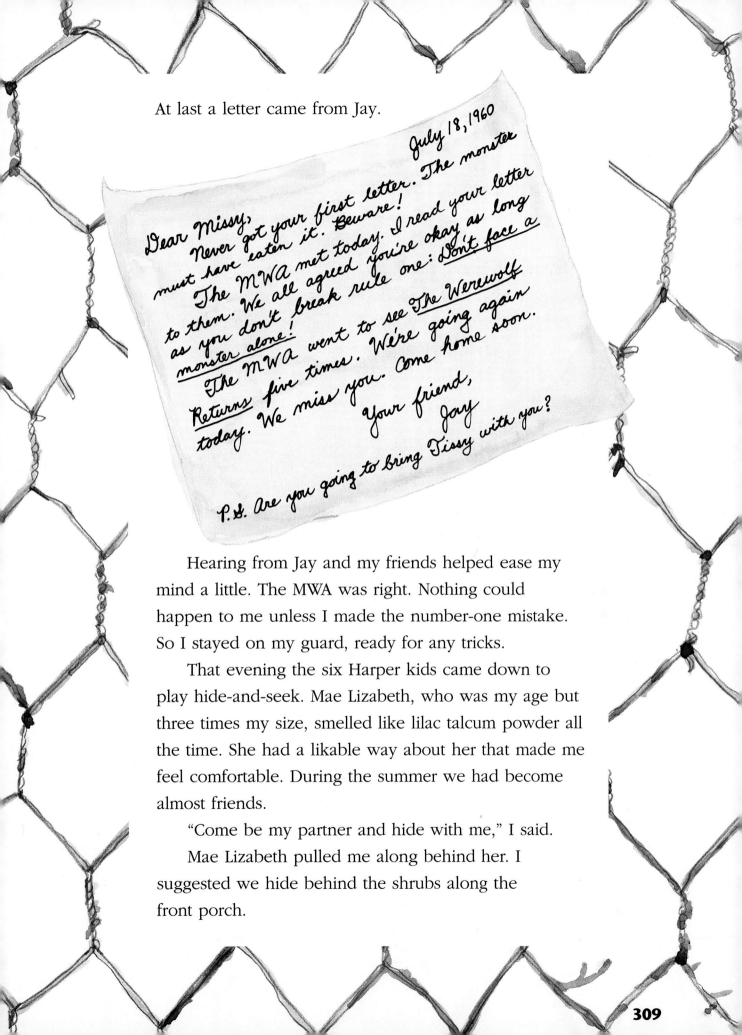

July 18, 1960

Dear Missy,

Never got your first letter. The monster must have eaten it. Beware!

The MWA met today. I read your letter to them. We all agreed you're okay as long as you don't break rule one: <u>Don't face a monster alone!</u>

The MWA went to see <u>The Werewolf Returns</u> five times. We're going again today. We miss you. Come home soon.

Your friend,
Jay

P.S. Are you going to bring Tissy with you?

Hearing from Jay and my friends helped ease my mind a little. The MWA was right. Nothing could happen to me unless I made the number-one mistake. So I stayed on my guard, ready for any tricks.

That evening the six Harper kids came down to play hide-and-seek. Mae Lizabeth, who was my age but three times my size, smelled like lilac talcum powder all the time. She had a likable way about her that made me feel comfortable. During the summer we had become almost friends.

"Come be my partner and hide with me," I said.

Mae Lizabeth pulled me along behind her. I suggested we hide behind the shrubs along the front porch.

"Come on," she said. "Let's hide in the chicken coop!"
I jerked away. "No! Don't . . ."

"Why? It's the perfect place to hide." Suddenly my almost-friend rushed toward that dreaded spot.

I could feel the monster's excitement. My warnings didn't stop Mae Lizabeth from going inside. When she disappeared into the darkness, I started screaming. At the same time Mae Lizabeth let go a bloodcurdling cry. I knew without a doubt my friend had been devoured.

Daddy James, moving like a man half his age, reached the backyard first. Ma Franky puffed along behind him fussing, "We're too old to be going through this, James."

Mae Lizabeth staggered forward, terror and pain twisting her face. She was holding her arm. Blood oozed from a deep gash and trickled down her hand.

Well, the monster hadn't swallowed Mae Lizabeth, but he'd taken a good-size bite out of her arm. Actually, I felt relieved. Now everybody would know that I'd been right all along.

Ma Franky scooted me off to the house to get the first-aid kit. "Seems this nail scratched you," she was saying when I got back. And Daddy James looked and nodded his agreement.

A nail? Oh, no! They couldn't be faked out by that old monster trick. No nail had attacked Mae Lizabeth. I moved in close to get a good look at the wound. "It was the monster!" I shouted. "I bet he did this with his sharp claws. Tell them, Mae Lizabeth. Tell them!"

Mae Lizabeth's eyes opened wide. "Huh? Oh, yes, I saw it . . . It got me."

The monster was hiding deep in the shadows, but I felt it stir. Oh, no, I thought. I was breaking monster rule seven: *Never lie about seeing a monster.* I hadn't lied, but I'd made my friend lie.

"Stop, Mae Lizabeth. You didn't really see anything, did you?" said Daddy James.

The girl shook her head.

"And neither did you, Missy," Ma Franky put in. "Tell me the truth. Have you ever really *seen* anything in that coop?"

"No," I answered, but hurried on to add, "That's how they fool you."

"Hush! Hush this minute," Ma Franky said sternly. "There's nothing in that old coop to hurt anybody."

"Oh yeah?" I sassed back. "Well, what's that running down Mae Lizabeth's arm? Tomato juice?"

Daddy James pulled me behind him. "Don't speak to your grandmama that way," he said in a stern voice.

"I'm sorry for sassing Ma Franky." And I really was sorry. Lies. Sassing. None of this was me! That thing in the coop had made my summer miserable. I wanted to hate it, but that would break rule eight.

The Harper children stared in wide-eyed amazement while Ma Franky bandaged Mae Lizabeth's arm. Then Daddy James and I walked them home.

Rule#7: Never lie about seeing a monster.

"It's a water moon," he said on the way back, pointing out how hazy the full moon looked. "It'll rain 'fore morning."

Most of the time Daddy James was right about things like that. He had his own way of understanding the world, and he'd taught me how to see things differently, too.

For a while we walked in silence. "Missy," he said at last. "Tell me about the monster in your grandmama's chicken coop."

What? Was my very own grandfather a believer? I tested him. "Ma Franky doesn't think it exists."

"I know. But monsters are sneaky like that," he said. "They want people not to believe in them."

How lucky could a kid get? My grandfather knew about monster tricks. He listened while I talked about Jay, the MWA, and all ten monster rules.

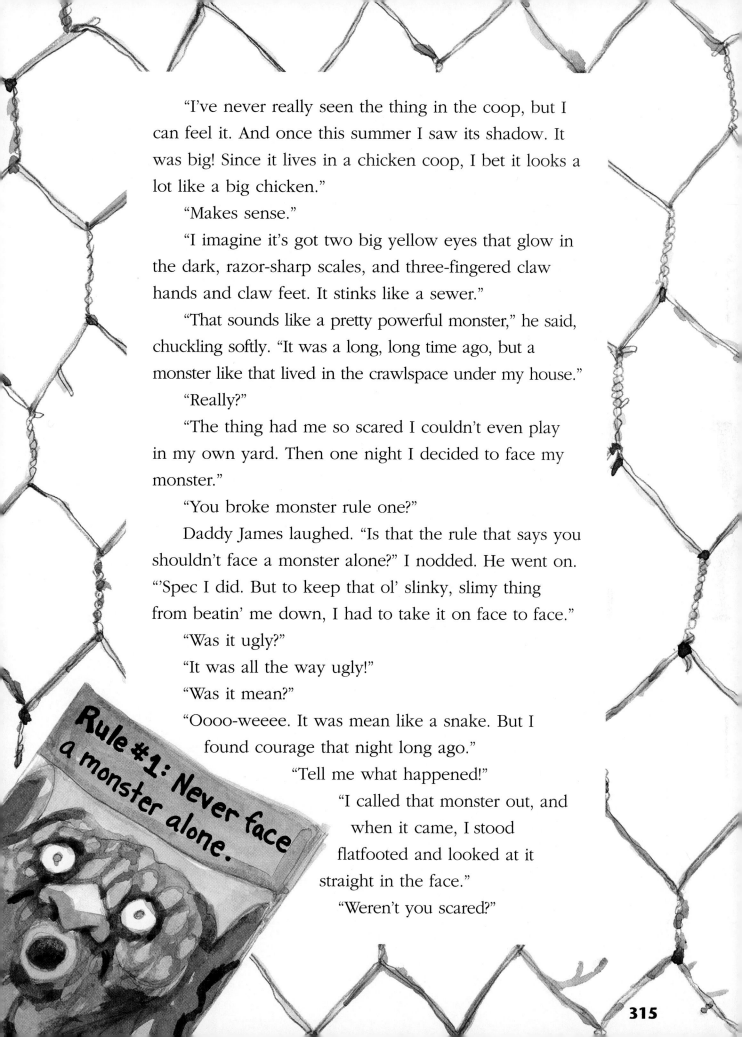

"I've never really seen the thing in the coop, but I can feel it. And once this summer I saw its shadow. It was big! Since it lives in a chicken coop, I bet it looks a lot like a big chicken."

"Makes sense."

"I imagine it's got two big yellow eyes that glow in the dark, razor-sharp scales, and three-fingered claw hands and claw feet. It stinks like a sewer."

"That sounds like a pretty powerful monster," he said, chuckling softly. "It was a long, long time ago, but a monster like that lived in the crawlspace under my house."

"Really?"

"The thing had me so scared I couldn't even play in my own yard. Then one night I decided to face my monster."

"You broke monster rule one?"

Daddy James laughed. "Is that the rule that says you shouldn't face a monster alone?" I nodded. He went on. "'Spec I did. But to keep that ol' slinky, slimy thing from beatin' me down, I had to take it on face to face."

"Was it ugly?"

"It was all the way ugly!"

"Was it mean?"

"Oooo-weeee. It was mean like a snake. But I found courage that night long ago."

"Tell me what happened!"

"I called that monster out, and when it came, I stood flatfooted and looked at it straight in the face."

"Weren't you scared?"

Rule #1: Never face a monster alone.

"At first. But as I held my ground I got stronger and it got weaker. Then I said, 'I'm not afraid of you. Now git gone!' Next thing I knew, it had run off hollering."

"Did it ever come back?"

"Oh, every now and then one tries to scare me. But that monster long ago must have told all its friends that I wasn't easy to scare, 'cause I ain' been bothered too much down through the years . . . till now, that is."

I was so excited. Daddy James was a monster fighter. "Good! Then will you chase the creepy thing in the chicken coop away?"

"I could. But it ain' troubling me. If I run it off, it'll just come back and devil you some other way. To be rid of it forever, you must call it out and face it by yourself."

"You mean break monster rules one and two? That'd be like facing Dracula in his castle, at night, all by myself! I wouldn't have a chance."

"You can do it. You're my granddaughter, and that makes you very special."

The short walk home had taken over an hour. Ma Franky had homemade peach ice cream waiting. I didn't feel much like eating, knowing what was before me.

Mustering my courage, I hugged Ma Franky and Daddy James, just in case I didn't get back. "There is no fear in love," he whispered.

Breaking every rule in the monster manual and trusting my grandfather completely, I went to face the creature within.

"You Chicken Creep. Come out and face me."

Heat lightning zippered across the sky. Thunder grumbled in the distance. Slowly the coop door creaked

open. The monster's foul odor sprang at me from its dark hole. The wind picked up, sending wind eddies scampering in the dust. All at once a scratchy moan followed by an awful commotion chilled me to the bone. "Ssss-flip-kkkkk-flop, ssss-flop-kkkkk-flop!" The thing was at the door. I waited breathlessly, not knowing what to expect. Running crossed my mind, but Daddy James's words helped me stand firm. And I did.

What a surprise to see Ma Franky's rooster flap and flutter out of the dark hole with one of his feet stuck in a tin can.

"Another trick," I said boldly. "You can't distract me."

The wind whipped and churned the trees. The thing's anger roared out of the dark gaping hole. It wanted to get

me. Why wouldn't it come? Suddenly I realized it couldn't! I was getting stronger and it was getting weaker.

Armed with the powerful weapon my grandfather had given me, I yelled over the whistling wind, "I'm not afraid of you. You're just a lot of hot stinky air."

I heard scurrying about inside the darkness. I waited and waited, hardly noticing that it had started to rain.

Then calling upon the growing courage within me, I turned my back on the monster, saying with confidence, "I am the oldest granddaughter of James Leon Russell. He loves me, and I know it!"

And that's when I knew that my monster was gone!

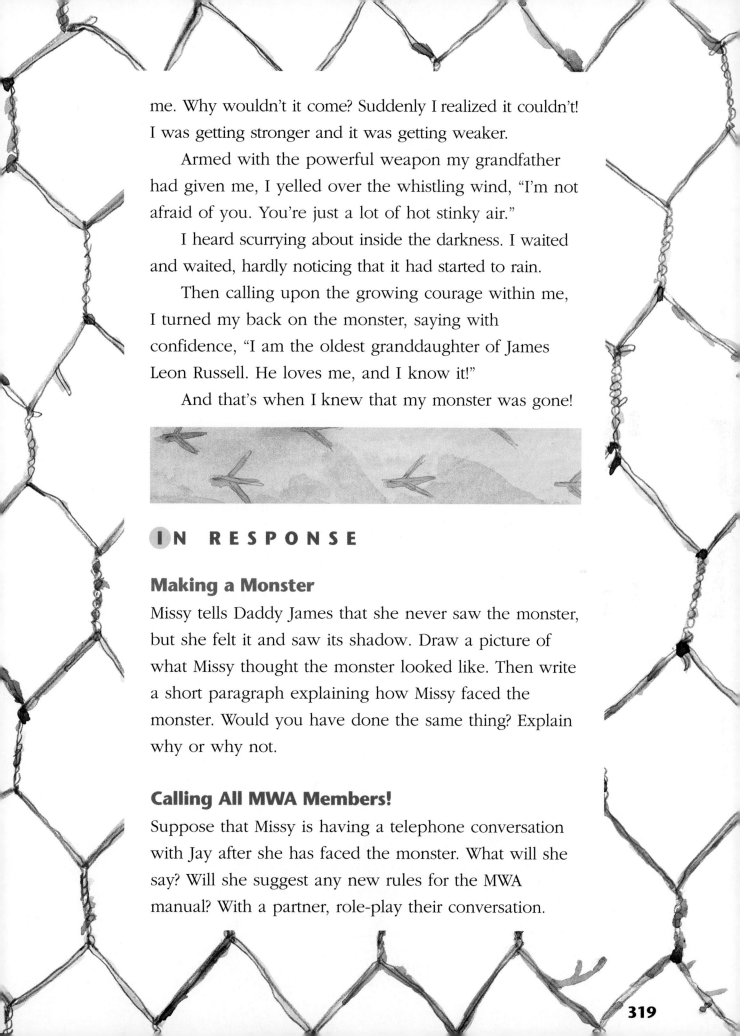

IN RESPONSE

Making a Monster
Missy tells Daddy James that she never saw the monster, but she felt it and saw its shadow. Draw a picture of what Missy thought the monster looked like. Then write a short paragraph explaining how Missy faced the monster. Would you have done the same thing? Explain why or why not.

Calling All MWA Members!
Suppose that Missy is having a telephone conversation with Jay after she has faced the monster. What will she say? Will she suggest any new rules for the MWA manual? With a partner, role-play their conversation.

AUTHOR AT WORK

Patricia C. McKissack

Patricia C. McKissack has had many careers—elementary school teacher, children's book editor, college instructor, and award-winning writer. As an author, she has written biographies of African American heroes, folk tales of American Indians, and stories about children. Her husband is an author, too. Like most good writers, they share a love for reading.

Ms. McKissack's love for reading began when she was growing up in Nashville, Tennessee. As a child, she spent much of her time at the library. When talking about libraries and librarians, she says, "I have a love of and loyalty to them. They opened up a world to me I otherwise wouldn't have had." Reading books by other authors has helped her writing, too.

Writing is "a kind of freedom," says Ms. McKissack. It lets us "do something positive with our experiences." How does she write about those experiences? Ms. McKissack says that it takes her one year to create a story in her head and two weeks to write it. When the story is in her head, she sees pictures moving. "I see the people talking and doing stuff," she says. Her goal is to write in a way that today's children will understand. When talking about her writing, Ms. McKissack says she tries "to enlighten, to change attitudes, to form new attitudes— to build bridges with books."

★ **Award-winning Author**

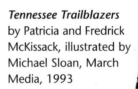

Patricia McKissack talks with elementary school students in Cincinnati.

Patricia C. McKissack

Zora Neale Hurston: Writer and Storyteller by Patricia and Fred McKissack, illustrated by Michael Bryant, Enslow, 1992

Tennessee Trailblazers by Patricia and Fredrick McKissack, illustrated by Michael Sloan, March Media, 1993

Library Link "The Chicken-Coop Monster" was taken from *The Dark-Thirty*, a collection of stories by Patricia C. McKissack. If you enjoyed this story, you might want to read more of her mysterious tales.

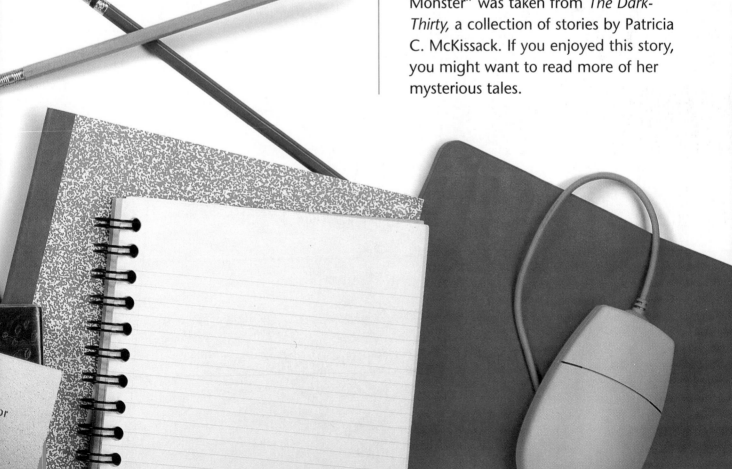

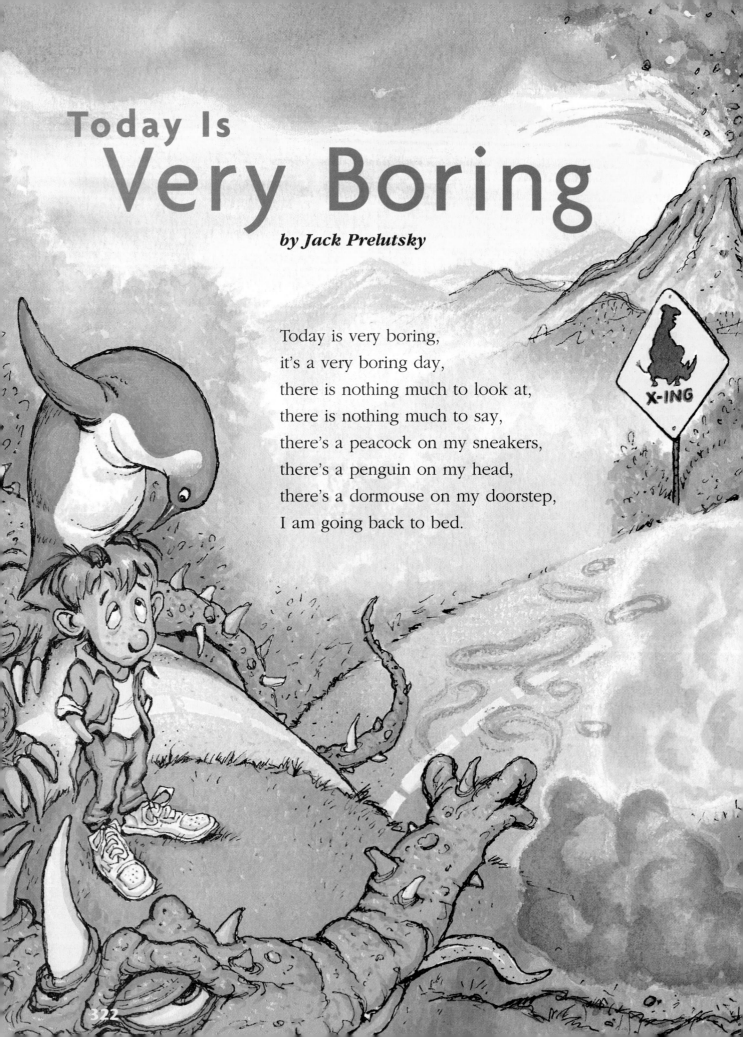

Today Is Very Boring

by Jack Prelutsky

Today is very boring,
it's a very boring day,
there is nothing much to look at,
there is nothing much to say,
there's a peacock on my sneakers,
there's a penguin on my head,
there's a dormouse on my doorstep,
I am going back to bed.

X-ING

Today is very boring,
it is boring through and through,
there is absolutely nothing
that I think I want to do,
I see giants riding rhinos,
and an ogre with a sword,
there's a dragon blowing smoke rings,
I am positively bored.

Today is very boring,
I can hardly help but yawn,
there's a flying saucer landing
in the middle of my lawn,
a volcano just erupted
less than half a mile away,
and I think I felt an earthquake,
it's a very boring day.

323

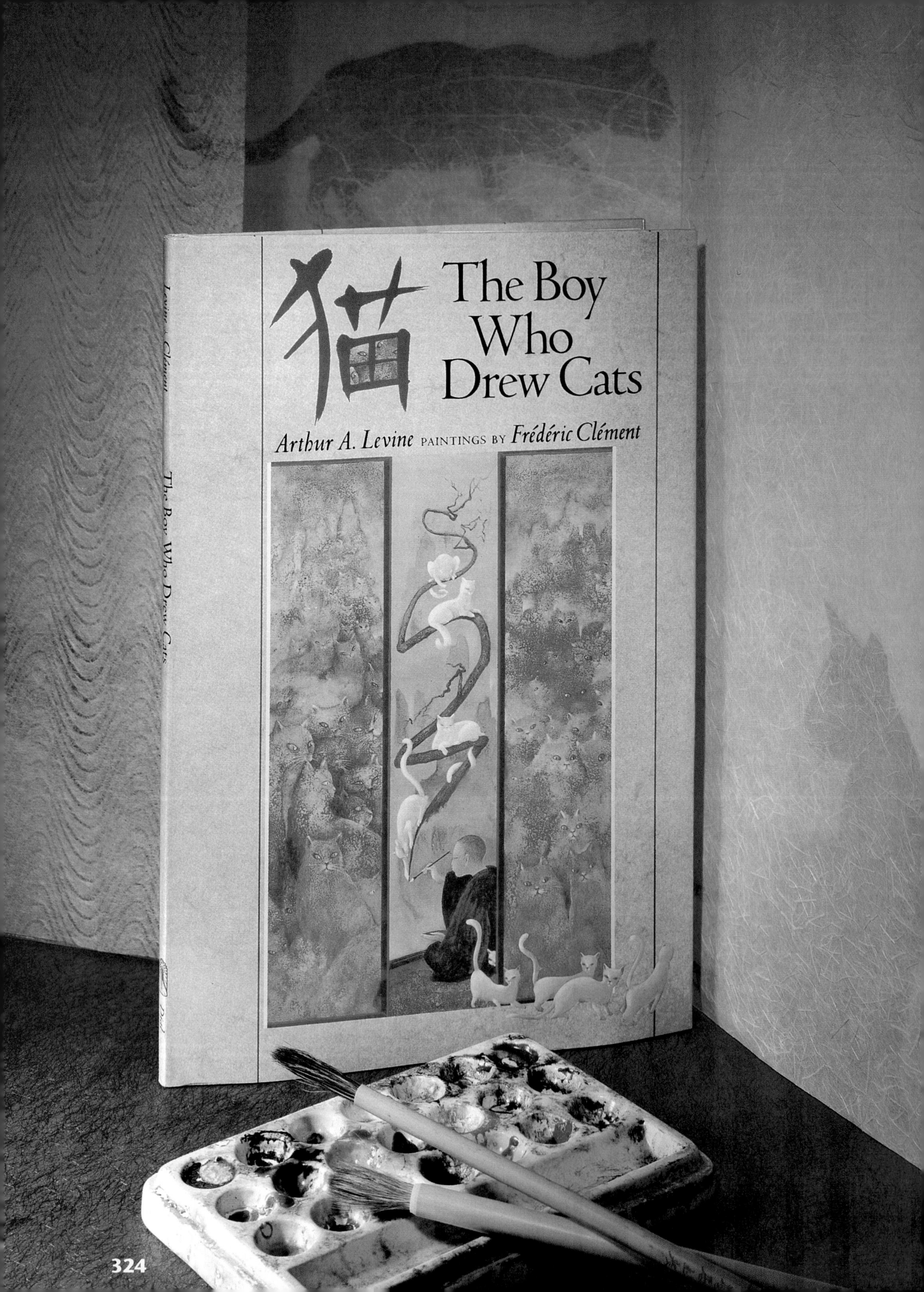
猫
The Boy Who Drew Cats
Arthur A. Levine PAINTINGS BY Frédéric Clément
Levine · Clément
The Boy Who Drew Cats

There was a time, long ago, when no winds blew, no rain fell, and the fields of Japan became parched and cracked. In this time lived a boy named Kenji, with his mother and four older brothers. They all worked hard in the fields each day, but there was not enough to eat. Small Kenji was frail, and tired easily. Try as he might, he could never help for long.

"Never mind, little one," his mother Matsuko said gently. "You can draw us some of your beautiful pictures instead." They all knew how much Kenji loved to draw.

So every day he drew cats and birds and bamboo stalks. He drew flowers that bloomed in the dried-out earth. He drew heaping plates of rice.

His brothers watched him draw at the edge of the field. "Make us something gold, Kenji!" they called.

Matsuko's worry mounted. On the farm, she feared, her youngest son would never eat well and grow strong. So she swallowed her sorrow, wrapped up Kenji's things, and took him to the village monastery.

At the dark wooden gate they were met by two priests. One was old and solemn with a beard that hung like an icicle from his chin. The other was younger and quiet too, but light danced merrily in his eyes.

"Please, sirs," Matsuko pleaded, "won't you take my youngest son for an acolyte? He will be respectful, and learn his lessons well."

"Do you wish to be a priest?" the older man asked. And the words fell like sleet on the young boy's ears.

"I wish not to be a burden," Kenji said, looking down. The older priest frowned, but the younger one whispered in his ear.

At last he nodded.

"Come," said the younger priest kindly, "my name is Takada." And together they entered the monastery, leaving Matsuko alone on the step.

Kenji struggled to please the priests. Yet the scrolls he copied grew whiskers and wings. And his mind never stayed in the gardens he was supposed to tend.

Instead he would sit near a stream of white pebbles and sketch as he always had. Takada loved Kenji's drawings, especially the ones of cats, so whenever he could, Kenji drew a cat for Takada.

But the older priest, Yoshida, remained stern as stone. It seemed that whenever Kenji stopped work for a moment and picked up his paper, Yoshida appeared overhead like a thundercloud, staring coldly.

One rainy day as Kenji swept the courtyard, he had an idea for a present to give Takada. Quickly he drew a lovely Siamese cat dancing in the rain. A few more strokes gave the cat a partner, and soon the whole page was filled with splashing, frolicking cats. Suddenly a shadow crossed the page.

"Deceitful boy!" Yoshida hissed. "I have no place in my temple for laziness. Be gone by morning." Kenji knew not to argue.

Takada appeared as Kenji was leaving. They looked at each other sadly. "Farewell, Kenji," Takada said. "You were meant to be an artist, not a priest." Then, from behind his back he brought out a delicate paper box tied in the cloth Kenji's mother had sent with him. Kenji gently untied the knot. The box contained the most beautiful set of brushes and inks he had ever seen. Kenji knew he would cry if he said so much as thank you.

"Go now," said Takada, "but remember this: AVOID LARGE PLACES AT NIGHT—KEEP TO SMALL."

Kenji wanted to ask what this meant, but he was still too close to tears. So he chanted the warning over and over to himself, down the winding path from the monastery, "Avoid large places at night. Keep to small," puzzling over its meaning.

Kenji was too ashamed to return to his family's farm. Instead he headed in the opposite direction, hoping to find another temple where he could try again to be an acolyte.

But in the next village he came to, the people were strange. When Kenji asked directions, they grew pale and stared at him, or they quickly pointed the way and scurried on.

Now it happened that there was a large and wealthy temple high at the top of a nearby mountain, where for months not a soul had entered or left. Villagers whispered that a terrible Goblin Rat, possessed of a magical sword and a fearsome tail, had claimed the temple as his own.

Kenji, however, knew none of this when he discovered the long staircase winding steeply up the mountain.

He climbed thousands of steps and reached a great gate. Then he caught his breath with a gasp of terror. On the gate, in the faintest of marks, someone had painted the Goblin Rat with his sword raised and the words "AVOID LARGE PLACES AT NIGHT. KEEP TO SM. . . ." Whoever had begun the message had not been able to finish.

Kenji looked back, but the sun had nearly set, and he knew he couldn't risk climbing down in the dark. So he turned toward the temple, shaking.

His steps crumbled ash-white leaves at the threshold. They filled the air with dust as he pushed the door open, then settled into an awful stillness. Not a breeze stirred the stench of decay in the air.

At the end of a hallway Kenji saw a candle glowing and he crept toward it on the balls of his feet. When he had almost reached the light, Kenji thought he heard scratching behind him and he hurried into an open room.

There he found a large hall filled with white screens. They stood in a row like servants, waiting for the priests to file in for prayer. Kenji felt a little better. Maybe someone would return if he just waited a while.

Up and back Kenji paced in front of the tall white screens. Suddenly he remembered Takada's gift. He could decorate the screens while he waited! Then when the priests returned, they would see that he was worthwhile. Kenji began to paint, and what came was truly magical. In honor of Takada he painted cats. Powerful cats with broad, majestic shoulders. Sleek cats with sharp claws and quivering whiskers. Alert cats with twitching tails and watchful eyes. By the time he was done, every screen was filled and Kenji was exhausted.

Sleep pressed against his eyes, but fear kept them open. The priests had not returned, and now he heard the scratching noise again. Takada's warning came back to him with a shiver: AVOID LARGE PLACES AT NIGHT—KEEP TO SMALL. Kenji spied a small cabinet and squeezed inside. He slid the door shut and slowly, slowly his eyes began to close.

Suddenly a horrible growling and screaming woke Kenji. He heard the clash of claw and metal. The floor rumbled and a piece of the cabinet splintered off, but Kenji was too terrified to move.

At sunrise the temple was quiet again. Yet something had changed. It was the breeze! Even before he slid the door open, Kenji could feel a fresh wind sweeping through the rooms, and he could hear the cry of a crane. Still, he was unprepared for the sight that met his eyes when he finally stepped out.

The room was covered with shattered screens. Bits of wood and paper littered the floor. And as Kenji looked closer, he saw that the broken screens were empty and white. Where had all his cats gone? Kenji heard a thump and spun around. In front of him stood the one screen still intact. On it sat the King of Cats, tall and proud, with the sword of the Goblin Rat at his feet.

Kenji ran to tell the villagers the news, but they were already climbing the steps to the temple. "We felt the breeze! We heard the cranes!" they shouted. "The Goblin Rat must be dead!"

The villagers were so grateful that they invited Kenji to live and paint at the newly reopened temple. There he worked in peace and happiness, becoming a great and famous artist.

And his specialty was cats.

IN RESPONSE

What Happened Here?

Kenji could hear loud noises the night he slept inside the cabinet. What was happening in the temple hall? How do you know? Write or draw your answer.

Monster Solutions

Kenji and Missy ("The Chicken-Coop Monster") each overcame a real or imagined monster. In writing, compare how Missy and Kenji solved their problems. Could they have used each other's solutions? Explain why or why not.

AUTHOR AT WORK

In fourth grade, author Arthur A. Levine wrote his first book—a joke recipe book that won a school contest. Winning this contest made him realize that he would like to be a writer when he grew up. Now that he is a writer, he advises children to follow their dreams. "Do what you love. Stick with it."

Other Books by . . .

Arthur A. Levine

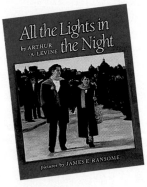

All the Lights in the Night by Arthur A. Levine, illustrated by James E. Ransome, Tambourine Books, 1991

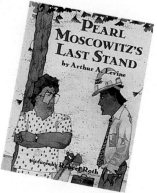

Pearl Moscowitz's Last Stand by Arthur A. Levine, illustrated by Robert Roth, Tambourine Books, 1993

Writing With Pictures

Japanese writing uses both Chinese characters and *kana* symbols. *Kana* symbols stand for syllables. The Japanese word *haiku* is made with two *kana* symbols. One symbol stands for the syllable *hai* and the other for *ku*. Chinese characters like the ones below stand for whole words. A Chinese character cannot be sounded out like an English word can. So Japanese students must memorize the word each Chinese character stands for. In fact, Japanese students have to memorize thousands of these characters before they can even read a newspaper!

Character	Japanese Pronunciation	Meaning
童	**warabe** (*wah rah beh*)	child
願	**negai** (*neh gah ee*)	request, wish
別	**wakare** (*wah kah reh*)	farewell, parting
靈	**rei** (*ray ee*)	goblin, spirit
門	**mon** (*mohn*)	gate
猫	**neko** (*neh koh*)	cat
勝	**kachi** (*kah chee*)	victory
福	**fuku** (*foo koo*)	happiness

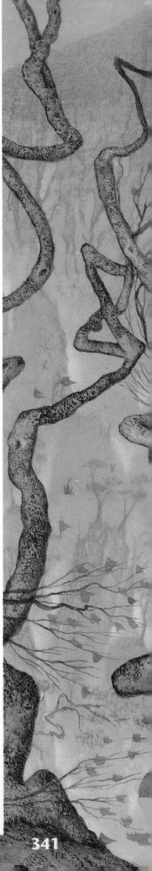

Art That Works

When artists put their imagination to work, tools, machines, and other items can be made pleasing to the eye.

What's the use?

This chopper could be used to chop food. What makes it different from an ordinary knife? If you saw this in your kitchen, would you know how to use it? Explain how.

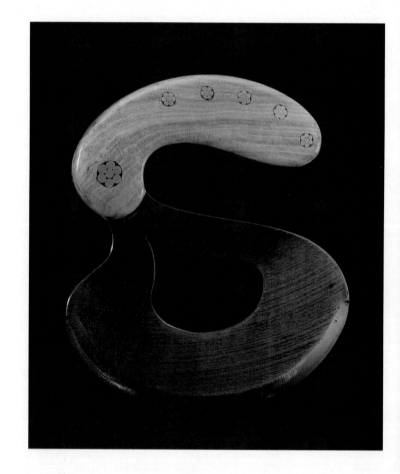

Free-form chopper with applewood handle by Vernon and Helen Raaen (United States), late 1900's

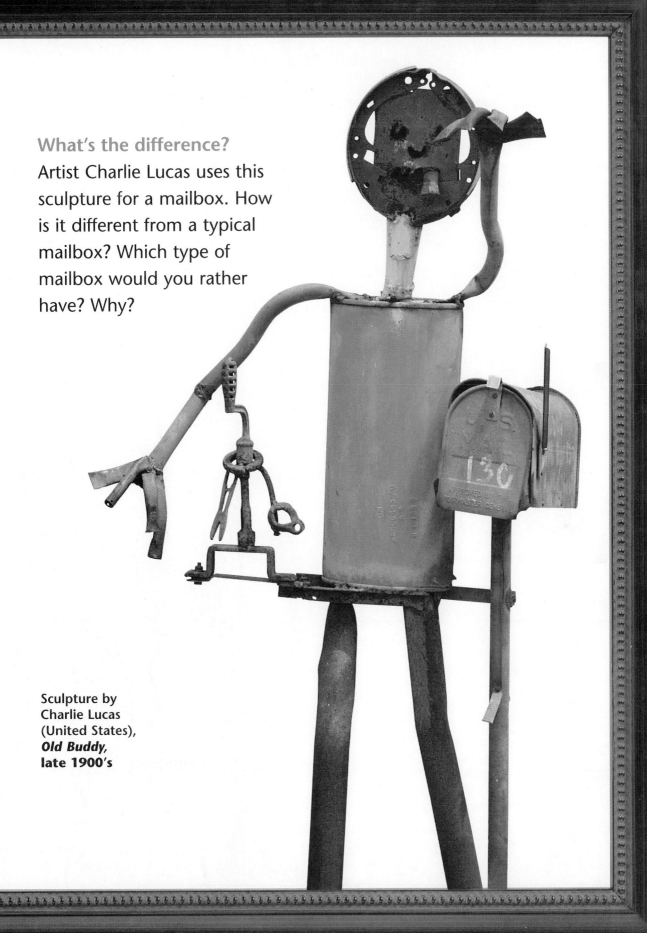

What's the difference?
Artist Charlie Lucas uses this sculpture for a mailbox. How is it different from a typical mailbox? Which type of mailbox would you rather have? Why?

Sculpture by
Charlie Lucas
(United States),
Old Buddy,
late 1900's

343

Garrett Morgan,
Inventor

from *Take a Walk in Their Shoes,* By Glennette Tilley Turner veryone who has ever crossed a street safely with the help of a traffic light can thank Garrett A. Morgan. He is the inventor who thought of a way for people and cars to take turns crossing at intersections.

Garrett A. Morgan was born in Paris, Tennessee, on March 4, 1875. His parents, Sydney and Elizabeth Reed Morgan, had ten other children. Times were hard and at age fourteen Morgan struck out on his own—heading for nearby Cincinnati, Ohio. He found a job as a handyman.

Four years later he moved to Cleveland, Ohio. He arrived with only a quarter to his name, but he had a talent for fixing mechanical things—and for saving his money. He got a job as a sewing machine adjuster at the Roots and McBride Company. Before long he had thought of an idea. It was a belt fastener for sewing machines.

Garrett Morgan soon saved enough money to buy his own sewing machine business and purchase a home. His father had died by that time and he invited his mother to move to Cleveland. A year later he married Mary Anne Hassek. They enjoyed a long, happy marriage and were the parents of three sons.

Morgan was a good businessman. Before long he was able to open a tailoring shop in which he hired thirty-two employees. His shop made suits, dresses, and coats with sewing equipment he had built.

Although planning was important to his success, his next business venture came about by accident. He was trying to find a liquid chemical that he could use to polish sewing machines. While he was experimenting, his wife called him to dinner. Hurriedly, he wiped his hands on a pony-fur cloth on his workbench and the wiry fur hairs straightened out. Curious to see how this liquid would affect other kinds of hair, he tried it out on the Airedale dog next door. The dog's hair got so straight that his owner hardly recognized him. After a bit more experimenting, Morgan put the chemical on the market as a product to straighten hair.

His next invention was a safety hood or "breathing device." In more recent years it has been called a gas mask. Morgan received a patent for it (U.S. Patent No. 1,113,675) and as he stated: "The object of the invention is to provide a portable attachment which will enable a fireman to enter a house filled with thick suffocating gases and smoke and to breathe freely for sometime therein, and thereby enable him to perform his duties of saving life and valuables without danger to himself from suffocation."

The safety hood won a first prize gold medal from the International Exposition for Sanitation and Safety. The judges at the exposition immediately recognized its value. Morgan wanted to market his invention, but he believed prejudice would limit his sales if his racial identity was generally known. He knew that some fire departments would rather endanger their firemen's lives than do business with a black inventor. He attempted to solve this problem

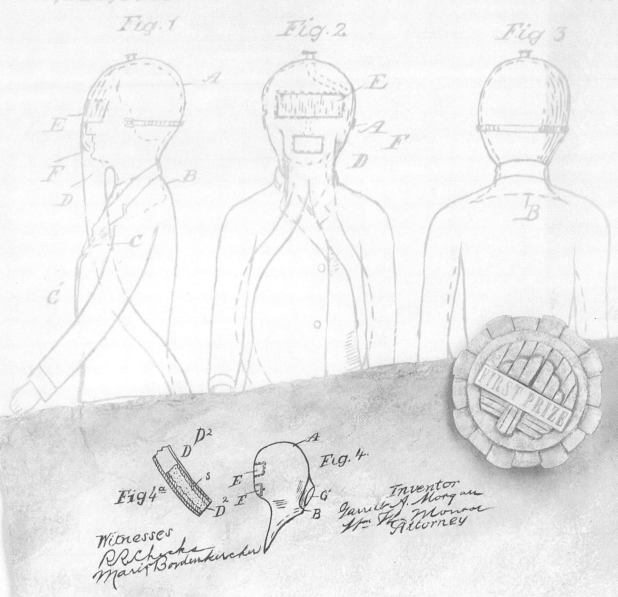

G. A. MORGAN.
BREATHING DEVICE.
APPLICATION FILED AUG. 19, 1912.

1,113,675.

Patented Oct. 13, 1914.

Fig. 1

Fig. 2

Fig. 3

Fig. 4

Fig. 4ᵃ

Inventor
Garrett A. Morgan
Wm. K. Monroe
Attorney

Witnesses
R. R. Hicks
Mary Bordenkircher

in a most unusual way. He formed the National Safety Device Company. He was the only nonwhite officer. The other officers—one of whom had been the director of public works for the city of Cleveland— would arrange for demonstrations of the device and set up a canvas tent in the demonstration area. They would set a fire in the tent with an awful-smelling fuel

made of tar, sulphur, formaldehyde, and manure. Once the fire was roaring, Morgan would appear disguised as an Indian chief. He'd put on the gas mask and go in and remain up to twenty minutes while he extinguished the flames. He would come out as good as new. This might have gone on indefinitely, but the night of July 25, 1916, changed everything. Morgan became a hero overnight.

That night there was a violent explosion at the Cleveland Waterworks. Approximately thirty workmen were trapped in a tunnel five miles out and more than 225 feet beneath Lake Erie. Smoke, natural gases, and debris kept would-be rescuers

from entering the tunnel where the workmen were trapped. Family and friends didn't know whether anyone had survived the blast.

Finally, someone at the site of this disaster remembered that Garrett Morgan had invented a gas mask. It was about two o'clock in the morning when Morgan was called in. He, his brother Frank, and two volunteers put on gas masks and entered the tunnel. They were able to save the surviving workmen, including the superintendent, whom Morgan revived with artificial respiration.

Newspaper wire services picked up the story. The account of Morgan's heroism appeared in papers across the country. This turned out to be a mixed blessing. The city of Cleveland awarded Morgan a diamond-studded gold medal for heroism. Safety hoods or gas masks were ordered by the U.S. government. Many American, English, and German veterans of World War I owe their lives to the gas masks. Chemists, engineers, and other people working with noxious fumes could work more safely.

At first, many fire departments ordered gas masks for use in their work, but because of racial prejudice, the number of orders dwindled, and some orders were cancelled when it became known that Morgan was a black man. Meanwhile, Thomas A. Farrell, Cleveland's Director of Public Utilities, wrote to the Carnegie Hero Fund Commission to inform them of Morgan's heroic deed. The Commission had been endowed by Andrew Carnegie to reward people who had shown great heroism. Instead of awarding Garrett Morgan, the Commission gave the hero medal to the project superintendent whose life Morgan had saved. People who knew that Morgan deserved this honor realized this was very unfair.

Instead of being discouraged, Garrett Morgan went back to his drawing board. Without the disappointment of the gas mask, he might never have developed his next invention, the stoplight. While the gas mask saved the lives of people who did dangerous work, the traffic light has saved the lives of drivers and pedestrians—of all ages, all across the world.

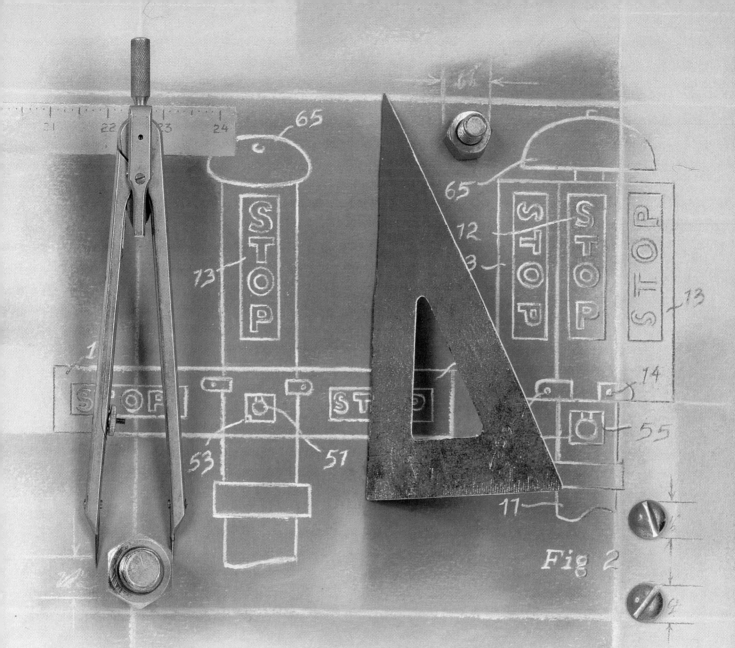

Fig 2

Reportedly, Morgan was the first black person in Cleveland to own a car. As the number of cars increased, there was a need for an effective way to control the flow of traffic. Intersections were especially dangerous. Morgan put his problem-solving skills to work and invented the three-way automatic electric stoplight. It didn't look like today's stoplight, but it provided the concept on which modern stoplights are based. For some time, railroads had used a semaphore or signaling system.

Train engineers could look straight down the track and tell from the position of the semaphore whether to stop or proceed. Since city streets intersect, Morgan had to come up with a way to signal drivers on side streets as well as main thoroughfares. He received his patent (U.S. Patent No. 1,475,024) on November 20, 1923. At first, Morgan marketed the invention himself, but then decided to sell rights to the General Electric Company for $40,000. He not

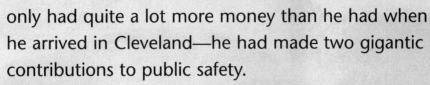

only had quite a lot more money than he had when he arrived in Cleveland—he had made two gigantic contributions to public safety.

Even though Garrett Morgan's contributions made life easier for everyone, regardless of race, he had been the victim of racism. Believing that no one should be denied opportunities because of their race, he worked to try to keep other people from having the kind of bad experiences he had had. He went about solving this problem in several different ways. He was concerned that the local newspapers didn't contain much news about the black community and things that were being accomplished there, so he started the *Cleveland Call* newspaper. (It is now known as the *Call and Post* and has a large circulation.) He was active in civil rights organizations. And feeling that black citizens were not properly represented in local government, he ran for City Council. Although he did not win that election, Cleveland later became the first large American city to elect a black man as mayor.

For the last twenty years of his life, Morgan suffered from glaucoma. This resulted in near-blindness, but it didn't slow down his sharp mind. Although he had hoped to attend the Emancipation Centennial to be held in Chicago in August, 1963, Garrett Morgan died less than a month before that event. But he had lived to receive a well-deserved honor. Six months before his death he was cited by the United States government for having invented the first traffic signal.

Father of Invention

Write a paragraph describing the problems Garrett Morgan saw and how his inventions solved those problems. Which invention do you think was the most important? Explain why you think so.

Never Give Up

Garrett Morgan and Kenji ("The Boy Who Drew Cats") both faced people who tried to discourage them from reaching their goals. With a partner, role-play a conversation between Kenji and Mr. Morgan. Discuss how you succeeded even though people tried to discourage you.

AUTHOR **A**T **W**ORK

Learning has always been a part of Glennette Tilley Turner's life. Her father was a college president and civil rights leader, and her mother was a nursery school teacher. It's no surprise, then, that Ms. Turner chose to become a teacher and writer. She has written books for children and for adults. Writing for children has helped her understand how connected life and learning are.

★ Award-winning Author

Another Book About . . .

Inventors

9 African American Inventors by Robert C. Hayden, illustrated by Richard Loehle, Twenty-First Century Books, 1992

Library Link "Garrett Morgan, Inventor" was taken from *Take a Walk in Their Shoes* by Glennette Tilley Turner. You might enjoy reading the entire book for more stories of African Americans who made their dreams a reality.

Meet the Inventor of the Light

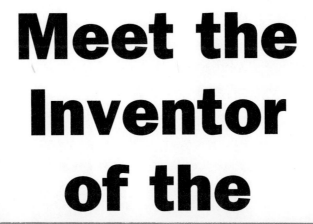

from *Take a Walk in Their Shoes* by Glennette Tilley Turner

CAST

FIRST NARRATOR   REPORTER

SECOND NARRATOR   STUDENT

GARRETT MORGAN

FIRST NARRATOR: It is rush hour on a Friday evening in a large city.

SECOND NARRATOR: A radio reporter and Mr. Garrett A. Morgan, inventor of the stoplight, are standing at a

busy corner. They watch as cars stop on the red light, then drive away when the light turns green.

FIRST NARRATOR: It is time for a radio program to begin.

SECOND NARRATOR: The reporter adjusts his earphones and speaks into his microphone.

REPORTER: Hello, this is (*child playing this part gives his or her own name*), your roving reporter. My guest today is Mr. Garrett A. Morgan, the inventor of the stoplight.

REPORTER: (*speaking to the guest*) Mr. Morgan, how does it feel to know that your invention makes it possible for rush hour traffic to move smoothly and safely?

GARRETT MORGAN: I'm very pleased.

REPORTER: How did you happen to think of the idea?

GARRETT MORGAN: Well, I knew that trains used light signals, and I saw that every year there were more and more cars on the streets. There were sure to be more and more accidents, so I set out to design a signal that could . . .

REPORTER: . . . make drivers take turns?

GARRETT MORGAN: (*laughingly*) Yes! Sometimes drivers are in such a big hurry to get where they're going, they don't remember whether it is their turn or not.

REPORTER: I've heard that you invented the stoplight after an unhappy experience. Is that true?

GARRETT MORGAN: (*pausing as if he really doesn't want to talk about this*) Yes, it is. I had invented the safety hood or gas mask.

REPORTER: Is it true that you had not only invented the gas mask, but you personally rescued many of the workmen at the Cleveland Waterworks explosion?

GARRETT MORGAN: Yes, that's true.

REPORTER: You're modest, Mr. Morgan. Please tell our listeners what happened.

GARRETT MORGAN: Well, the blast trapped workmen more than 200 feet below Lake Erie. Tunnel Number Five was filled with smoke and gas.

REPORTER: Luckily, you lived in the same city and someone at the Waterworks had heard of your invention.

GARRETT MORGAN: Yes, I was called in about two o'clock in the morning. My brother and I put on gas masks and went down with two volunteers. And we brought up all the workmen who were still alive.

STUDENT: (*who has walked up in time to hear about this rescue*) Wow! You all were heroes!

GARRETT MORGAN: We were just glad to do what we could.

REPORTER: I would have thought that every fire department in the world would have bought gas masks after they heard you'd gone through all that smoke and gas unharmed.

GARRETT MORGAN: They did at first, but when they found out that the gas mask was invented by a black person, they stopped buying the masks.

REPORTER: Even though it might have saved their lives?

STUDENT: Oh, Mr. Morgan, really?

GARRETT MORGAN: Yes, but I didn't let it get me down. By that time I started working on the stoplight.

REPORTER: And your stoplight has made such a great contribution. Cities couldn't have handled all the traffic they have today without the stoplight.

STUDENT: Well, at least you do get recognized for inventing the stoplight. I'm really glad I stopped here today and got to meet you.

GARRETT MORGAN: Thank you.

REPORTER: Thank you, Mr. Morgan, for being with us today. Thank you even more for using your inventive genius to save so many lives.

The Fabulous Fork!

by Don L. Wulffson

Often inventions result from planned experiments. Sometimes, though, inventions happen by accident. The use of the fork was actually a surprise. Whether an invention is designed or discovered, though, one thing is certain. Trying new ideas can lead to interesting solutions.

Forks are funny things: more than a thousand years passed between the time they were first invented and the time people began eating with them.

The first forks were put to many uses, but eating was not one of them. It is known, for example, that ancient people used big wooden forks for farming. They used small, sharp-pointed forks for fishing. They even took their forks to war: the English had a vicious weapon called a fork which had prongs covered with little hooks.

The people of the Middle East were the first to come up with the idea of eating with a fork. Not until the eleventh century did the idea spread to Europe. At that time a woman from Constantinople married a man in Italy. When the woman moved to her husband's homeland she brought a little two-pronged fork with her. Instead of eating with her fingers as everyone else did, she cut her meat in little pieces and ate it with her fork.

The first table fork on record in England is one that belonged to King Edward I in the late thirteenth century. It was made of glass and was considered a great treasure.

By the fifteenth century, the custom of eating with a fork was widespread in many parts of Europe. Of all Europeans, it was the English who resisted this custom the longest. Instead of a fork, the English used a pair of knives to eat their meat. One was for cutting, the other for spearing the pieces.

Not until the seventeenth century did the use of forks become general throughout the western world. By that time even the English had started using the things.

*Wayne Grover has been diving with his friends for years.
Using scuba equipment and their special training, they
regularly explore the peaceful underwater beauty of the
Atlantic Ocean along the coast of Florida. One morning,
as they are preparing to dive, Wayne gets a strange feeling
that something unusual is about to happen.*

Geared up and ready to dive, I held the end of
the rope in my hand, and when we got to the
place I felt was right, I rolled over the side of
the boat and into the water.

As I drifted down, I had the distinct feeling that
something was happening over which I had no control.
I tried to relax, but the feeling would not go away.

After swimming along the deep outer reef edge at
eighty feet, I suddenly heard a loud clicking noise in
the water. It grew louder with each passing second.

Underwater

I stopped and held on to a large rock as I tried to see what was making the noise. I looked in every direction.

The clicking became so loud, I could feel it against my eardrums. There was something familiar about the noise, but I could not place it.

Then I saw them!

Racing through the clear water, three dolphins were coming from the deep side of the reef, knifing through the water with graceful speed.

Rescue

from *Dolphin Adventure: A True Story* by Wayne Grover

I had been diving for many years, but never before had wild dolphins come near me in the water. As I watched, the three swam closer to me.

There was a large male, a smaller female, and a baby dolphin. As the three circled me, I could see the baby was bleeding from a deep wound near its tail where a long string of clear plastic fishing line trailed for several feet behind.

The male and female dolphins were making a clicking noise as they swam nearer to me. Then they stopped and hovered.

The clicking noise also stopped.

The baby was between its mother and father. All three looked at me with their little eyes over upturned mouths, reminding me of a human grin.

I could see the baby had become tangled in a fishing line with a big hook that had snagged it between the dorsal fin on its back and the tail fluke.

The shaft of the hook was sticking out of the bleeding wound, making a trail of green in the depth.

Because all colors are filtered out in the ocean depth, the baby's red blood looked green eighty feet below the surface. My first reaction was one of awe. My second thought was worry for the baby. I knew it would either get snagged and drown or be tracked down and eaten by a shark.

Dolphins are very intelligent and are abundantly happy in their wild domain. They are loving and loyal and have close family ties, taking care of their young and their older, less able peers.

They seldom approach people in the sea and with good reason. Humans are dangerous and can cause them harm. But these dolphins were desperate.

The baby dolphin looked scared and in pain. Its little eyes rolled in their sockets as it watched me. It was afraid of me, but its parents had brought it near.

I looked into the eyes of each of them as they hovered just three feet away, and thought about all the dolphins that had been needlessly killed by fishermen and their nets or caught on their hooks. All my life I have loved animals and have done my best to see they are respected and protected. Perhaps the dolphins had sensed that I was a friend. There were four other divers in the water, all armed with weapons. I was alone and unarmed.

Now we were face-to-face. This dolphin family had an injured baby. Could they have come to me for help?

I knew something most unusual was happening.

The baby dolphin would probably die without help, but what could I do? How could I do anything about the fishing hook and the plastic line?

I had only my big diving knife and no one to help me. If I didn't help, the baby was doomed. I decided I must try.

I reached out to touch the big male, who was nearest me, and all three suddenly shot away, swimming out of sight.

I felt a great surge of disappointment, thinking I'd never see them again. Had I done something wrong?

Then, within seconds, they were back. They swam around me, clicking again, but more softly. They kept their eyes on me every moment. Now I was convinced the dolphins had chosen me to help them.

I tied the rope from the float ball to a nearby rock and let myself sink to the seafloor, where I sat on my knees.

I could sense the dolphins were trying to communicate with me. As I sat there on the sea bottom looking at the three creatures, I knew it was a rare moment. They were trusting me and I was trusting them. With their great speed and strength, they could easily injure me.

They needed help, but they could not speak. I wanted them to know I would help, but I could not communicate in their dolphin language. There must be a way, but how?

The clicking increased in frequency and then stopped. The three dolphins moved very slowly toward me. With their strong tail flukes barely moving up and down, they inched nearer and nearer until they were close enough for me to reach out and touch them.

The mother and father dolphin were slightly above the baby and were holding it between their flippers as they tried to place it on the sand right in front of me. At last they pushed the baby to the bottom.

The baby was frightened, and I could see it trembling. Its eyes never left mine. I slowly reached out to touch it, but when I did, it freed itself and swam rapidly away. The two parent dolphins immediately swam after it. In moments they were back, holding the baby tightly between them.

The father dolphin, hovering just inches from me, placed his nose under my arm and pushed up. My arm lifted, and I let it fall back in place. Again the big dolphin lifted it. I looked at his upturned mouth and bright eyes and couldn't help smiling. The impatient father dolphin wanted me to "get to work."

I took off my diving gloves and slowly reached out to touch the trembling baby. Its skin was smooth and silky as I ran my hand from just behind its breathing hole on the top of its head to the base of its dorsal fin in the middle of its back. I used my fingers to stroke its nose very gently, then ran them up and between its eyes.

The trembling stopped as the little dolphin began to sense that I had no intention of harming it. After petting it for a couple of minutes, I slowly ran my hand to the wounded area near its tail. The clear fishing line was wrapped around the thin part of its body, embedded into the skin, causing blood to ooze out.

The shaft of the fishhook stuck out from a bloody hole in its back that had been ripped open when the baby broke the line, freeing itself from the fisherman above.

It was in great pain and frightened. Instinctively it understood that a shark could sniff along the blood trail and find it. That would be the end of the baby dolphin, and all four of us knew it.

I knew that getting the hook out and the line loose would be painful for the baby, but it had to be done.

All I had to work with was the big diving knife I wore strapped to my right leg. It was about a foot long, and it was not very sharp.

I gently touched the hook shaft, and the baby made a high-pitched cry. It was going to be hard to help it.

Suddenly all three dolphins swam away, climbing toward the surface above. I had forgotten they had to breathe every few minutes.

Within a minute they were right back to me, this time with the baby coming along on its own. I knew I had to work fast so they could breathe when they needed to.

I gently held the baby on the sea floor, then cut the trailing fishing line free until all that was left was the part embedded under the baby's tender skin. Getting it out with as little pain for the baby as possible was going to be the hard part.

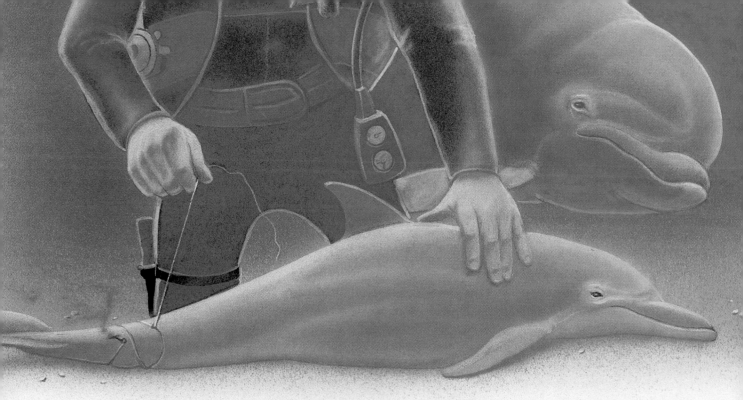

Then, bit by bit, I started pulling the embedded line loose so l could cut it with my knife. As I pulled it up, more blood flowed out.

I looked around for sharks, not wanting to get in the way if the parent dolphins needed to protect their baby from an attack.

Seeing no sharks, I gently continued to pull some line free.

The baby cried out in pain, and the big dolphin clicked several times. It seemed as though the parent dolphins were working with me, encouraging their baby to cooperate.

Finally, all the line was cut free except for a short piece attached to the hook. This was going to be the hardest part. I touched the hook shaft, and the baby jumped and trembled. I carefully ran my finger into the deep wound, feeling its body heat within the flesh. The baby struggled to get away, but I placed my left hand on its back and pushed it down against the sand.

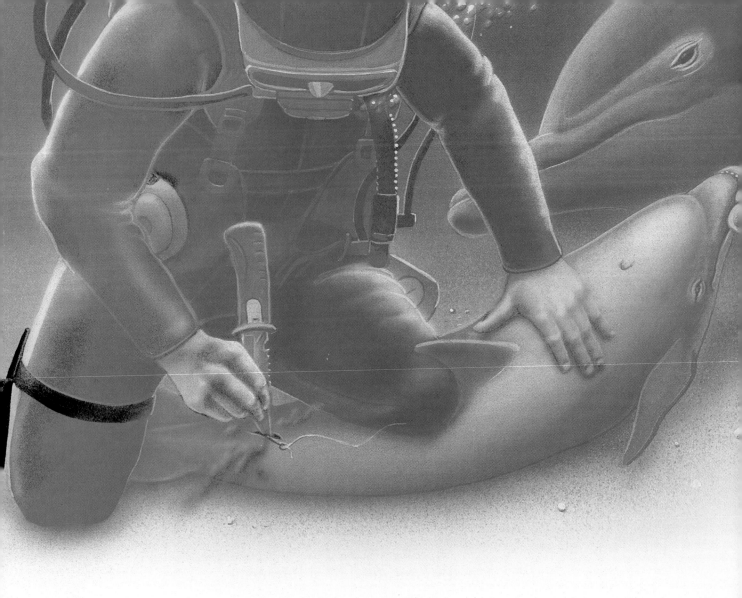

I felt so bad to be hurting it, but I knew if I didn't help, it would probably die.

Holding the baby dolphin with my left hand, I stuck one finger down the hook shaft until I felt the place where it turned up to form the barbed hook.

It was stuck tight, hooked into the muscle tissue in the baby's tail.

I tried to wiggle it free, but it would not budge.

As the baby cried out, the mother dolphin used her nose to stroke the baby, calming its struggle. She watched my hands closely and seemed like a nurse hovering over a doctor at the operating table.

The hook had to be cut free, and I dreaded using the big diving knife to do it, but there was no choice.

Placing the blade between my fingers the way you would hold a pencil to write, I very carefully put the point into the hole above the embedded hook.

The baby cried and struggled. I could not hold it with my hand, so I placed my left leg over its body and held it down gently. I stroked its whole body for a few moments, trying to calm it.

Impatient, the big dolphin again nudged me with his bottle nose. They would need to breathe soon.

Taking a deep breath from the regulator in my mouth, I slipped the knife into the wound and gently ran it down along the hook shaft. I used my left hand to feel into the wound as I pushed the knife in. Then I hit the muscle tissue that held the hook in place. It was now or never.

I cut the barb loose, and the hook was free. I withdrew the knife and took the hook out. Blood flowed from the baby's tail, and I pushed my palm down hard on the open wound to slow the bleeding.

The two big dolphins clicked excitedly about me. I felt a great surge of relief. I had done it. My heart was filled with joy. I was unbelievably happy.

Then the big dolphin suddenly darted away downcurrent. Something had caught his attention. A pair of bull sharks were coming straight for the baby, sniffing the blood trail as it flowed toward them in the fast Gulf Stream.

The father dolphin saw them and raced for them head-on. He was so fast that even the speeding sharks could not get out of his way.

Wham! The father dolphin hit the bigger shark right behind its gill slits, knocking it aside.

Wham! He hit it again. The shark swam away with a trail of blood pouring from its gills. It wanted no more fight with the protective father dolphin.

The other shark continued swimming straight toward the baby and me. The mother dolphin exploded into action. She tore through the water and met the shark with a fierce bump to its side.

A second later the father dolphin hit it from the other side. It swam away, also trailing blood.

The father dolphin followed, making repeated attacks, ensuring they would not return to harm the bleeding baby.

The sharks were no match for the enraged parent dolphins who had saved their baby and probably me, too.

I lifted my hand from the baby, and the bleeding
had almost stopped. The mother dolphin had
returned. She looked at the hole in its body and then
at the hook lying on the sand nearby. She clicked
loudly, and I heard more clicking from farther away.
It was the father dolphin coming back.

He had chased the sharks far away. He was there
in an instant, swimming rapidly back to his family.

I let the baby up, and it joined the parent dolphins.
They all swam around me, making clicking sounds.

The father dolphin swam right up to me and
looked into my eyes behind the diving mask. He
nodded his head up and down in a rapid motion and
then gently pushed me with his nose.

I reached out to touch his head, and he let me do so. For that brief moment, whether it was my imagination or it was really happening, I had the strong impression that he was thanking me, one father to another.

Then he made the clicking sound again, and the three swam rapidly toward the surface, leaving me alone on the bottom. I knew it was time for them to breathe again.

I looked at my air gauge and saw I had enough air to swim awhile longer. The experience that I will never forget had all happened in about ten minutes.

I kept looking for the dolphins to return that day, but they didn't.

As I climbed into the boat after I surfaced, I felt a happiness that I have never known before. The dolphins had left me with a sense of peace and a strong feeling of love.

All the way back from the day's dive, I could not stop feeling the dolphins were still communicating with me from someplace out there in the sea.

For the next couple of weeks I kept thinking about the baby dolphin, wondering if the sharks had gotten it or if it had survived. I couldn't get the dolphins out of my mind.

Then Amos called to see if I wanted to dive the next morning, and I said yes.

It was a different kind of morning from that last time. The sky was overcast, and the sea was much rougher with a cool northeastern wind blowing whitecaps toward shore. Only Amos and one other diver were along as we sped down the coast to our selected diving area.

I was working on my diving equipment when Amos shouted, "Hey, look over there. Dolphins!"

I looked up, and sure enough, several dolphins were racing with our boat, jumping from the water right by our bow wake. Suddenly I had that same feeling I had experienced on the day I helped the dolphin family.

Then I saw a small dolphin. It was in the midst of six other dolphins with a scar clearly visible on its back. It was the baby I had helped. I cheered and laughed until the tears rolled down my cheeks. The baby dolphin had survived.

It swam close to the boat, easily keeping pace with our speed, jumping high out of the water. It seemed its upturned mouth had an even bigger grin on it than before.

For a few minutes the dolphins stayed with us. Then they swam away, jumping and enjoying just being alive in the sea.

As I watched them go, I knew I had experienced something very special.

It's been some time now since my dolphin adventure, but I often think about that dolphin family. I shall never forget the feeling of happiness I felt in their presence.

I look forward to swimming with the dolphins again. It could happen anytime now.

IN RESPONSE

Dolphin Headlines

What might the headlines in a newspaper say about the unusual happening the diver described? Write three headlines that tell of the dolphin rescue.

Problems and Solutions

In a group, discuss problems the diver faced and how he solved them. Next, discuss the problems Garrett Morgan's inventions solved. What made the diver and Mr. Morgan want to solve these problems? Give examples from the selections.

AUTHOR AT WORK

"I write my books and articles to let people know they can make a difference," says Wayne Grover. In keeping with his lifelong concern for animals, *A Dolphin Adventure* tells how he made a difference for one baby dolphin.

Through the years, Mr. Grover's writing has appeared in newspapers and magazines. Today, he writes about how people can take care of the earth. Mr. Grover believes that people "can work together to create a new world, dedicated to natural balance and returning to the earth what we take from it."

Another Book About . . .

Dolphins

Dolphins at Grassy Key by Marcia Seligson, photographs by George Ancona, Macmillan, 1989

Library Link "Underwater Rescue" was taken from *Dolphin Adventure: A True Story* by Wayne Grover. You might enjoy reading the entire book to learn more about his adventure.

Express Yourself

In Creative Solutions, you read about characters who found new ways to solve problems, both real and imagined. You also learned that, just as problems are sometimes in our imagination, so are their solutions.

Imagining a Solution

Imagination can be a helpful tool for identifying and solving problems. Write a paragraph explaining how the diver ("Underwater Rescue") and Garrett Morgan ("Garrett Morgan, Inventor") used their imagination to solve problems.

Understanding Themselves

In the Understanding Ourselves Theme, you read about characters who discovered their special talents. Which characters from the Creative Solutions theme also discovered their special talents? In writing, explain your choices. Be sure to describe the special talents.

Finding a Way

"There must be a way, but how?" asked the diver in "Underwater Rescue." By not giving up and trying different solutions, the diver was able to find a way to help the dolphins. Choose another character from this theme who tries different solutions. Which of his or her strategies were successful? Which were not? How have the characters in these theme helped you learn about problem solving?

Real or Imagined

In "The Chicken-Coop Monster" and "The Boy Who Drew Cats," Missy and Kenji both feared something. Was what they feared real or imaginary? Why do you think so? Discuss your answer with a classmate. Be sure to use examples from the story to support your answer.

Places and Problems

Sometimes it is harder to solve a problem when you are in an unfamiliar place. For "Underwater Rescue," "The Boy Who Drew Cats," or "The Chicken-Coop Monster" explain how this is true. Discuss your answer with a partner.

The Silver Bookcase

Tanya's Big Green Dream
by Linda Glaser, illustrated by
Susan McGinnis, Macmillan, 1994

Earth Day is only a week away, and
Tanya needs a project. All the other
fourth graders think her idea—to plant
a tree—is impossible. But Tanya is
determined to see her dream come true.

Coaching Ms. Parker
by Carla Heymsfeld, illustrated by
Jane O'Connor, Bradbury Press, 1992

Mike is having a hard time in fourth
grade, especially with reading and
book reports. Then he learns that Ms.
Parker is dreading the annual baseball
game between the teachers and the
sixth graders because she can't play
very well. Together, they come up with
a solution to help them both succeed.

Morgan's Zoo
by James Howe, illustrated by Leslie Morrill, Atheneum, 1984

Morgan takes care of the animals at the city zoo. They are his only family. Now that the zoo is going to close, what will happen to the animals and the kindly old gentleman who loves them?

The Stone Lion
by Alan Schroeder, illustrated by Todd L. W. Doney, Charles Scribner's Sons, 1994

Drashi is a kind and honest boy who lives in Tibet. When he and his mother are forced to leave their village, they must struggle to survive. One day while searching for firewood, Drashi finds a stone lion, and wonderful things happen.

Making Musical Things
by Ann Wiseman, Charles Scribner's Sons, 1979

This book contains dozens of ideas for making musical instruments from ordinary household items. Use these intruments to play music from all over the world.

Transformations

THEME

5

"Each day my world
shows
one more change;
each day I see another
one in me."

—Michael Spooner
"Changes"

Transformations

CONTENTS

Imaginary Changes

Personal Changes

Theme Trade Books

New Providence:
A Changing Cityscape

by Renata von Tscharner
and Ronald Lee Fleming
Like a person, a city struggles as
it grows and changes. Follow the
town of New Providence as it
changes from a sleepy town to
a thriving city.

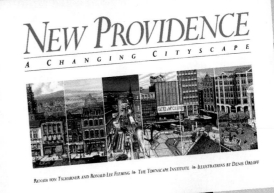

A Boy Becomes a Man
at Wounded Knee

by Ted Wood with Wanbli
Numpa Afraid of Hawk
One hundred years after most of
his ancestors were killed by
soldiers, eight-year-old Wanbli rides a
dangerous six-day journey
to help heal his people.

See a tree trunk turn into a totem pole in Carving Culture.

Theme Magazine

Are they buffalo or bison? How
many Cinderellas are there? How
can a car turn into a growling
tiger? The Theme Magazine
Transforma Zone can help you
figure it out.

Buffalo
Woman

retold and illustrated by Paul Goble

There was a young man who was already a great hunter. Even coyotes and the crows and magpies followed him to pick up the scraps from his hunting. He felt a wonderful harmony with the buffalo. The people knew he could find the herds when they needed meat. When they had hunted, the young man gave thanks that the buffalo had offered themselves.

One early morning the young man went to a place at the stream where the buffalo came to drink. He waited, hidden among the bushes, watching the butterflies opening and closing their wings in the warming sun.

After a while the young man saw a buffalo cow plodding through the tall weeds toward the water. He tightened an arrow against his bowstring.

The buffalo was coming very slowly.

The young man did not know whether he fell asleep, or what happened, but when he looked again the buffalo was not there. Instead, a beautiful young woman stepped from the weeds onto the pebbles at the water's edge and took a drink. She was not one of his people; her clothes were different and her hair was not braided. She smelled of wild sage and prairie flowers. He knew at once that he loved her.

"I come from the Buffalo Nation," she told him. "They have sent me because you have always had good feelings for our people. They know you are a good and kind man. I will be your wife. My people wish that the love we have for each other will be an example to both our peoples to follow."

The young man and the beautiful young woman were married. They had a son and named him Calf Boy. Their life together was good.

But the young man's relatives did not like his wife. They often said unkind things among themselves: "He has married a woman without a family," they said. "Her ways are different; she's like an animal. She will never be one of our family." One day when the young man was away hunting, his relatives came and said to his wife: "You should never have come here; go back to wherever you came from. You are nothing but an animal, anyway." At that she immediately picked up Calf Boy and ran out of the tipi.

The young man was returning home when he saw his wife and child hurrying away from the camp. He was angry when he found out what had happened, and set out at once to bring them back.

Their trail led across rolling country. He followed all day, hearing the grasshoppers calling again and again from the sagebrush on every side. Evening was coming when he saw in the distance a painted tipi with smoke rising from a cooking fire.

The young man was surprised to see his son playing outside the tipi. When Calf Boy saw his father he ran to meet him. "I am glad you have come, Father. Mother has your meal ready." He took his father's hand and they went inside. The lodge was filled with the good smell of cooking. His wife placed a bowl of soup before him. "I am going home," she

said. "I cannot live with your people. Do not follow us or you will be in great danger." "I love you," the young man said, "And wherever you and our son go, I am going too."

The young man awoke next morning looking up into the sky. The tipi was gone! There was nobody anywhere. Yet, it had not just been a dream, because he could see the circle in the dew-soaked grass where the tipi had stood, and the tracks of his wife and child leading away.

The young man followed their trail until he again came to the tipi. His son ran out to meet him.

"Mother does not want you to come any farther. Tomorrow she will make the rivers dry, but when you are thirsty, look for water in my tracks."

That evening his wife told him: "My people live beyond that distant high ridge. They know I am coming home. They are angry because your relatives were unkind to me. Do not follow any farther or they will kill you." But the young man replied: "It does not matter when I die. I shall not turn back. I do this because I love you both."

When his wife was asleep he buckled his belt through hers and wrapped her long hair around his arm.

Again the young man awoke alone. The only tracks in the dew were those of a buffalo and her calf walking side by side. While he was wondering about the tracks, a flock of little birds flew around him excitedly: "They have gone home! They have gone home!" He then knew that the tracks were of his wife and child.

The tracks led toward the high ridge. Thin lines of trees marked the winding rivers. They were dry, but just as Calf Boy had told him, he found water in his hoof-prints in the baked mud of the river-beds.

From the top of the high ridge the young man looked out in wonder over the multitude of the Buffalo Nation.

As he walked down toward them a calf came running out. "Father, go back! They will kill you! Go back!"

But the young man answered: "No, Son, I shall always stay with you and Mother."

"Then you must be brave," Calf Boy said. "My Grandfather is chief of the Buffalo Nation. Do not show fear or he will surely kill you. He will ask you to find me and Mother. But you think we all look alike! When he lines us up, you will know me because I

shall flick my left ear. You will find Mother because I
shall put a cockle-burr on her back. You must pick us
out and then you will be safe. Be attentive!"

The old bull bellowed and charged out from the
herd. The ground trembled under his thundering
hoofs. He stopped just in front of the young man. He
pawed the earth into dust clouds, hooked his horns
into clumps of sagebrush and tossed them aside in
anger. The young man stood still. He showed no fear.

"Ah, this Straight-up-Person has a strong heart,"
breathed the old bull. "By your courage you have
saved yourself. Follow me."

The old bull led the way. The silent multitude
parted and joined again behind. At the center was the
painted tipi. The whole Buffalo Nation formed into

radiating circles. The calves made the inner ring; the yearlings the next, the cows and bulls, all according to their ages.

"Straight-up-Person," said the old bull in a voice which all could hear, "your relatives insulted my daughter. But you have come among us because you love your wife and child. Then *find* them! If you cannot, we shall trample you until not even a stain of your blood remains."

The young man passed in front of the little calves. They looked alike, but one flicked his ear as if troubled by a fly. He laid his hand on the calf's head. "My Son," he said, and a sound of surprise came from the multitude. "This must be a wonderful Person," they said.

He then walked around the circle formed by the cows. Again, they all looked alike, but he came to one with a cockle-burr on her back; "My Wife," he said. Once more a sound of surprise came from the Buffalo Nation: "Ah, he calls her 'Wife'."

"This Straight-up-Person loves his wife and little child," the old bull announced. "He was willing to die for them. We shall make him one of us. We shall all join in with our thoughts while we do this."

The young man was led inside the tipi and they tied the door shut. His only covering was a buffalo robe with the horns and hoofs attached.

For three days and nights the buffalo surrounded the tipi, filling the air with their continuous grunts and bellowing.

On the fourth day the bulls made a sudden rush and pushed the tipi over. They rolled and rolled the young man in a wallow until he was covered all over with dirt. They squeezed the breath from his body and breathed new breath into him. They licked him and rubbed against him until his man-smell was gone. He tried to stand but he could not. He felt the robe become a part of him. When the bulls heard him grunting they worked even harder, tumbling him over and over.

And at last, he stood up on his own four legs—a young buffalo bull.

That was a wonderful day! The relationship was made between the People and the Buffalo Nation; it will last until the end of time. It will be remembered that a brave young man became a buffalo because he loved his wife and little child. In return the Buffalo People have given their flesh so that little children, and babies still unborn, will always have meat to eat. It is the Creator's wish.

Mitakuye oyasin[1]—We are all related.

---

1 **mitakuye oyasin** (*mee tah KWAY uh oh YAH seh*)

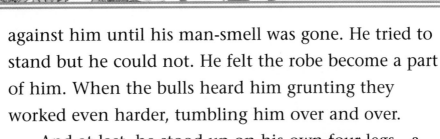

IN RESPONSE

Read All About It!
Write a letter to a friend about the story "Buffalo Woman." Give a short description of the characters in the story. Would you recommend "Buffalo Woman" to your friend? Why or why not?

What Does It Mean?
Think about the saying *"Mitakuye oyasin*—We are all related." How do the Buffalo Nation and the People become related? As a group, list the events that lead to the young man becoming a member of the Buffalo Nation.

Paul Goble

Paul Goble grew up in London, England, thousands of miles from the setting of "Buffalo Woman." When he was a child, his mother read him stories about Native Americans. Soon he began collecting every picture, magazine article, and book he could find.

After Mr. Goble graduated from design school in 1959, he took his first trip to an Indian reservation. He traveled to reservations in South Dakota and Montana, where the Native Americans shared their people's stories with him. During his trip, Mr. Goble was accepted by the Yakima and Sioux peoples. He was given the name *Wakinyan Chikalai*, which means "Little Thunder," by a

★ Award-winning Author and Illustrator

Sioux chief. After many visits to the reservations, Mr. Goble moved from London to the Black Hills of South Dakota in 1977.

Now Mr. Goble writes children's books based on the stories he learned while visiting the reservations. In his illustrations, Mr. Goble tries to include symbols from Native American culture. His story writing and illustrations have won many awards.

The Black Hills of South Dakota provide inspiration for Mr. Goble's paintings and books.

YOU—TÚ

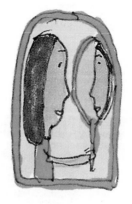

You are you.
Not me,
But you.
Look in the mirror
Peek-a-boo
The face that you see
Isn't me—
It's you.

Tú eres tú.
No yo,
Pero tú.
Mira al espejo
Peek-a-boo
La cara que miras
No soy yo—
Eres tú.

—Charlotte Pomerantz

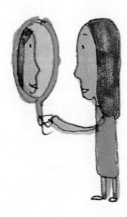

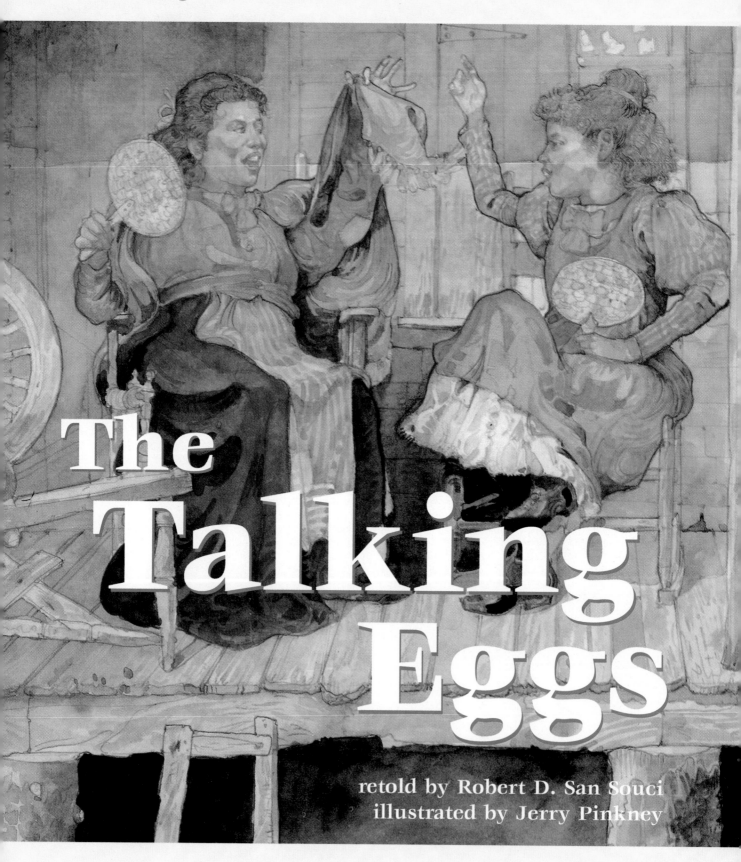

The Talking Eggs

retold by Robert D. San Souci
illustrated by Jerry Pinkney

Back in the old days there was a widow with two daughters named Rose and Blanche. They lived on a farm so poor, it looked like the tail end of bad luck. They raised a few chickens, some beans, and a little cotton to get by.

Rose, the older sister, was cross and mean and didn't know beans from birds' eggs. Blanche was sweet and kind and sharp as forty crickets. But their mother liked Rose the best, because they were alike as two peas in a pod—bad-tempered, sharp-tongued, and always putting on airs.

The mother made Blanche do all the work around the place. She had to iron the clothes each morning using an old iron filled with hot coals, chop cotton in the afternoon, and string the beans for supper.

While she'd be doing these chores, her mama and sister would sit side by side in rocking chairs on the shady porch, fanning themselves and talking foolishness about getting rich and moving to the city, where they could go to fancy balls wearing trail-train dresses and lots of jewels.

One hot day the mother sent Blanche to the well to fetch a bucket of water. When the girl got there, she found an old woman wrapped in a raggedy black shawl, near fainting with the heat.

"Please, child, give me a sip of water," the old woman said. "I'm 'bout to die of thirst."

"Yes, aunty," said Blanche, rinsing out her bucket and dipping up some clean, cool well water. "Drink what you need."

"Thank you, child," said the old woman when she'd taken swallow after swallow of water. "You got a spirit of do-right in your soul. God is gonna bless you." Then she walked away down the path that led to the deep woods.

When Blanche got back to the cabin, her mother and sister hollered at her for taking so long.

"This water's so warm, it's near boilin'," shouted Rose, and she dumped the bucket out on the porch.

"Here your poor sister's near dyin' for a drop of cool water," her mother screamed, "and you can't even bring her that little thing."

Then the two of them scolded and hit Blanche until the frightened girl ran away into the woods. She began to cry, since she didn't have anywhere to go, and she was scared to go home.

Suddenly, around a bend in the path came the old woman in the raggedy black shawl. When she saw Blanche, she asked kindly, "What's made you cry so, you poor child?"

"Mama and sister Rose lit into me for something that wasn't my fault," said Blanche, rubbing tears off her cheek. "Now I'm afraid to go home."

"Hush, child! Stop your crying. You come on home with me. I'll give you supper and a clean bed. But you got to promise you won't laugh at anything you see."

Blanche gave her word of honor that she wouldn't laugh. Then the old woman took her by the hand and led her deep into the backwoods. As they walked along the narrow path, bramble bushes and tree branches opened wide in front of them, and closed up behind them.

Soon they came to the old woman's tumbledown shack. A cow with two heads, and horns like corkscrews, peered over a fence at Blanche and brayed like a mule. She reckoned it was a pretty strange sight, but she didn't say anything, not wanting to hurt the old woman's feelings.

Next, she saw that the yard in front of the cabin was filled with chickens of every color. Some were hopping about on one leg, some running about on three or four or even more. These chickens didn't cluck, but whistled like mockingbirds. But strange as all this was, Blanche stuck by her promise not to laugh.

When they got inside the cabin, the old woman said, "Light the fire, child, and cook us some supper." So Blanche fetched kindling from the woodpile outside the back door.

The old woman sat down near the fireplace and took off her head. She set it on her knees like a pumpkin. First she combed out her gray hair, then she plaited it into two long braids. Blanche got pretty scared at this. But the woman had been nothing but kind to her, so she just went on lighting the fire.

After a bit the old woman put her head back on her shoulders and looked at herself in a sliver of mirror nailed to the cabin wall. " Um-m-m-hum!" she said, nodding. "That's better."

Then she gave Blanche an old beef bone and said, "Put this in the pot for supper.

Now Blanche was near starving, and the bone looked like a pretty sad meal for the two of them, but she did what the old woman said. "Shall I boil it for soup, aunty?" she asked.

"Look at the pot, child!" the old woman said, laughing.

The pot was filled with thick stew, bubbling away.

Next the woman gave Blanche only one grain of rice and told her to grind it in the stone mortar. Feeling mighty foolish Blanche began to pound the grain with the heavy stone pestle. In a moment the mortar was overflowing with rice.

When they had finished supper, the old woman said, "It's a fine moonshiny night, child. Come with me."

They sat themselves down on the back porch steps. After a time dozens of rabbits came out of the underbrush and formed a circle in the yard. The men rabbits all had frock-tail coats, and the lady rabbits had little trail-train dresses. They danced, standing on their hind feet, hopping about. One big rabbit played a banjo, and the old woman hummed along with it.

Blanche kept time by clapping along. The rabbits did a square dance, a Virginia reel, and even a cakewalk. The girl felt so happy, she never wanted to leave. She sat and clapped until she fell asleep, and the old woman carried her inside and put her to bed.

When Blanche got up the next morning, the old woman told her, "Go milk my cow."

The girl did what she was told and the two-headed cow with the curly horns gave her a bucket of the sweetest milk she'd ever tasted. They had it with their morning coffee.

"You gotta go home now, child," the old woman said to Blanche, who was washing the breakfast dishes. "But I tell you, things will be better from here on out. And since you are such a good girl, I got a present for you."

"Go out to the chicken house. Any eggs that say, 'Take me,' you go ahead and take. But if you hear any say, 'Don't take me,' you leave them be. When you get near home, throw those eggs one after another over your left shoulder so they break in the road behind you. Then you'll get a surprise."

When Blanche got to the little chicken house, she found all the nests filled with eggs. Half were gold or silver or covered with jewels; half looked no different from the eggs she got from her chickens back home.

All the plain eggs told her, "Take me." All the fancy ones cried, "Don't take me." She wished she could take just *one* gold or silver or jeweled egg, but she did what the old woman told her and only scooped up the plain ones.

She and the old woman waved good-bye to each other, then Blanche went on her way. Partway home she began to toss the eggs one at a time over her left shoulder. All sorts of wonderful things spilled out of those eggs: now diamonds and rubies, now gold and silver

coins, now pretty silk dresses and dainty satin shoes.
There was even a handsome carriage that grew in a
wink from the size of a matchbox—and a fine
brown-and-white pony that sprouted from the size
of a cricket to draw it.

Blanche loaded all these lovely things into the
carriage and rode the rest of the way home like a
grand lady.

When she got back to the cabin, her mother and sister just gawked at her new finery. "Where did you get all these things?" her mother asked, making Rose help Blanche carry the treasures inside. That evening the mother cooked dinner for the first time since Blanche was old enough to hold a skillet. All the time telling Blanche what a sweet daughter she was, her mama got the girl to tell about the old woman and the cabin in the woods and the talking eggs.

When Blanche was asleep, the mother grabbed Rose and told her, "You gotta go into the woods tomorrow mornin' and find that old aunty. Then you'll get some of those talkin' eggs for yourse'f so's you can have fine dresses and jewels like your sister. When you get back, I'll chase Blanche off and keep her things myse'f. Then we'll go to the city and be fine ladies like we was meant to be."

"Can't we just run her off tonight so's I don't have to go pokin' through the woods lookin' for some crazy ol' aunty?" Rose whined.

"There's not near enough for two," her mother said, getting angry. "You do as I say and don't be so contrary."

So the next morning Rose set out drag-foot into the woods. She dawdled mostly, but soon met the old woman in her raggedy black shawl.

"My sweet little sister Blanche tol' me you got a real pretty house an' all," said Rose. "I'd 'preciate to see it."

"You can come with me if you've a mind to," said the old woman, "but you got to promise not to laugh at whatever you see."

"I swear," said Rose.

So the old woman led her through the bramble bushes and tree branches into the deep woods.

But when they got near the cabin and Rose saw the two-headed cow that brayed like a mule and the funny-looking chickens that sang like mockingbirds, she yelled, "If there ever was a sight, that's one! That's the stupidest thing in the world!" Then she laughed and laughed until she nearly fell down.

"Um-m-m-hum," said the old woman, shaking her head.

Inside, Rose complained when she was asked to start the fire, and she wound up with more smoke than flame. When the old woman gave her an old bone to put in the pot for supper, Rose said crossly, "That's gonna make a mighty poor meal." She dropped it in the pot, but the old bone remained a bone, so they only had thin soup for supper. When the old woman gave her one grain of rice to grind in the mortar, Rose said, "That sad speck won't hardly feed a fly!" She wouldn't lift the pestle, so they had no rice at all.

"Um-m-m-hum!" the old woman muttered.

Rose went to bed hungry. All night long she heard mice scratching under the floor and screech-owls clawing at the window.

In the morning the old woman told her to milk the cow. Rose did, but she made fun of the two-headed creature and all she got was a little sour milk not fit for drinking. So they had their breakfast coffee without cream.

When the old woman lifted her head off her shoulders to brush her hair, quick as a wink Rose grabbed that head and said, "I'm not gonna put you back t'gether 'til you give me presents like my sister got."

"Ah, child, you're a wicked girl," said the old woman's head, "but I got to have my body back, so I'll tell you what to do.

"Go to the chicken house and take those eggs that say, 'Take me.' But leave be the ones that cry, 'Don't take me.' Then you toss those eggs over your right shoulder when you're on your way home."

To be sure the old woman wasn't playing her a trick, Rose set the old woman's head out on the porch while her body sat groping around the cabin. Then she ran to the chicken house. Inside, all the plain eggs cried, "Take me," while all the gold and silver and jeweled ones said, "Don't take me."

"You think I'm fool enough to listen to you and pass up the prettiest ones? Not on your life!" So she grabbed all of the gold and silver and jeweled eggs that kept yelling "Don't take me," and off she ran into the woods with them.

As soon as she was out of sight of the old woman's cabin, she tossed the eggs over her right shoulder as fast as she could. But out of the shells came clouds of whip snakes, toads, frogs, yellow jackets, and a big, old, gray wolf. These began to chase after her like pigs after a pumpkin.

Hollering bloody murder Rose ran all the way to her mother's cabin. When the woman saw the swarm of things chasing her daughter, she tried to rescue her with a broom. But the wasps and wolf and all the other creatures wouldn't be chased off, so mother and daughter hightailed it to the woods, with all the animals following.

When they returned home, angry and sore and
stung and covered with mud, they found Blanche had
gone to the city to live like a grand lady—though she
remained as kind and generous as always.

For the rest of their lives Rose and her mother tried
to find the strange old woman's cabin and the talking
eggs, but they never could find that place again.

The Old Woman's Opinion

Rose and Blanche are as different as can be. Write a paragraph in which the old woman describes the two sisters. How do you think the old woman feels about what happens to Rose and Blanche? Explain.

Sudden Changes

Blanche and the young man ("Buffalo Woman") are both transformed as a reward for good actions. With a partner, describe how each character's life changes. How are these changes alike? What does each character do to make the change come about?

ILLUSTRATOR AT WORK

Author Robert D. San Souci got a lot of help from illustrator Jerry Pinkney in the retelling of the folk tale "The Talking Eggs." To create his illustrations, Mr. Pinkney often photographed real people acting out the story. Then he used the photographs to help him draw the characters.

Mr. Pinkney is a well-rounded artist who illustrates in many different styles. Even though his teachers, family, and friends all greatly admire his work, he has never stopped trying to improve it.

Another Book Illustrated by . . .

Jerry Pinkney

Mirandy and Brother Wind by Patricia C. McKissack, illustrated by Jerry Pinkney, Alfred A. Knopf, 1988

★ Award-winning Illustrator

Changing **Art**

Artists' styles may change over time. Sometimes an artist decides to try something new. Other times, an artist may be forced to change.

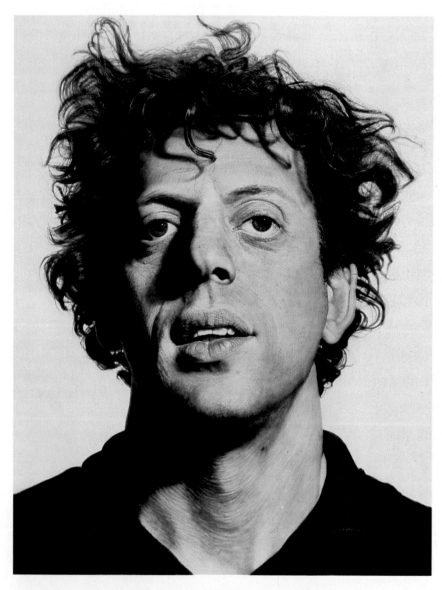

Painting by Chuck Close (United States), *Phil,* **1969**

What has changed?

After becoming ill and losing full control of his hands, Chuck Close was forced to change his style of painting. He painted *Phil* before becoming ill and *April* afterward. How are these paintings different?

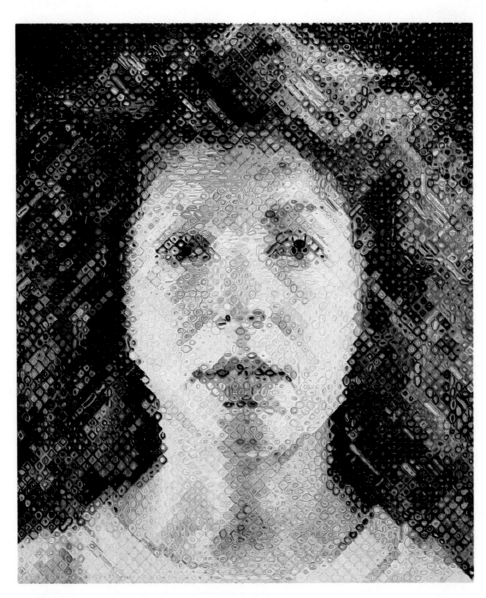

Painting by Chuck Close (United States), *April,* **1991**

The Gold Coin

written by Alma Flor Ada,
illustrated by Neil Waldman
translated by Bernice Randall

Juan[1] had been a thief for many years. Because he did his stealing by night, his skin had become pale and sickly. Because he spent his time either hiding or sneaking about, his body had become shriveled and bent. And because he had neither friend nor relative to make him smile, his face was always twisted into an angry frown.

One night, drawn by a light shining through the trees, Juan came upon a hut. He crept up to the door and through a crack saw an old woman sitting at a plain, wooden table.

What was that shining in her hand? Juan wondered. He could not believe his eyes: It was a gold coin. Then he heard the woman say to herself, "I must be the richest person in the world."

Juan decided instantly that all the woman's gold must be his. He thought that the easiest thing to do was to watch until the woman left. Juan hid in the bushes and huddled under his poncho, waiting for the right moment to enter the hut.

---

1 Juan (*hwahn*)

Juan was half asleep when he heard knocking at the door and the sound of insistent voices. A few minutes later, he saw the woman, wrapped in a black cloak, leave the hut with two men at her side.

Here's my chance! Juan thought. And, forcing open a window, he climbed into the empty hut.

He looked about eagerly for the gold. He looked under the bed. It wasn't there. He looked in the cupboard. It wasn't there, either. Where could it be? Close to despair, Juan tore away some beams supporting the thatch roof.

Finally, he gave up. There was simply no gold in the hut.

All I can do, he thought, is to find the old woman and make her tell me where she's hidden it.

So he set out along the path that she and her two companions had taken.

It was daylight by the time Juan reached the river. The countryside had been deserted, but here, along the riverbank, were two huts. Nearby, a man and his son were hard at work, hoeing potatoes.

It had been a long, long time since Juan had spoken to another human being. Yet his desire to find the woman was so strong that he went up to the farmers and asked, in a hoarse, raspy voice, "Have you seen a short, gray-haired woman, wearing a black cloak?"

435

"Oh, you must be looking for Doña Josefa,"[2] the young boy said. "Yes, we've seen her. We went to fetch her this morning, because my grandfather had another attack of—"

"Where is she now?" Juan broke in.

"She is long gone," said the father with a smile. "Some people from across the river came looking for her, because someone in their family is sick."

"How can I get across the river?" Juan asked anxiously.

"Only by boat," the boy answered. "We'll row you across later, if you'd like." Then turning back to his work, he added, "But first we must finish digging up the potatoes."

The thief muttered, "Thanks." But he quickly grew impatient. He grabbed a hoe and began to help the pair of farmers. The sooner we finish, the sooner we'll get across the river, he thought. And the sooner I'll get to my gold!

It was dusk when they finally laid down their hoes. The soil had been turned, and the wicker baskets were brimming with potatoes.

---

2 Doña Josefa (*DOHN yah hoh SAY fah*)

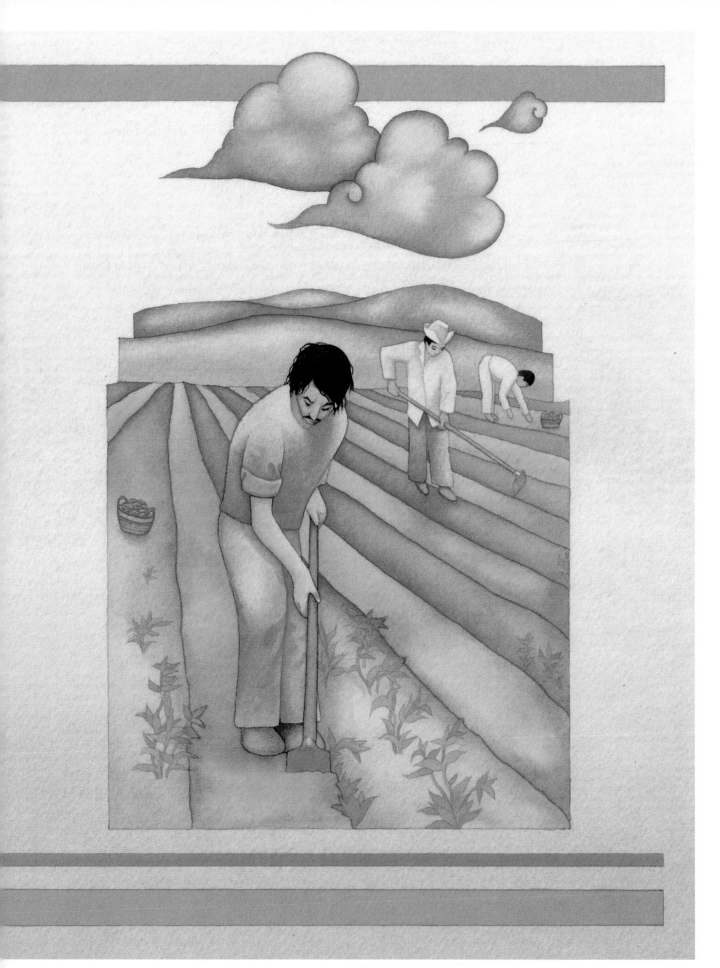

"Now can you row me across?" Juan asked the father anxiously.

"Certainly," the man said. "But let's eat supper first."

Juan had forgotten the taste of a home-cooked meal and the pleasure that comes from sharing it with others. As he sopped up the last of the stew with a chunk of dark bread, memories of other meals came back to him from far away and long ago.

By the light of the moon, father and son guided their boat across the river.

"What a wonderful healer Doña Josefa is!" the boy told Juan. "All she had to do to make Abuelo better was give him a cup of her special tea."

"Yes, and not only that," his father added, "she brought him a gold coin."

Juan was stunned. It was one thing for Doña Josefa to go around helping people. But how could she go around handing out gold coins—*his gold coins*?

When the threesome finally reached the other side of the river, they saw a young man sitting outside his hut.

"This fellow is looking for Doña Josefa," the father said, pointing to Juan.

"Oh, she left some time ago," the young man said.

"Where to?" Juan asked tensely.

"Over to the other side of the mountain," the young man replied, pointing to the vague outline of mountains in the night sky.

"How did she get there?" Juan asked, trying to hide his impatience.

"By horse," the young man answered. "They came on horseback to get her because someone had broken his leg."

"Well, then, I need a horse, too," Juan said urgently.

"Tomorrow," the young man replied softly. "Perhaps I can take you tomorrow, maybe the next day. First I must finish harvesting the corn."

So Juan spent the next day in the fields, bathed in sweat from sunup to sundown.

Yet each ear of corn that he picked seemed to bring him closer to his treasure. And later that evening, when he helped the young man husk several ears so they could boil them for supper, the yellow kernels glittered like gold coins.

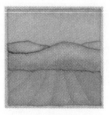

While they were eating, Juan thought about Doña Josefa. Why, he wondered, would someone who said she was the world's richest woman spend her time taking care of every sick person for miles around?

The following day, the two set off at dawn. Juan could not recall when he last had noticed the beauty of the sunrise. He felt strangely moved by the sight of the mountains, barely lit by the faint rays of the morning sun.

As they neared the foothills, the young man said, "I'm not surprised you're looking for Doña Josefa. The whole countryside needs her. I went for her because my wife had been running a high fever. In no time at all, Doña Josefa had her on the road to recovery. And what's more, my friend, she brought her a gold coin!"

Juan groaned inwardly. To think that someone could hand out gold so freely! What a strange woman Doña Josefa is, Juan thought. Not only is she willing to help one person after another, but she doesn't mind traveling all over the countryside to do it!

"Well, my friend," said the young man finally, "this is where I must leave you. But you don't have far to walk. See that house over there? It belongs to the man who broke his leg."

The young man stretched out his hand to say goodbye. Juan stared at it for a moment. It had been a long, long time since the thief had shaken hands with anyone. Slowly, he pulled out a hand from under his poncho. When his companion grasped it firmly in his own, Juan felt suddenly warmed, as if by the rays of the sun.

But after he thanked the young man, Juan ran down the road. He was still eager to catch up with Doña Josefa. When he reached the house, a woman and a child were stepping down from a wagon.

"Have you seen Doña Josefa?" Juan asked.

"We've just taken her to Don Teodosio's,"[3] the woman said. "His wife is sick, you know—"

"How do I get there?" Juan broke in. "I've got to see her."

"It's too far to walk," the woman said amiably. "If you'd like, I'll take you there tomorrow. But first I must gather my squash and beans."

So Juan spent yet another long day in the fields. Working beneath the summer sun, Juan noticed that his skin had begun to tan. And although he had to stoop down to pick the squash, he found that he could now stretch his body. His back had begun to straighten, too.

Later, when the little girl took him by the hand to show him a family of rabbits burrowed under a fallen tree, Juan's face broke into a smile. It had been a long, long time since Juan had smiled.

Yet his thoughts kept coming back to the gold.

---

3 Don Teodosio (*dohn tay oh DOH syoh*)

444

The following day, the wagon carrying Juan and the woman lumbered along a road lined with coffee fields.

The woman said, "I don't know what we would have done without Doña Josefa. I sent my daughter to our neighbor's house, who then brought Doña Josefa on horseback. She set my husband's leg and then showed me how to brew a special tea to lessen the pain."

Getting no reply, she went on. "And, as if that weren't enough, she brought him a gold coin. Can you imagine such a thing?"

Juan could only sigh. No doubt about it, he thought, Doña Josefa is someone special. But Juan didn't know whether to be happy that Doña Josefa had so much gold she could freely hand it out, or angry for her having already given so much of it away.

When they finally reached Don Teodosio's house, Doña Josefa was already gone. But here, too, there was work that needed to be done. . . .

Juan stayed to help with the coffee harvest. As he picked the red berries, he gazed up from time to time at the trees that grew, row upon row, along the hillsides. What a calm, peaceful place this is! he thought.

The next morning, Juan was up at daybreak. Bathed in the soft, dawn light, the mountains seemed to smile at him. When Don Teodosio offered him a lift on horseback, Juan found it difficult to have to say good-bye.

"What a good woman Doña Josefa is!" Don Teodosio said, as they rode down the hill toward the sugarcane fields. "The minute she heard about my wife being sick, she came with her special herbs. And as if that weren't enough, she brought my wife a gold coin!"

In the stifling heat, the kind that often signals the approach of a storm, Juan simply sighed and mopped his brow. The pair continued riding for several hours in silence.

Juan then realized he was back in familiar territory, for they were now on the stretch of road he had traveled only a week ago—though how much longer it now seemed to him. He jumped off Don Teodosio's horse and broke into a run.

This time the gold would not escape him! But he had to move quickly, so he could find shelter before the storm broke.

Out of breath, Juan finally reached Doña Josefa's hut. She was standing by the door, shaking her head slowly as she surveyed the ransacked house.

"So I've caught up with you at last!" Juan shouted, startling the old woman. "Where's the gold?"

"The gold coin?" Doña Josefa said, surprised and looking at Juan intently. "Have you come for the gold coin? I've been trying hard to give it to someone who might need it," Doña Josefa said. "First to an old man who had just gotten over a bad attack. Then to a young woman who had been running a fever. Then to a man with a broken leg. And finally to Don Teodosio's

448

wife. But none of them would take it. They all said, 'Keep it. There must be someone who needs it more.'"

Juan did not say a word.

"You must be the one who needs it," Doña Josefa said.

She took the coin out of her pocket and handed it to him. Juan stared at the coin, speechless.

At that moment a young girl appeared, her long braid bouncing as she ran. "Hurry, Doña Josefa, please!" she said breathlessly. "My mother is all alone, and the baby is due any minute."

"Of course, dear," Doña Josefa replied. But as she glanced up at the sky, she saw nothing but black clouds. The storm was nearly upon them. Doña Josefa sighed deeply.

"But how can I leave now? Look at my house! I don't know what has happened to the roof. The storm will wash the whole place away!"

And there was a deep sadness in her voice.

Juan took in the child's frightened eyes, Doña Josefa's sad, distressed face, and the ransacked hut.

"Go ahead, Doña Josefa," he said. "Don't worry about your house. I'll see that the roof is back in shape, good as new."

The woman nodded gratefully, drew her cloak about her shoulders, and took the child by the hand. As she turned to leave, Juan held out his hand.

"Here, take this," he said, giving her the gold coin. "I'm sure the newborn will need it more than I."

IN RESPONSE

The Woman's Riches

Doña Josefa in "The Gold Coin" says, "I must be the richest woman in the world," What does she mean? List three of the woman's actions in the story that help make her life rich.

Sharing Stories

Role-play a meeting between Juan and Blanche ("The Talking Eggs"). Have them share their experiences and describe how their lives have changed and why.

Golden Gift

Each time Doña Josefa helps a person, she offers him or her a gold coin. Everyone she helps returns the coin to her. What reason do they all give for returning the gold coin? Using details from the story, explain why each person believes there is someone who needs the gold coin more than he or she does.

AUTHOR AT WORK

The idea for "The Gold Coin" came to Alma Flor Ada when she was driving home after talking with some migrant farm workers in California. She was struck by their generosity and kindness. All of a sudden, the entire story came to her. "It was as if the story was there, waiting for me to write it down," Ms. Ada said.

The character Doña Josefa in "The Gold Coin" is based on a real person. Her name is María Josefa Canellada. Alma Flor Ada has always considered her to be "one of the most generous and kindest" people she has known.

Ms. Ada has been interested in writing books since she was a child. When she was in fourth grade, she thought the books she read at school were boring compared with the ones she read at home. Ms. Ada promised herself that when she became a writer, she would write books that were fun and exciting. So far, she has written over a hundred books.

 Award-winning Author

Other Books by . . .

Alma Flor Ada

My Name Is María Isabel by Alma Flor Ada, illustrated by K. Dyble Thompson, Atheneum, 1993

The Unicorn of the West by Alma Flor Ada, illustrated by Abigail Pizer, Atheneum, 1994

Changes

The earth sheds its winter quilts
and hurries on toward summer,
    as if it, too, is restless
    for the tree house and the bicycle.

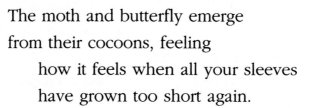

The moon looks rounder
than it did last night;
    I think it knows that I am growing too.

The moth and butterfly emerge
from their cocoons, feeling
    how it feels when all your sleeves
    have grown too short again.

Each day my world shows
one more change;
    each day I see another one in me.

The earth rolls out of hibernation.
The moon slips through its phases in the sky.
The butterfly will try its wings today,

    and so will I,
    and so will I.

—Michael Spooner

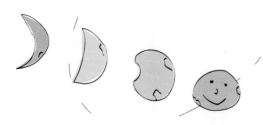

The phase I'm going through

I asked my mother
    why the moon is full sometimes
    and dark sometimes and sometimes in between.
She smiled a silly half-moon smile
    and said, "It's all
    a matter of which phase it's in."

I asked my father
    why the baby screams sometimes
    or laughs and wipes his supper in his hair.
He said that children go through phases.
    "Not to worry;
    he'll be through this in a year."

So if I turn my
    dark face to the world sometimes,
    or eat my hat with ketchup and with glue,
or yowl with cats when the moon is full,
    think nothing of it—
    it's just the phase I'm going through.

—Michael Spooner

SATO
and the
Elephants

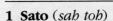

written by Juanita Havill
illustrated by Jean and Mou-sien Tseng

Sato[1] was a happy man. From morning to night he did what he wanted to do. He carved figures from creamy white pieces of ivory. Rabbits and monkeys. Turtles and fish. Dragons with smooth, delicate scales, and birds that looked as if they would fly right out of his hand.

As a boy, Sato had watched his father work. A master carver of netsuke[2] and okimono,[3] he was famous for the beauty and precision of his ivory figures. One day he carved a netsuke of happy, round-bellied Hotei[4] and gave the figure to Sato. Sato was so pleased that he hung the figure on a cord and wore it always around his neck. Whenever he touched the smooth, polished figure, he told his father, "Someday I will be a great ivory carver like you."

SATO
and the Elephants
JUANITA HAVILL --- JEAN AND MOU-SIEN TSENG

---

1 **Sato** (*sah toh*)
2 **netsuke** (*neh tsoo keh*) decorative buttonlike fastener
3 **okimono** (*oh kee moh noh*) something for display
4 **Hotei** (*hoh tay ee*) one of the seven Japanese gods of luck

Sato learned much from his father about the secrets of ivory. He learned that the best ivory was hard and dense and fine-grained. He learned how to saw and file the ivory, and to shave and pare it with knives. He learned how to sand, then polish a figure until it shone.

But he was young when his father died. It would take many more years of hard work before Sato could carve with his father's skill. Someday, he promised himself, he *would* be a master ivory carver.

Whenever Sato finished a carving, he took it to Akira,[5] the dealer. Akira admired Sato's work and always sold the figures for a good price. With the money Sato was able to buy more ivory from Akira.

One Saturday after Akira paid him, Sato asked, "What piece do you have for me to carve?"

---

5 Akira (*ah kee rah*)

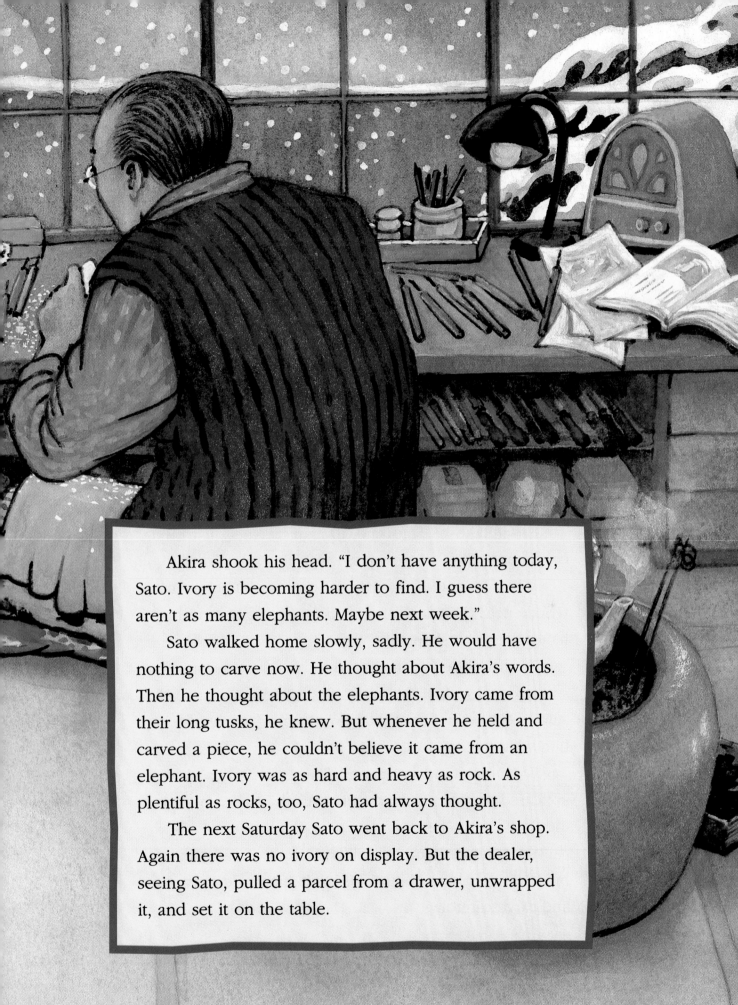

Akira shook his head. "I don't have anything today, Sato. Ivory is becoming harder to find. I guess there aren't as many elephants. Maybe next week."

Sato walked home slowly, sadly. He would have nothing to carve now. He thought about Akira's words. Then he thought about the elephants. Ivory came from their long tusks, he knew. But whenever he held and carved a piece, he couldn't believe it came from an elephant. Ivory was as hard and heavy as rock. As plentiful as rocks, too, Sato had always thought.

The next Saturday Sato went back to Akira's shop. Again there was no ivory on display. But the dealer, seeing Sato, pulled a parcel from a drawer, unwrapped it, and set it on the table.

"Oh," Sato gasped. It was a beautiful piece, the size of his two fists, and creamy as foam on the sea. His hands shook as he picked it up and felt its strength and firmness. From this ivory he hoped to carve a masterwork.

"This is the piece I have been waiting for!" he shouted.

The price was high. "It's very rare," said Akira.

"I will take it," Sato said, though he knew it would cost almost all of his savings.

When he got home, Sato sat on his mat before his workbench. He turned the block over and over in his hands, eager to shape and smooth it. What should he carve? This piece was too large to become a netsuke strung on a cord. He didn't want to waste any of it. He studied the ivory. It would speak to him. It would tell him what to carve.

For a long time Sato stared. Then suddenly a vision appeared to him, as clear as if magic had already carved the figure: a big head, wide ears, powerful legs.

Sato's heart thumped wildly. He closed his eyes and breathed deeply to control his excitement. He must plan and carve carefully.

First he made a small clay model of the figure he would carve. Then he began to pencil light marks on the ivory to guide his hands. But the image was so distinct that he soon dropped his pencil and picked up a small saw.

He cut away the edges and corners and chiseled a rough shape. With a knife he grated the ivory, making a rhythmic, scritching sound. Then he smoothed the ivory and began to carve again. From time to time, he lay down his knife to flex his hand. But when he turned back, the image still shone in the ivory like a beacon.

Sato forgot about everything but the figure. He ate only handfuls of rice, drank tepid green tea, and slept hardly at all. Week after week he worked, often past midnight, stopping only when he could no longer make his hands obey his mind.

Then late one night, his knife slipped and cut a thin streak across his finger.

"Ai!" Sato cried out.

Only a small cut, he thought. I'm tired. I should rest before I make some horrible mistake.

But as he got up, he noticed something dark within the ivory. What was it? Only a shadow, Sato was certain. But he sat back down to look more closely. The shadow remained. A flaw? In this perfect piece? Sato's body felt weak, his chest so heavy he could hardly breathe. How could he carve a masterwork from a flawed piece of ivory? Hope drained from his heart.

In shock Sato began to cut tiny chips from around the flaw. He had never before seen anything so strange. Why, the flaw wasn't even part of the ivory. It was something else. Hard. Corroded. Metallic.

Suddenly Sato realized what it was: a bullet. A cry filled his mind, eerie and strange, like the trumpeting of elephants mourning their dead. Elephants who had died so that Sato might have ivory to carve.

Sato set his tools down. He bent his head before the unfinished figure, covered his face with his hands, and wept.

465

After a while he began to carve again. As if in a trance, he carved all night. By morning he was covered with a fine, white dust. He wiped the figure with a soft cloth and cleaned and polished the "flaw." Then he set it on the low table beside his futon and lay down to rest. The figure glowed as if sunlight shone within it. It was just as he had imagined, except for one thing. A dark, shiny bullet was buried in its forehead like a jewel.

Exhausted, Sato gazed at the figure. Its white sides seemed to breathe, and with each breath the elephant grew. Its trunk swayed, and its huge ears spread like sails.

Sato rubbed his eyes. He raised himself on his elbow, then rose to his knees. The elephant towered above him. Slowly it bowed, and Sato understood that he was to climb onto its back. As the elephant stood, Sato felt his stomach lurch. He was afraid to look down.

"Where are you taking me?" he cried out.

The elephant trudged on in silence. Sato felt the wind in his face, first cool, then warm, then hot. The sun drummed down upon him.

Across the African savannah, he saw a herd of elephants. The largest raised its trunk and trumpeted. The white elephant kneeled, and Sato slid off its back. Then it became small and hard, an ivory figure again. Sato picked it up and put it inside his shirt, next to his skin.

Sato walked toward the herd. As he drew near, the elephants parted, forming a clear path to their leader. Sato trembled, but he had no choice. He had to follow the path. How small and helpless he felt, and how ashamed and sorrowful!

When he looked up at last, he was staring at the giant elephant's tusks, as smooth and graceful as stony carvings. He looked into its small eyes. Then he reached inside his shirt for the ivory statue. He held it up for the elephant to see.

The elephant closed its eyes and nodded. Then it raised its front legs. Sato covered his face with his arms, terrified that the elephant would crush him.

Instead, it backed away to join the others, who now encircled Sato. Their huge bodies swayed from sided to side, and their trumpeting echoed as they marched around him, slowly at first, then faster and faster. Dust rose in clouds as their massive feet pounded the earth. Sato felt the ground shake, and he shuddered with fear.

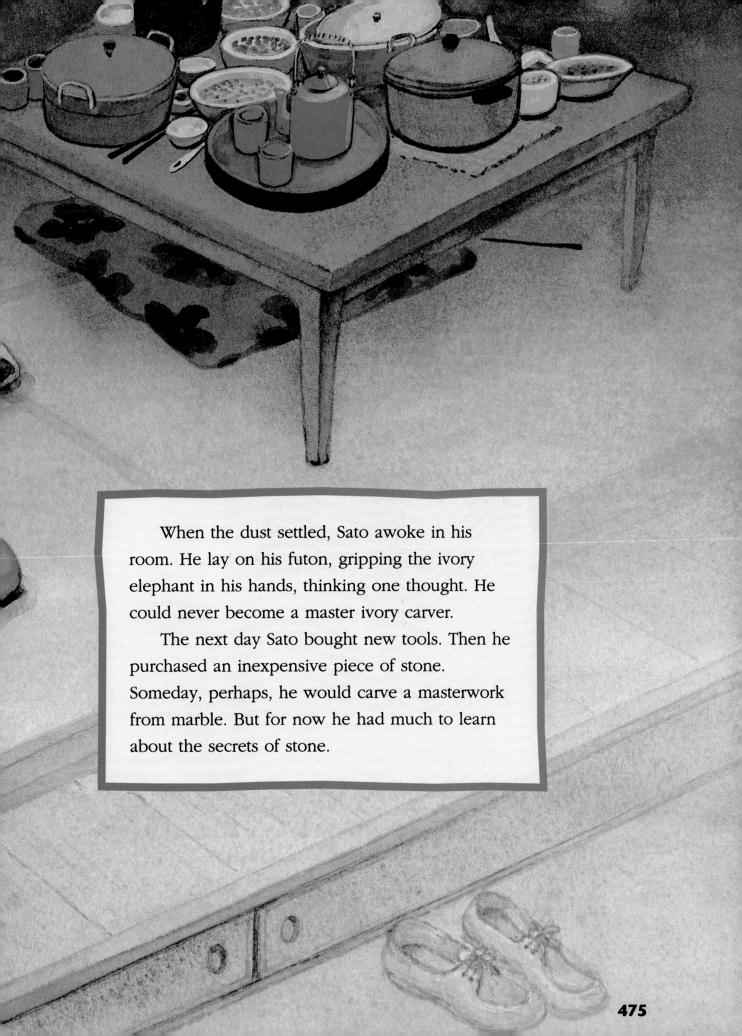

When the dust settled, Sato awoke in his room. He lay on his futon, gripping the ivory elephant in his hands, thinking one thought. He could never become a master ivory carver.

The next day Sato bought new tools. Then he purchased an inexpensive piece of stone. Someday, perhaps, he would carve a masterwork from marble. But for now he had much to learn about the secrets of stone.

Sato never sold the ivory elephant. He kept it on the table by his futon so that he would see it each day when he awoke and each night before he went to sleep.

IN RESPONSE

A Change of Art

Make a list of the important events in Sato's life. Discuss how these events lead him to carve stone instead of ivory.

Buffalo and Elephants

Imagine you and a classmate are Sato and the young man in "Buffalo Woman." Role-play a discussion in which these characters share what they have learned about animals. How are their experiences similar? How are they different? How have their opinions about these animals changed?

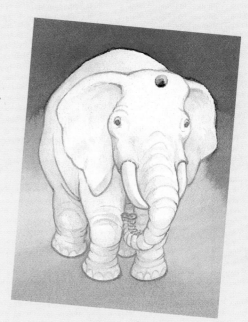

AUTHOR AT WORK

Juanita Havill has been writing since she was a young girl. She discovered she loves writing books for children.

After reading a magazine article about African elephants and a Japanese ivory carver, Ms. Havill knew she had to write a story about ivory. The article described how sad the carver was to learn that ivory comes from the tusks of dead elephants. The carver's sadness inspired Ms. Havill to ask herself what might happen to the carver. She wrote the book *Sato and the Elephants* to answer the question.

★ Award-winning Author

Another Book by . . .

Juanita Havill

It Always Happens to Leona by Juanita Havill, illustrated by Emily A. McCully, Crown Publishing, 1989

Express **Yourself**

In Transformations you've read about some of the changes people go through. You have read about imaginary changes that taught lessons. You have seen how people can change as they learn from their experiences.

Transforming a Quote

In his poem "Changes," Michael Spooner talks about change. "Each day my world shows/one more change;/each day I see another one in me," he said. Think about how this quote applies to the characters in this theme. Choose one character and explain how he or she changes. If you like, write your answer as a poem.

Time to Transform

All the characters in this theme undergo some kind of change. Compare the ways Juan ("The Gold Coin") and Sato ("Sato and the Elephant") change. What events in their lives help them change? Do they change all at once or over time? Role-play a discussion between these two characters. Take turns telling their stories. Be sure to explain how your character used to be and how he changes.

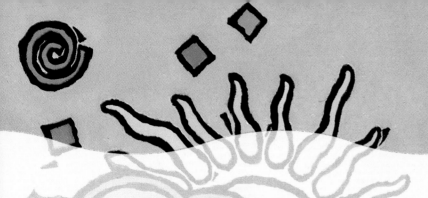

Give Them a Hand

Several of the characters in this theme help others. Working in a small group, choose a character whom you agree should be honored for good deeds. With your group, list this character's good deeds. Work together to write a brief speech explaining why your character was selected. Then choose someone from your group to read the speech to the class.

Advice From Experience

Blanche ("The Talking Eggs") and Juan ("The Gold Coin") both change in their stories. With a partner, discuss how Blanche and Juan feel about changing. Are they happy about their change? Each pretend to be Blanche or Juan. Write a letter explaining how your character feels about change. Use experiences from the stories to help explain his or her feelings.

Making Connections

In the theme Sharing the Earth, you explored ways to protect and save the environment. Do you think "Buffalo Woman" or "Sato and the Elephants" would be good stories to add to Sharing the Earth? Write a brief paragraph telling what you think and why. You may want to discuss your ideas with a classmate first.

The Silver Bookcase

The Girl Who Loved Wild Horses
written and illustrated by Paul Goble,
Macmillan, 1978

A girl cares for her tribe's horses until
one day a thunderstorm drives her
and her horses away from the tribe
to the place where wild horses live.
This beautifully illustrated story is
based on a Plains Indian legend.

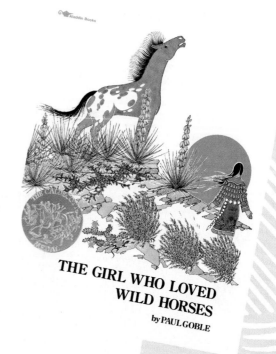

THE GIRL WHO LOVED
WILD HORSES
by PAUL GOBLE

Why Spiders Spin:
A Story of Arachne
retold by Jamie and Scott Simons,
illustrated by Deborah Winograd,
Silver Press, 1991

Arachne was a fine weaver who lived in
ancient Greece. Unfortunately, Arachne
thought she weaved better than the
goddess Athena. Her boasting angered
Athena, who challenged Arachne to a
contest, with startling results.

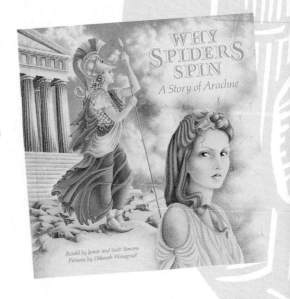

Stinker from Space

by Pamela F. Service, Charles Scribner's Sons, 1988

After crashing his spaceship on Earth, Tsynq Yr has to find a way to escape his enemies. He hides in the body of a skunk, but he won't be able to get off Earth without help from space buffs Karen and Jonathan.

The Big Tree

written and illustrated by Bruce Hiscock, Macmillan, 1991

This is the story of a very special tree, which began as a small seed in 1775 and grew to be a majestic sugar maple that is still living today. In its lifetime, it has witnessed many important events in American history.

Tales from the Bamboo Grove

by Yoko Kawashima Watkins, illustrated by Jean and Mou-sien Tseng, Bradbury Press, 1992

In these six folk tales from Japan, you will learn why the sea is salty, and why you should take care when wishing. You will read about love, trickery, and revenge.

Discovering
Hidden Worlds

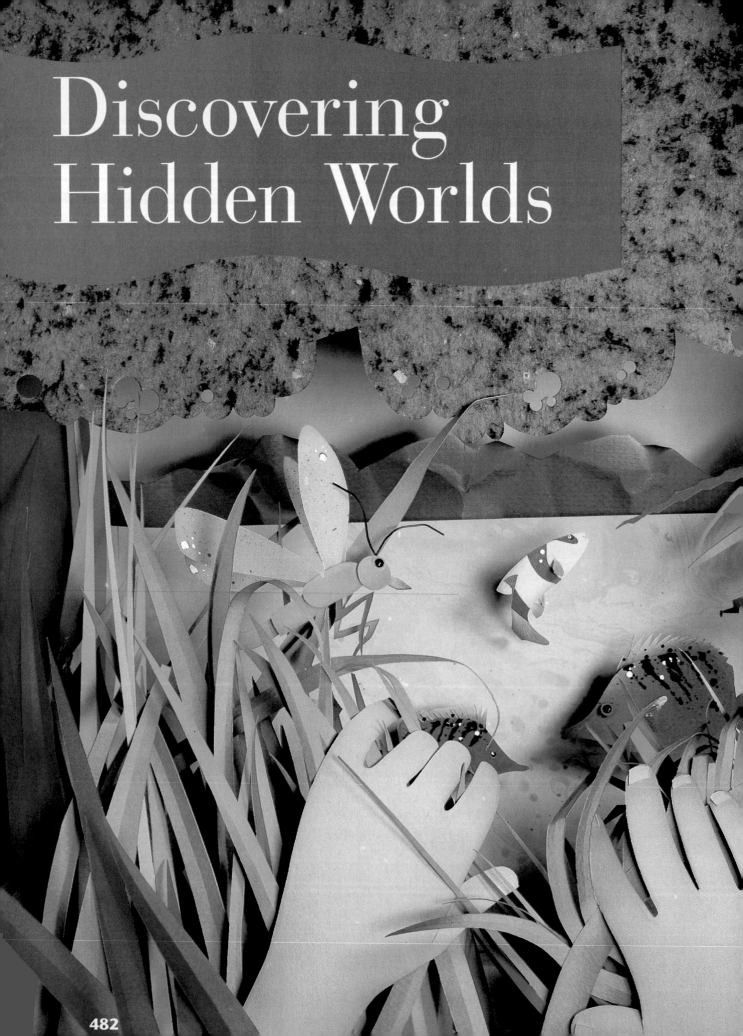

"He has watched stories unfold that other people have never dreamed of."

—Kathryn Lasky
"Entering Animal Worlds"

Discovering Hidden Worlds

CONTENTS

Looking Beneath the Surface

Techniques of Discovery

Theme Trade Books

The Mysterious Rays of Dr. Röntgen

by Beverly Gherman
Dr. Röntgen becomes famous by accidentally discovering X-rays. Everyone is excited about these mysterious rays until doctors realize that X-rays can be dangerous.

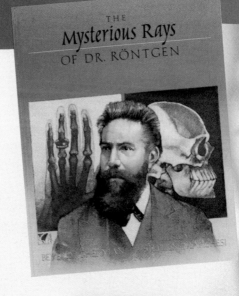

Compost Critters

by Bianca Lavies
Rather than fill her trash can with food and yard scraps, Bianca Lavies creates a compost pile. Little critters work in their own way to turn her garbage into materials that help plants grow.

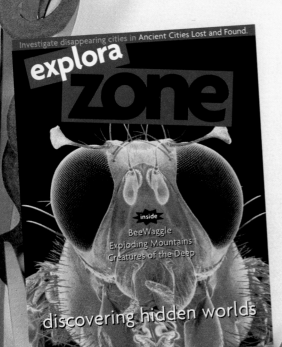

Theme Magazine

What kinds of strange creatures might you find in a coral reef? What makes a volcano erupt? Read about these and other hidden worlds in the Theme Magazine *Explora Zone.*

DARK

NIGHT DIVE

ANN McGOVERN
PHOTOGRAPHS BY
MARTIN SCHEINER AND JAMES B. SCHEINER

DEPTHS

Going on a Night Dive

I must be crazy. It's nighttime and here I am on this dive boat, in total darkness. And I'm scared to death.

The sky above me is black except for a half-moon. The sea around me is black. I see lights twinkling on the distant shore. Land seems far away. But land is where most twelve-year-old girls should be. So what am I doing on the sea?

I'm going on a night dive, that's what I'm doing. In just a few minutes, I'll be in that black sea, and it's too late to do anything about it.

How did I get myself into this? By opening up my big mouth, that's how.

Mom and I have been scuba diving on this beautiful Caribbean island for a week now. We've been diving every day. It's been great.

When Jim, who is in charge of diving, first met me, he asked to see my "C" card—my scuba certification card. It proves I've had the proper diving training. You have to be twelve before you can be certified. I went to the local "Y" for my course.

Brain coral by night

Yesterday Mom told Jim about her work as a marine biologist and about her interest in parrotfishes.

"There are lots of different parrotfishes on our reefs," he said.

Then I blew it. Why don't I think before I speak, like Mom is always telling me to do?

"Really?" I said. "Do you have the kind of parrotfish that spins a cocoon around itself at night?"

Jim grinned. "Sure, kid," he said. "Since you're such a hotshot diver, how about a night dive to see for yourself?"

So that's why I'm on Jim's boat tonight with Mom and the other divers. About to take a plunge into inky waters. I'll probably never even see a parrotfish sleeping in its cocoon. I'll probably be eaten alive by a shark as soon as I hit the water.

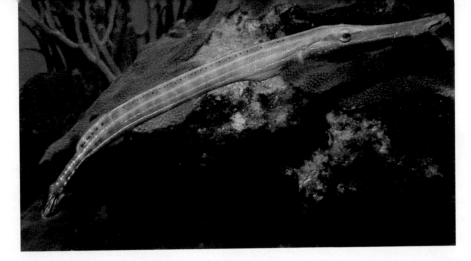

Trumpetfish

Nighttime Wonders

It's so different at night! The fish I see by the hundreds during the daytime are nowhere to be seen. Some fish sleep deep on the reef, deeper than divers can safely go. Some bury themselves in the sand at night. Others fit into tiny cracks and crevices of the coral and hide till daybreak.

The most common night fishes seem to be the red ones—the squirrelfish, the bigeye, and the soldierfish. Their big eyes help them find their prey. During the day I see them hiding under ledges in the coral, watching me. At night, they swim around freely. The little cardinalfish, too, are out in the open.

Squirrelfish

I see so many new things. My light seeks out a slow-moving trumpetfish. Whenever I get too close to this fish in the daytime, it swims away so quickly I hardly see it leave. But this trumpetfish is sleepy. It's moving very slowly toward the coral reef. It uses its fins as feelers, guiding itself away from the sharp spines of spiny sea urchins.

Cardinalfish

Blue tang by night

Blue tang by day

Here's a sleepy blue tang in its night colors. It has stripes that I never see on a day dive.

I feel a tap on my arm. I turn to see Jim holding a spiny porcupinefish. He rubs it and it puffs up. It looks like a balloon with spines sticking out all over. I've seen porcupinefish on day dives with their spines flat against their bodies. Jim hands it to me. It feels a little squishy. When a porcupinefish is disturbed, it takes in water and blows up to almost three times its normal size. Its eyes are open wide. Its spines are sharp.

The photographer, Joe, swims up to me and begins taking pictures of the porcupinefish. Every time he takes a picture, his underwater flash goes

Jim with porcupinefish

off, blinding me for a second. The poor porcupinefish must be blinded, too. Joe swims away to take pictures of other creatures. I say good-bye to the spiny fish and let it go. It bumbles slowly off into the dark, getting flatter and flatter by the minute until it is a normal-sized fish again.

I see a bright red crab. And more brittle starfish.

Spiny lobsters are out from under their ledges. Their hiding places protect them from creatures of the sea but sometimes not from divers who catch them for food. When I shine my light on them, their eyes glow green. I follow a slipper lobster along the reef. Slipper lobsters don't have claws or pincers. They move quickly over the reef.

Porcupinefish puffed up

Mom and I see a stoplight parrotfish sleeping, wedged tight against a sponge. Parrotfish are large and come in many colors. They have sharp teeth that chomp on coral and help turn it into sand. The mouth of the parrotfish looks like a beak of a parrot and is just as strong.

491

Rainbow parrotfish

I see a parrotfish with black spots on its side. Mom sees me looking at it and points to a spiny sea urchin. I know what she means. Poor parrotfish— it probably crashed into a spiny sea urchin when it was blinded by a diver's light.

I check my air. How could it get that low so fast? I shine my light on Mom's gauge. She's used up most of her air, too. I look at my watch. It can't be! We've been under almost an hour. It seems like seconds.

Jim swims over and checks our gauges. Then he shines his light on his hand and gives a thumbs-up signal. Other divers are going up, too.

Just think. An hour ago, I hated the idea of a night dive. And now I don't even want to get out of the water.

The Last Dive

We have to wait an hour before we can dive again.

Randy and Sally hand out sandwiches. Jim has a cooler filled with cold drinks. Mom has brought apples and chocolate chip cookies.

While we eat, everybody tells diving stories. Oh, the places that Sally and Randy have dived! The Great Barrier Reef. The Galapagos[1] Islands. The Red Sea.

"My best night pictures are from the Red Sea!" Joe says. "I'll show you my pictures of lionfish and flashlight fish when we get back to shore."

Jenny wants to know about them. Joe tells us that the spines of the lionfish are poisonous, so its enemies keep away. The flashlight fish comes out only at night. A patch under its eye glows, flashing light signals to other flashlight fish. The light signals may keep the fish together or help one flashlight fish find its mate. Jim says he's seen a flashlight fish swimming near the *Rhone*[2] at night.

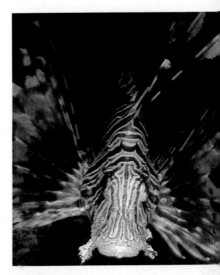

Lionfish

We've already seen three different kinds of parrotfish—the stoplight, the rainbow, and the midnight parrotfish. But Mom is still hoping to see the parrotfish sleeping in its cocoon.

Tonight is our last chance. We go home tomorrow. I hate to think about it. I wish I could dive every night of my life.

The hour passes. Now it's totally dark. We put on our dive gear. When we're ready, we sit on the edge of the boat.

---

1 Galapagos (*guh LAH puh gohs*) islands in the Pacific Ocean
2 Rhone (*rohn*) a ship that sank in the Caribbean in 1867

"Who wants to be first one in?" Jim asks.

Something comes over me. I can't explain it. Before I can stop myself, I say, "Me." I turn to Mom, who nods her okay.

Jim grins. "You're turning into a nocturnal creature. A mermaid of the night."

He slips the tank on my back and turns on the air. I check my air gauge. Plenty of air. I put the regulator in my mouth and begin to breathe.

"Over you go," Jim says. "Happy diving."

Before I can change my mind about being first in, I make my backward entry into the water.

I turn my light on, swim to the line, and start down. This time I remember to clear my ears.

I feel alone in this vast sea.

But I am not alone. I know there are zillions of fish and creatures below me. One minute I feel very much a part of this watery world. The next minute I feel I'm a lone outsider from another planet. My airtank is my spaceship.

Now I'm on the bottom. I shine my light around. I see the gold gleaming eyes of small shrimp. Some shrimp are cleaners. They pick off and eat tiny animals, called *parasites*, that grow on fish. I see night fish hunting for food. And two dotted snails on a sea fan—beautiful flamingo tongues. They feed on the polyps of soft sea fans. The orange and black spots on its mantle look like leopard spots. I get too close. One pulls its mantle back, exposing a creamy-rose shell.

Flamingo tongues

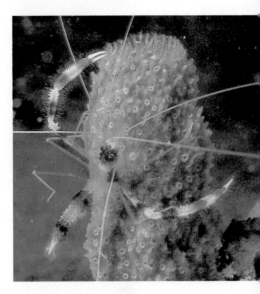

Banded coral shrimp

I hear splashes above me. The other divers will soon be down.

I wonder how much we scare the fish and the tiny creatures—the little striped shrimp, the sea stars and the crabs. We must look frightening to them. We are so much bigger.

Jim has warned us to be careful about our lights. He says that if a fish is blinded by a diver's light— even for a moment—it could crash into spiny sea urchins or into a hard coral and get hurt. Fish can't close their eyes because they have no eyelids. I remember the parrotfish I saw with spine marks on its side.

Parrotfish sleeping in its cocoon

So I try to be careful where I shine my light. I see a red spider star and a crab the size of a basketball. Jim lets me hold it.

And then I see it! A parrotfish sleeping in its see-through cocoon, wedged deep under a ledge. I look up at the divers swimming down. I can tell which diver is Mom by the glowing stick on the back of her tank.

I wave my light. Mom hurries over. I show her the sleeping parrotfish. She hugs me and settles down to study it. I feel I've given her the best present in the world. And it's not even her birthday. Mom has told me that the nighttime cocoon keeps in the parrotfish's smell—and keeps the moray eels from finding it. Jim thinks it might give the parrotfish a warning if an enemy breaks through.

Everyone gathers round to look at the parrotfish in its transparent cocoon. Joe takes a lot of pictures. Then Jim leads us to the *Rhone*.

We're not going as deep this time. Our second dive has to be shallow, for safety's sake. So we won't have a chance to see if that giant sea bass is still inside the *Rhone*.

But I see new wonderful things. A lizardfish that seems to blend into the sandy bottom. An orangeball anemone. A startled stingray. The stingray feeds on tiny creatures that dwell in the sand. It will uncover and scoop a creature out of the sand with its snout. A stingray will never go after a diver. But if I were to step on a stingray by mistake, it would defend itself. It might whip up its long tail with its stinging barb. Ouch!

Lizardfish

Stingray

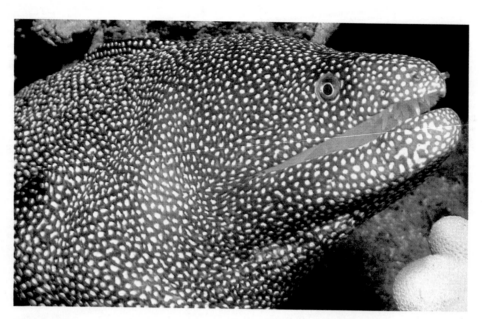

Moray eel

Suddenly my light goes out.

I see nothing in front of me! Nothing at all but inky blackness. I tell myself to calm down and swim toward Mom's glowing stick. She sees my problem and lights up the divers one by one till she finds Jim. Jim gives me his extra light. Now I can see again.

And just in time. My light shows up a big moray eel. It must be about four feet long. By day, I see only its head and a little of its body peering out from a cave in the coral. Its jaws open and close, showing sharp teeth. At night, eels swim freely over the reef. What if I had bumped into it without my light? How would the moray eel know I wouldn't harm it? It might have thought of me as an enemy and it would have had to defend itself. Maybe it would have bitten me.

Jim playing with an octopus

I swim away, even though the eel fascinates me. Jim is waving his light around. He's found an octopus. At first it's red, then green. Then it flashes white. Jim puts it on his arm and plays with it. He prods it with the tip of his light. The octopus wraps one of its eight arms around the light. I laugh into my regulator.

Next, Jim captures a squid. He holds it while Joe takes a close-up picture of its eye. Then he lets it go. It jets away, trailing a cloud of ink, the way the octopus does when it, too, is scared.

Though the squid and the octopus belong to the same family, they are different in many ways. A squid has ten arms; the octopus has eight. Squid swim in schools; the octopus is a loner. The octopus can crawl along the bottom of the reef, seeking crabs. When either is surprised or attacked, it can change its color to frighten and confuse the attacker. The squid can become transparent. The octopus changes color rapidly. In these warm waters, the octopus and the squid are small—nothing like the giant monsters I sometimes see on TV.

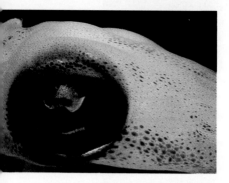

Eye of a squid

I feel I want to stay down here forever. There is something new to see around every corner, in every beam of my light.

The coral reef is always changing. In about ten hours, it will be daytime. Creatures who have hidden and slept all night will come out to feed in the bright daylight.

The night creatures will seek safe hiding places. All day, they will sleep or hide. And when darkness falls again, they will turn the coral reef into the strange and magical place I have come to love.

IN RESPONSE

List the Do's and Don'ts

To explore the sea at night, divers must pay extra attention to their surroundings. Make a list of do's and don'ts for diving at night on the coral reef. You could give safety tips and describe how to find sea creatures you read about in "Dark Depths."

Night and Day

Find descriptions in the story of how the creatures of the coral reef look and act. On one half of a piece of paper, write how the creatures look and act during the day. On the other half, write how the same creatures look and act at night. Discuss with a partner which time you would rather see the coral reef.

AUTHOR AT WORK

The first time Ann McGovern was to go scuba diving, she was so scared she sat on the beach for three days without putting on her scuba gear. When at last she found the courage to dive, she never wanted to stop. Eighty feet beneath the sea, she felt weightless. Tropical fish swam amid the coral on the sea floor. "It was magical!" she says.

Ms. McGovern has since gone diving all over the world and written several books for young people on underwater exploration. The idea for *Night Dive* grew from her longing to see the coral reef at night, when certain creatures that hide during the day are out and some fish change appearance. Her husband, Martin Scheiner, and their son, James Scheiner, took the photographs for her book.

Other Books by . . .

Ann McGovern

Swimming With Sea Lions and Other Adventures in the Galápagos Islands by Ann McGovern, Scholastic, 1992

The Desert Beneath the Sea by Ann McGovern and Eugenie Clark, illustrated by Craig Phillips, Scholastic, 1991

Library Link "Dark Depths" was taken from *Night Dive* by Ann McGovern. You might enjoy reading the entire book to find out more about night diving on the coral reef.

501

FIRE
MOUNTAIN

from *Volcano* by Patricia Lauber

For more than one hundred years, gas and melted rock had been building up beneath Mount St. Helens. Scientists watched as a bulge formed and grew on the volcano. On May 18, 1980, the bulge opened and Mount St. Helens erupted.

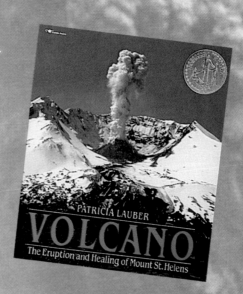

PATRICIA LAUBER

VOLCANO
The Eruption and Healing of Mount St. Helens

The Big Blast

The May 18 eruption began with an earthquake that triggered an avalanche. At 8:32 a.m. instruments that were miles away registered a strong earthquake. The pilot and passengers of a small plane saw the north side of the mountain rippling and churning. Shaken by the quake, the bulge was tearing loose. It began to slide, in a huge avalanche that carried along rock ripped from deep inside Mount St. Helens.

503

A gigantic column of ash and gas rose miles into the sky.

The avalanche tore open the mountain. A scalding blast shot sideways out of the opening. It was a blast of steam, from water heated by rising magma.

Normally water cannot be heated beyond its boiling point, which is 212 degrees Fahrenheit at sea level. At boiling point, water turns to a gas, which we call steam. But if water is kept under pressure, it can be heated far beyond its boiling point and still stay liquid. (That is how a pressure cooker works.) If the pressure is removed, this superheated water suddenly turns, or flashes, to steam. As steam it takes up much more room—it expands. The sudden change to steam can cause an explosion.

Before the eruption Mount St. Helens was like a giant pressure cooker. The rock inside it held superheated water. The water stayed liquid because it was under great pressure, sealed in the mountain. When the mountain was torn open, the pressure was suddenly relieved. The superheated water flashed to steam. Expanding violently, it shattered rock inside the mountain and exploded out the opening, traveling at speeds of up to 200 miles an hour.

The mountain disappeared in billowing clouds of hot gas, ash, and rock.

The blast flattened whole forests of 180-foot-high firs. It snapped off or uprooted the trees, scattering the trunks as if they were straws. At first, this damage was puzzling. A wind of 200 miles an hour is not strong enough to level forests of giant trees. The explanation, geologists later discovered, was that the wind carried rocks ranging in size from grains of sand to blocks as big as cars. As the blast roared out of the volcano, it swept up and carried along the rock it had shattered.

The result was what one geologist described as "a stone wind." It was a wind of steam and rocks, traveling at high speed. The rocks gave the blast its great force.

The blast leveled whole forests of huge firs. The tiny figures of two scientists (*lower left*) give an idea of scale.

Before it, trees snapped and fell. Their stumps looked as if they had been sandblasted. The wind of stone rushed on. It stripped bark and branches from trees and uprooted them, leveling 150 square miles of countryside. At the edge of this area other trees were left standing, but the heat of the blast scorched and killed them.

The stone wind was traveling so fast that it overtook and passed the avalanche. On its path was Spirit Lake, one of the most beautiful lakes in the Cascades. The blast stripped the trees from the slopes surrounding the lake and moved on.

Meanwhile the avalanche had hit a ridge and split. One part of it poured into Spirit Lake, adding a 180-foot

The avalanche poured material into Spirit Lake.

layer of rock and dirt to the bottom of the lake. The slide of avalanche into the lake forced the water out. The water sloshed up the slopes, then fell back into the lake. With it came thousands of trees felled by the blast.

The main part of the avalanche swept down the valley of the North Fork of the Toutle River. There, in the valley, most of the avalanche slowed and stopped. It covered 24 square miles and averaged 150 feet thick.

The blast itself continued for 10 to 15 minutes, then stopped. Minutes later Mount St. Helens began to erupt upwards. A dark column of ash and ground-up rock rose miles into the sky. Winds blew the ash eastward. Lightning flashed in the ash cloud and started forest fires. In Yakima, Washington, some 80 miles away, the sky turned so dark that street lights went on at noon.

The depth of the May 18, 1980, mudflow can be seen in the traces it left on trees along the Muddy River.

Ash fell like snow that would not melt. This eruption continued for nine hours.

Shortly after noon the color of the ash column changed. It became lighter, a sign that the volcano was now throwing out mostly new magma. Until then much of the ash had been made of old rock.

At the same time the volcano began giving off huge flows of pumice and ash. The material was very hot, with temperatures of about 1,000 degrees Fahrenheit, and it traveled down the mountain at speeds of 100 miles an hour. The flows went on until 5:30 in the afternoon. They formed a wedge-shaped plain of pumice on the side of the mountain. Two weeks later temperatures in the pumice were still 780 degrees.

Finally, there were the mudflows, which started when heat from the blast melted ice and snow on the mountaintop. The water mixed with ash, pumice, ground-up rock, and dirt and rocks of the avalanche. The result was a thick mixture that was like wet concrete, a mudflow. The mudflows traveled fast, scouring the landscape and sweeping down the slopes into river valleys. Together their speed and thickness did great damage.

The largest mudflow was made of avalanche material from the valley of the North Fork of the Toutle River. It churned down the river valley, tearing out steel bridges, ripping houses apart, picking up boulders and trucks and carrying them along. Miles away it choked the Cowlitz River and blocked shipping channels in the Columbia River.

The mudflow roared through a logging camp, overturning large pieces of equipment.

When the sun rose on May 19, it showed a greatly changed St. Helens. The mountain was 1,200 feet shorter than it had been the morning before. Most of the old top had slid down the mountain in the avalanche. The rest had erupted out as shattered rock. Geologists later figured that the volcano had lost three quarters of a cubic mile of old rock.

The north side of the mountain had changed from a green and lovely slope to a fan-shaped wasteland.

At the top of Mount St. Helens was a big, new crater with the shape of a horseshoe. Inside the crater was the vent, the opening through which rock and gases erupted from time to time over the next few years.

In 1980 St. Helens erupted six more times. Most of these eruptions were explosive—ash soared into the air, pumice swept down the north side of the mountain. In the eruptions of June and August, thick pasty lava oozed out of the vent and built a dome. But both domes were destroyed by the next eruptions. In October the pattern changed. The explosions stopped, and thick lava built a dome that was not destroyed. Later eruptions added to the dome, making it bigger and bigger.

During this time, geologists were learning to read the clues found before eruptions. They learned to predict what St. Helens was going to do. The predictions helped to protect people who were on and near the mountain.

On May 17, 1980, Mount St. Helens had a soaring, ash-stained peak and green forests climbing its slopes.

On May 18, 1980, the big eruption tore the top off the mountain and flattened the forests, as shown in this photograph, taken September 9, 1980.

Among these people were many natural scientists. They had come to look for survivors, for plants and animals that had lived through the eruption. They had come to look for colonizers, for plants and animals that would move in. Mount St. Helens had erupted many times before. Each time life had returned. Now scientists would have a chance to see how it did. They would see how nature healed itself.

Scientists sample the gases given off by magma. A sharp increase in sulfur dioxide often signals a coming eruption.

Survivors and Colonizers

In early summer of 1980 the north side of Mount St. Helens looked like the surface of the moon—gray and lifeless. The slopes were buried under mud, ground-up rock, pumice, and bits of trees. Ash covered everything with a thick crust. The eruption had set off thunderstorms that wet the falling ash. The ash became goo that hardened into a crust. The slopes looked like a place where nothing could be alive or ever live again. Yet life was there.

With the coming of warm weather, touches of green appeared among the grays and browns. They were the green of plants that had survived the force and heat of the eruption.

Sedge grew through a crust of ash.

Fireweed appeared through cracks in the ash.

Some plants had still been buried under the snows of winter on May 18. Huckleberry and trillium sprang up among the fallen forest trees. So did young silver firs and mountain hemlocks.

In other places, where the snow had melted, the blast swept away the parts of plants that were above ground. But roots, bulbs, and stems remained alive underground. They sprouted, and hardy shoots pushed up through the pumice and ash. Among these was fireweed, one of the first plants to appear after a fire.

Ground squirrels were other underground survivors

A few plants were even growing in blocks of soil that had been lifted from one place and dropped in another.

Some small animals had also survived under the snowpack or below ground. There were chipmunks, white-footed deer mice, and red squirrels. There were

Willow seeds traveled on wind-borne clouds of silky fluff.

pocket gophers, small rodents that carry food in fur-lined pockets in their cheeks.

Ants survived underground. So did eggs laid by insects. Many other small animals, such as springtails and mites, lived through the eruption in their homes of rotting logs.

Termites survived in rotting logs.

Snow and ice still covered a few lakes on May 18. Here fish, frogs, salamanders, crayfish, snakes, and water insects were alive on May 19.

Natural scientists also found many tiny living things. They found more kinds of bacteria than they could name. They found fungi, which are very simple plants. Fungi lack the green coloring matter called chlorophyll and cannot make their own food, as green plants do. They take their nourishment from other living things or from once-living things, like rotten wood. Fungi can reproduce in several ways. One is by making spores, which are as small as specks of dust. Fungus spores are everywhere. When conditions are right for them, they sprout and grow. In the summer of 1980 scientists at Mount St. Helens saw fire fungi, which often appear after forest fires. Their spores need great heat to sprout.

Both fungus spores and bacteria are very light, and they can travel thousands of miles on the wind. So no one could really tell which were survivors and which were colonizers. But even in that first summer, scientists could see many other colonizers arriving.

The earliest came by air. Light seeds of willow and cottonwood blew in. Insects blew or flew in. And then there were the spiders, which ballooned in. Many kinds of young spiders spin threads of silk that remain attached to their bodies. When the wind catches these threads, it lifts the spiders into the air and carries them for miles.

The scientists also saw animal visitors. Birds flew in. Coyotes, elk, deer, and other large mammals passed through, perhaps looking for food and water.

This herd of elk passed through a mudflow area.

That first summer there were not many plants and animals on the north slope. But there was a wide variety. So natural scientists were able to start studying the links among these forms of life, for no living thing exists all by itself. Each is linked to other living things and to its surroundings. All need food and places to live.

Scientists knew, for example, that over a year or so the crust of ash would break up and wash away. But they saw important small changes taking place in the summer of 1980. There were areas where snow lay under the ash. When the warmth of summer melted the snow, it no longer supported the ash. The ash slumped and broke up. Here surviving roots could send up shoots. Heavy rains sent water running down the slopes. The water cut channels in the ash. Here, too, roots could send up shoots.

Lupine provided food and shelter to insects and spiders.

Deer and elk wandered through. They fed on some of the plants. But their sharp hooves broke up more of the ash. Like other animal visitors, they brought in seeds. Some seeds had stuck in their coats. Others were in their droppings.

Hoofprints and broken ash made places that trapped seeds. They made places where seeds could sprout and get their roots into soil. They made places where plants could grow.

In time these plants would form seeds. The seeds would colonize other places. And every plant that grew would help still other forms of life.

Hoofprints made hollows that trapped seeds and offered a place where seeds could sprout and plants could grow.

IN RESPONSE

Notes on a Volcano

Imagine you are a scientist observing Mount St. Helens in 1980. Write notebook entries describing what you see on a day one month before the explosion, the day after the explosion, and several months after the explosion.

Look Again

The scientists who explored Mount St. Helens and the young diver ("Dark Depths") were both excited when they discovered things they had not expected to find. Make a list of some of the things that surprised the scientists and the diver. What surprised you about these two hidden worlds? Draw a picture of the thing that surprised you most about each world.

Patricia Lauber

A photograph of a plant growing in the ash-covered ground near Mount St. Helens gave Patricia Lauber the idea for writing *Volcano*. Ms. Lauber wanted to explain how plants and animals could return to a place that seemed as lifeless as the moon.

Patricia Lauber writes books about things that interest her— mummies, whales, volcanoes, outer space, her dog Clarence, kangaroos. She finds her ideas by looking at things and talking to people, and from reading a great deal.

She advises young people who want to be writers to read and write as much as they can. "Wanting to be a writer is like wanting to be a tennis player or anything else," she insists. "You have to get at it. It's like exercising a muscle. The more you do it, the better you get."

★ **Award-winning Author**

520

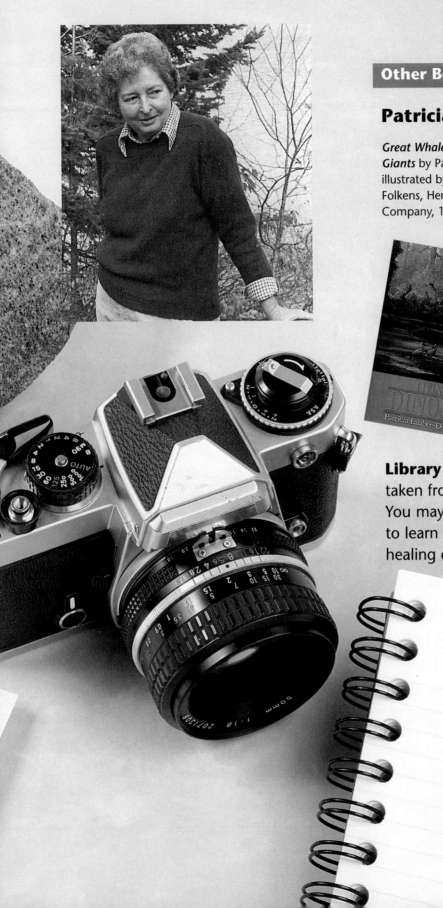

Other Books by . . .

Patricia Lauber

Great Whales: The Gentle Giants by Patricia Lauber, illustrated by Pieter Folkens, Henry Holt and Company, 1991

Living with Dinosaurs by Patricia Lauber, illustrated by Doug Henderson, Bradbury Press, 1991

Library Link "Fire Mountain" was taken from *Volcano* by Patricia Lauber. You may want to read the entire book to learn more about the eruption and healing of Mount St. Helens.

The Desert

by Eucario Mendez

As I walk in the desert
I see a coral snake passing by,
and the bright sun shines the day.

I hear birds singing on a
mesquite tree. I hear animals
crying for food and water.

I feel a strong breeze passing by,
and the animals come to me
so I can touch them.

So, next time you are in
a desert, like me, see things,
feel things, and hear things.

Eucario was a sixth-grade student when he wrote this poem about experiencing the desert. He is a member of the Yaqui people from Arizona.

Yaquis in the Desert

The Yaquis are a Native American people living in Arizona, California, and northwestern Mexico. Much of the land the Yaquis settled lies between two rivers. The soil along the rivers is rich enough to grow crops. The land between the rivers is dry and desertlike.

In earlier times, the Yaquis lived and farmed along the rivers but often visited the desert. In the desert, they cut down mesquite trees to build roofs for their houses. They gathered cactus fruits, seeds, and greens for food. They hunted small animals.

The Yaquis believed that ancient spirits lived in the desert. These spirits could give special power to a human being. This power, which could come through a desert animal such as a snake or a deer, would allow the person to help other people.

Today some Yaquis still farm along the rivers. Others live and work in nearby cities. Some, like Eucario, visit the desert just to walk and watch and listen.

Art Worlds

Like explorers of hidden worlds, artists need to be careful observers of the world around them. If you view art with a careful eye, you can sometimes find unexpected things hidden within the art.

Painting by Claude Monet (French), *Pool With Waterlilies, Harmony in Green,* **1899**

What's the difference?

Claude Monet observed that his subjects looked different depending on the time of day or year. These paintings show the same bridge at two different times. At what time of year do you think each picture was painted? What makes you think so?

Painting by Claude Monet (French), *Water Lily Pool,* **1900**

What's your view?

The person on the ladder is looking over the wall instead of plastering the wall like the others. What do you think this person sees? Explain why you think so.

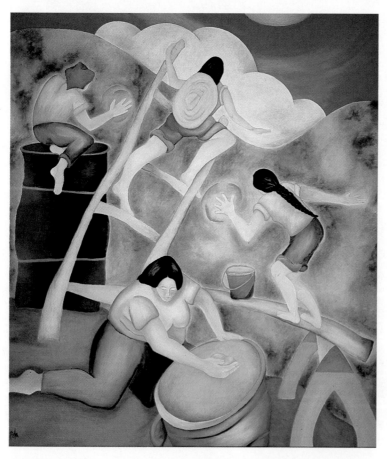

Painting by Pola Lopez de Jaramillo (United States), *Las Enjarradoras (The Mud Plasters),* 1990

Transformation mask (Kwakiutl), about 1900

What is hidden?

The two pictures above show the same mask opened and closed. This mask was used in a dance by the Kwakiutl, a native American people from near Vancouver, Canada. After first appearing wearing the mask closed, the dancer would pull the strings, revealing the face hidden inside. Do the two faces look like the same creature? How are they different?

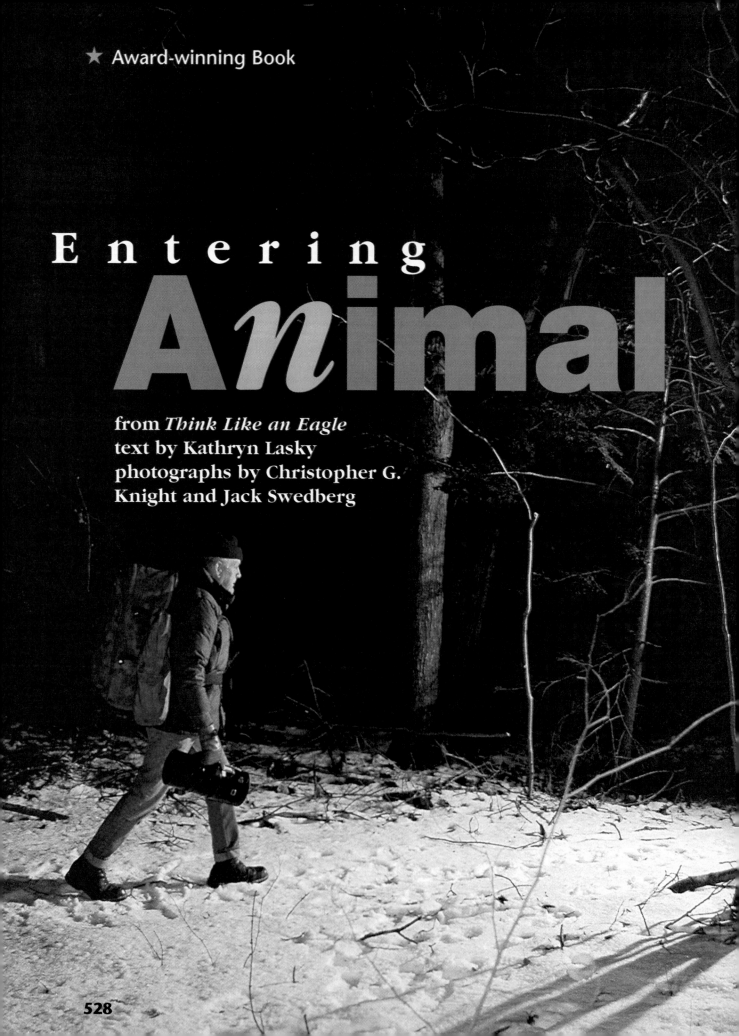

Entering
Animal

from *Think Like an Eagle*
text by Kathryn Lasky
photographs by Christopher G.
Knight and Jack Swedberg

A Walk Through the Night

He follows a silver thread of moonlight through the forest. The tangled shadows of bare-branched trees spread across the snowy ground. His breath comes in great clouds, and the only sound is the soft crunch of

Worlds

his boots in the snow. Over the past thirty years or more, he has often walked through these woods. He knows the way even on a moonless night. He is never lost. On his back he carries a pack, and in each hand he holds a cylindrical case. In the backpack and the cases are lenses and cameras and films. These are his tools. Jack Swedberg is a wildlife photographer.

Now Jack crosses a stream that feeds into the reservoir. The water slides like a black satin ribbon under snow bridges and curls around billowing white banks. He is coming near the edge of the forest, where the reservoir begins. Frozen solid and glistening white, the water reflects the moon's light like a huge shield of battered silver.

Jack is wrapped in the silence of the forest when suddenly from somewhere behind him, deep in the heart of the woods, comes the flat *hooo hoooo* of the great horned owl. *Hooo hoooo*. The call thrums through the forest.

On this bitterly cold February night, Jack is heading toward a secret shelter. It is on the edge of the vast frozen reservoir. The shelter is called a blind, because from it bird-watchers and photographers can observe animals without being seen.

Some people are happy to have a small, simple blind made out of plywood. Not Jack. He wanted his structure to look as though it really belongs, so that nobody, animal *or* human, would ever suspect it of being anything but a natural dwelling. So he sheathed the plywood walls of the structure with beaver cuttings gathered from the reservoir and nearby ponds. In fact, not more than two hundred feet away in the frozen reservoir, a real beaver lodge thrusts through the ice. Both lodges appear identical, except for one difference: a deer carcass lies stiffly on the ice in front of Jack's blind; it's been baited.

He found the dead deer days before in another section of the woods and brought it to this spot. First the blue jays came to the carcass, then the crows, and now he hopes the eagles will come, attracted by the activity of the other birds. That is why Jack has walked through the winter forest on this frozen night—to photograph eagles. The Quabbin Reservoir in western Massachusetts is one of their favorite winter feeding grounds on the East Coast. But eagles here are shy and wary. They do not care for people. Therefore, Jack must come quietly, under the camouflage of night.

The first thing Jack does when he gets to the blind is uncover a bucket of dried corn and scatter it on the

ice in front of the blind to attract smaller birds. The flittering movements of these birds will screen the movements of his large lenses, which protrude from the window slot in the blind—for even the smooth, silent movements of the camera lenses and the reflections of their glass eyes can frighten the eagles. Now he can look out and photograph while they are safely distracted—they do not seem to look beyond the frantic, small-scale activity of the tiny birds. It is one more way of concealing his presence, of becoming part of the world he studies.

Finally he crawls into the blind for the rest of the night, to wait until first light, when he will mount his cameras in the window slot and hope for eagles.

Inside the blind it is cozy. An adult cannot stand up, only sit or lie down. There is a bed made from two

A moment worth waiting for.

mattresses, with a sleeping bag slung across it. There is a small stove for coffee. There is carpeting to quiet sounds. But the most important part of the blind is the rectangular window slot. This slot is Jack's window on the world. He has spent as much time peering through it as many people spend in front of a television. He can't switch the channel. He can't change the scene. He must wait for the real-life action to happen in front of this small rectangle. It does.

The night melts into the dawn. Then out of the east, where a soft pink light begins to tinge the sky, he sees a speck. The speck becomes larger. Within minutes, an eagle is circling over the blind, its wings held in a nearly perfect horizontal plane until it folds them to descend. The big talons extend and appear like splayed stars as the wings scoop the air in front of them. The bird's powerful strokes break his forward motion. The air outside the blind seems tossed with drafts and eddies in a weather of its own. And then, as the bird lands, it is suddenly still.

Jack has waited all night for this moment. When the eagle came into view, he pushed the firing button, and both his still camera and his motion-picture camera are clicking and whirring. He swivels the cameras, following the eagle as it steps lightly across the deer carcass, its white head eager and curious. The eagle is hungry and focused entirely on the carcass. It tears at the fur to get to the meat with its beak and talons, but suddenly it stops, looks up. It senses a threat. Jack is ready as a second bird descends. To even hope for eagles, you have to learn how to think like an eagle.

A Key to the Forest

Jack Swedberg did not always think like an eagle, or a beaver or a grizzly bear or any of the animals he now photographs. Once he was a hunter.

"I bought a movie camera and tried to point and shoot it like a gun, but that didn't work." Jack chuckles as he recalls his early days trying to get a good picture of an animal. "With hunting, you either hit it or miss it, but photography is much more challenging."

Photography *is* different from hunting. A hunter stalks his prey. There is always an invisible wall between him and the animal he hunts. Compared to a photographer or an artist, a hunter is a stranger in the forest. A hunter can shatter the invisible wall with one shot, but he can never simply walk through it. The wall never seems to dissolve for the hunter as it does for the photographer, who can, if he or she is careful, enter that natural world and become a part of it.

When Jack started taking photographs, he didn't know about light meters, so much of his film was either underexposed or overexposed. His shots were often shaky because it is difficult to hold a camera with a long lens steady. And sometimes in framing a picture, he would accidentally chop off an animal's head or feet because the camera did not have a reflex viewfinder, which would have allowed him to see through the lens for precise framing. In fact, just getting an animal *into* the viewfinder was the most difficult challenge of all. During long hours of hiking, he saw deer that ran off, beavers that submerged, and foxes that disappeared into their dens. He was still on the other side of the invisible wall. He had to figure out how to move through it without shattering it, so he could be with the animals quietly and unnoticed.

To become a great wildlife photographer, Jack had to become a student of animal behavior and figure out how to be at the right place at the right time, without being detected by the animals.

The eagles in New England are wary of humans because people, especially farmers, used to shoot them. At one time some people even thought that eagles could steal babies. It was not true. There was not a single report of an eagle attacking a human, but there were plenty of instances of humans attacking eagles. It does not take any animal very long to know who its enemies are and how to avoid them. Jack

Ready for action.

soon figured out that he must come into the Quabbin at night and stay hidden throughout the day if he hoped to get near these cautious birds that could see him from miles away.

Since the Quabbin Reservoir was built, over fifty years ago, every measure has been taken to ensure that the water remains as clean and pure as possible. No pesticides are allowed. Gradually, because of the undisturbed land, the pure water, and the lack of human visitors, wildlife began to flourish. To enter, a person must pass through a locked gate.

Jack has had a key for many years. He had been a carpenter, but as he became expert in his hobby of wildlife photography, he found a job that would allow him to watch the world he had come to love. He was appointed official photographer for the state Fisheries and Wildlife Division, and the Quabbin Reservoir was the focus of his work.

He has become a watcher in the wild. Through the window of his blind, Jack has seen animals fight

Talons clash over
the deer carcass.

over food and mates. He has seen them desperately protect their young from danger. From behind the camouflage curtains, he has watched stories unfold that other people have never dreamed of, and he has been close to living creatures that most of us can only hope to see from afar.

The eagle he has been photographing in the early dawn light has ceased tearing at the fur of the deer. The threat it sensed now materializes as another bird appears overhead. It is a younger eagle, full of nerve, and hungry, too. The first eagle pulls itself from the carcass, its talons still bloody, ready to confront this young intruder. Within seconds Jack has shot thirty frames of this confrontation with his motor-driven camera unit. The younger eagle finally backs away and lifts off into the clear winter sky, hungry still. The first eagle returns to its meal. It feasts for almost an hour before taking off.

Jack will wait in the blind all day until he is sure that this eagle as well as the younger one are nowhere nearby. If they were to see him emerge, his hiding place would be revealed and Jack might lose his chance to photograph eagles in the future.

When Jack finally leaves the blind, it is late afternoon. Already the sun is low and crashes like shards of glass on the frozen surface of the water. The sedges and cattails, which looked like silver reeds in the moonlight, are licks of fire in the setting sun. By the time Jack reaches the other edge of the ice, where the forest begins, there is one last golden yawn of the sun as twilight begins to steal into the winter sky.

Thinking Like a Beaver

It has been three months since Jack was last in the woods of the Quabbin. The ice shield of winter has melted. The dark water sparkles in the sunshine of the bright spring day. The streams, once still, now gurgle madly, swollen from the spring rains. There is the new soft green of spring, and leaves curled tightly as babies' fists are about to open. Everything seems new, fresh, and ready to grow.

The last trace of ice has been gone for nearly a month. Grassy hummocks released from the frozen grip of winter blow in the spring breeze, moving as slowly as snails across the water. These hummocks are free-floating mats of grassy vegetation. They look like little mountains on the surface of the water.

The beavers are hard at work, and Jack is working just about as hard. He has driven his van almost to the edge of the reservoir and has unloaded his hummock blind in hopes of photographing the beavers and other wildlife. He is busy now cutting cattails to camouflage the blind.

Jack devised the hummock blind some years ago and built it in his basement. A dome of chicken wire is mounted on a set of Styrofoam pontoons covered with plywood. Between the pontoons is a detachable board from which he suspends a pair of waders to protect him from leeches and the cold water. Another piece of plywood, facing front, provides a platform for his cameras. There is even room inside to carry some small waterproof bags for lunch and film and camera filters. A camouflage cover fits over the chicken-wire dome. To make this cover look natural, Jack ties cattails over it, interlaced with freshly cut grasses and twigs.

He stands back and studies the blind. It looks good. Beavers are smart but not that smart. And they don't have very good eyesight. They won't notice that the cattails are upside down. But they do hear well, and they do have a good sense of smell. They are not as shy as deer, but they tend to be nocturnal in their work habits. When Jack started taking pictures of beavers, he began by poking a hole in one of their dams so they would have to come out and repair it. But they would just wait for dark and then start to work—making it impossible for Jack to film them.

Jack slips the canvas cover over his hummock blind.

The blind becomes more "hummocky" as Jack weaves in the cattails.

Getting ready to vanish.

So he started poking the hole in the dam earlier and earlier during the day. Soon the beavers started moving their work time up toward the better hours for picture making. When Jack had lured them into daylight, he put a glass box containing his camera into the hole and operated it by remote control from a nearby tree. It worked beautifully until the third time. When he came back to his tree, the beavers had chewed it down.

Now he tucks a last reed into his blind and pulls it down to the water's edge. He climbs into the waders, slips between the pontoons, and flips the dome down over his head. He begins to move away from the shore to join the other floating hummocks. Within a few feet he is in deep water, his wader boots are off the bottom, and he is paddling along at a stately pace.

He glides through a small population of hummocks, indistinguishable from them except for his motion and the black gleaming eye of the camera that pokes out from his hummock's small opening.

The only hummock with a photographic eye.

Soon he is in the open water of the beaver pond, moving determinedly toward a beaver lodge several hundred feet away. He slows abruptly as he spots a beaver directly ahead. Jack must be careful not to propel himself too fast and leave

a wake, which might spook the beavers. But this beaver seems curious and keeps swimming rapidly

Swimming the hummock toward a beaver lodge.

A beaver grooms itself in the late afternoon sun.

542

toward Jack. Suddenly the beaver turns. With a loud *smack*, it slaps the water with its tail. A big splash rains down on Jack's hummock. "So long!" Jack mutters as he watches the beaver dive. The beaver can stay underwater for up to three minutes. Membranes slide over its eyes, others close off its ears, and an inner membrane in its mouth comes right over its teeth so the animal can chew under the surface without taking in a drop of water.

The day has turned sunny and warm. Jack carefully paddles into a cove. Straight ahead he sees a hummock not far from the shore, and on the side facing him, he finds himself eye to eye with a turtle.

For the next half hour Jack seeks out the smaller, skittering life of the cove—skater beetles, dragonflies, and damselflies. He watches everything very closely— no movement is too minute, no action too quiet to intrigue him. The great advantage of the hummock blind is that it gives Jack a special view of this small-scale life since his head is only a foot or so above the water. He stops the blind and watches a sliver of green. On top of it there appears to be a twig. But is it? A transformation is occurring before his eyes. Jack switches to his macro lens, which allows him to shoot close-up pictures of very small creatures. He catches the first steps of the damselfly as it drags itself out of its larval case. Before its adult life, which is about to begin, this insect spent its larval or immature stage at the bottom of the reservoir, perhaps under a stone. But Jack has arrived at the moment just after it has swum to the top and is in the process of hatching. It is exhausted but crawls out farther onto the green sliver, leaving the split case behind. Its wings, wet and folded, have never been used. The insect will wait for a while, gathering energy and letting its wings dry before trying them in its first flight.

A few hours later, in the narrow slot of time and light at the end of the day, just before the sun is whisked away and the cool gray of dusk gathers, deer come to the water's edge to feed. The wading birds stalk the shore, and beavers make their way along their underwater paths to their lodges. It is the best time for making pictures. It is that time between times called twilight. It is almost dark when Jack pulls the hummock blind onto shore.

⬤ N RESPONSE

Your Best Shot

Draw a picture of the blind that Jack Swedberg uses to photograph beavers. Label each of its parts and write a paragraph explaining how the blind allows him to successfully take his pictures.

Some Good Advice

Imagine you are Jack Swedberg or the young diver from "Dark Depths." In the story about your character, find three tips for hidden-world explorers. Then pair up with a classmate who chose the other character and role-play a discussion in which you share your tips.

AUTHOR AT WORK

As a child, Kathryn Lasky did not like reading nonfiction. To her, it was just a lot of facts. When she set out to write nonfiction, she wanted to let

her readers know that nonfiction is more than facts. It is also mystery and discovery. To achieve this goal, she tries to "bring the feeling of people, drama, and personality to nonfiction." When writing *Think Like an Eagle,* Ms. Lasky went along with Christopher Knight and Jack Swedberg on their photographing trips. The night they spent in the blind waiting for the eagles, her fingers were so cold she could barely write. That night, Ms. Lasky realized how patient Mr. Swedberg has to be. When the eagles appeared, she knew that the long night of waiting was worth it.

★ Award-winning Author

Other Books by . . .

Kathryn Lasky

The Librarian Who Measured the Earth by Kathryn Lasky, illustrated by Kevin Hawkes, Little, Brown and Company, 1994

Sugaring Time by Kathryn Lasky, photographs by Christopher G. Knight, Macmillan, 1983

Dinosaur Dig by Kathryn Lasky, photographs by Christopher G. Knight, Morrow Junior Books, 1990

Library Link This story was taken from *Think Like an Eagle: At Work with a Wildlife Photographer* by Kathryn Lasky. You might enjoy reading the entire book to learn more about the animals Jack Swedberg has photographed.

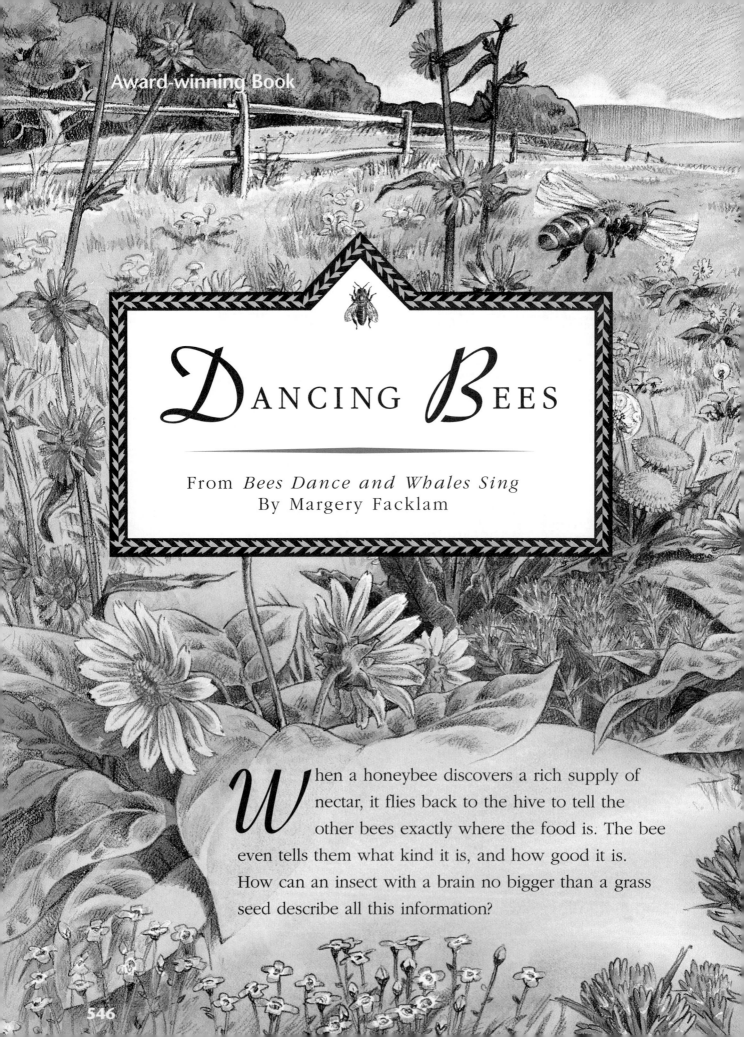

Dancing Bees

From *Bees Dance and Whales Sing*
By Margery Facklam

When a honeybee discovers a rich supply of nectar, it flies back to the hive to tell the other bees exactly where the food is. The bee even tells them what kind it is, and how good it is. How can an insect with a brain no bigger than a grass seed describe all this information?

Dr. Karl von Frisch[1] was the first person to find out.
He put a dot of red dye on a worker bee and watched
as she flew off and returned to the hive. (Worker bees
are always female.) As he watched thousands of bees,
Dr. von Frisch discovered how they sent their messages.
They danced!

_____

1 Frisch (*frihsh*)

547

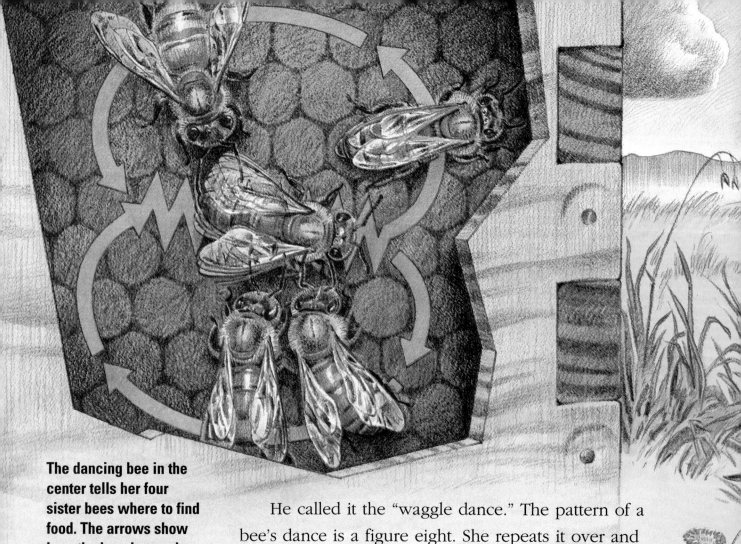

The dancing bee in the center tells her four sister bees where to find food. The arrows show how the bee dances in a figure-eight pattern. The zigzag lines show where she waggles her body.

He called it the "waggle dance." The pattern of a bee's dance is a figure eight. She repeats it over and over again as her sister bees watch. The most important part of the dance is the straight run through the middle of the figure eight. That shows the direction from the hive to the food. If the bee is dancing outside the hive on a flat surface, she lines up with the sun, then turns to point toward the food. If the bee is inside, on the wall of the dark hive, her head points up, as if the sun were overhead. Then she turns right or left to show where the food is.

As she runs through the figure eight, the bee waggles her head and tail from side to side. The farther away the food is, the faster she dances. Different kinds of bees have different waggle signals. For German honeybees, one waggle means the food is about fifty

yards away. Italian bees, which are favored by beekeepers in the United States, use one waggle to mean about twenty-five yards.

As she dances, the bee's wings vibrate so fast that they buzz. The other worker bees touch the dancer with their antennae to feel the vibrations. They also sample a drop of the nectar she has found. In a few minutes, the first bees to figure out where the food is fly away. Then the others move up to touch the dancer bee, and they leave the hive as soon as they know the directions, too. Before each bee flies off, she lines up facing the sun and turns in the direction that the waggle dancer pointed.

The information given by a dancing bee is so accurate that scientists can follow the bee's directions and find the same flowers.

A robot bee gives real bees directions to the sugar water.

In 1988, a team of scientists from Denmark and Germany built a tiny electronic robot honeybee that was run by a computer. The robot bee was designed to "talk" to a hive full of bees and give them instructions to fly to a specific spot. The robot doesn't look much like a real bee, but it doesn't have to, because a bee hive is dark. All the robot has to do is send signals the bees can understand—and offer a sample of the food.

Before the scientists could test the robot, they had to get real bees to taste the peppermint-scented sugar water they would use as bait. They put a dish of sugar water almost a mile away from a hive, and let a worker

bee from that hive taste it. (They had marked the worker bee so they could recognize her.) When the worker bee flew back to the hive, she danced and gave samples of the food, and almost three hundred bees followed her instructions. They found the peppermint-scented sugar water a mile away.

The next step was to program the robot bee to dance the directions to the sugar water, which had been moved to a new spot. In the hive, the bees gathered around and paid attention to the robot bee. But could they follow the robot's directions? That was the big test. When the dancing robot bee buzzed and waggled and gave samples of the food (the scientists released a drop of the sugar water through a tiny brass tube above the robot's head), almost a hundred bees found the sugar water. The robot wasn't quite as successful as the real bee—but the robot was obviously working.

Then they tried some other experiments. For example, when the robot gave samples but didn't dance, only ten bees found the food. When the robot danced but didn't give samples, or when it danced and gave samples but didn't whir its wings, very few bees found their way to the sugar water. Finally the scientists knew that the bees needed the whole message—the waggle dance, the whirring wings, and a taste of the food.

The keepers of the robot bee can hardly wait to find out what else it will tell them. They are ready for surprises.

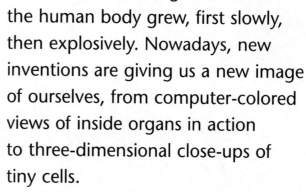

What did early people know about the human body? They could easily see the skin, hair, fingers, and toes. They could feel the movement of a muscle, the hardness of a bone. But they knew very little about the inside of the body.

As instruments such as the microscope and X-ray machines were invented, knowledge of the inside of the human body grew, first slowly, then explosively. Nowadays, new inventions are giving us a new image of ourselves, from computer-colored views of inside organs in action to three-dimensional close-ups of tiny cells.

This picture was taken inside the stomach of a living person. It shows a sore, called an ulcer, in the lining of the stomach.

The photo was taken with the aid of fiber optics. Ninety thousand glass fibers, each about one-fifth the diameter of a human hair, are bundled together in a long, flexible tube half the thickness of a pencil.

The fiber-optic tube, along with a similar tube made of somewhat thicker glass fibers, is inserted down the throat and inside the stomach of the patient. Light travels through one of the tubes and the photograph is taken through the other.

Hidden Worlds Inside Your BODY

from *Hidden Worlds*
by Seymour Simon

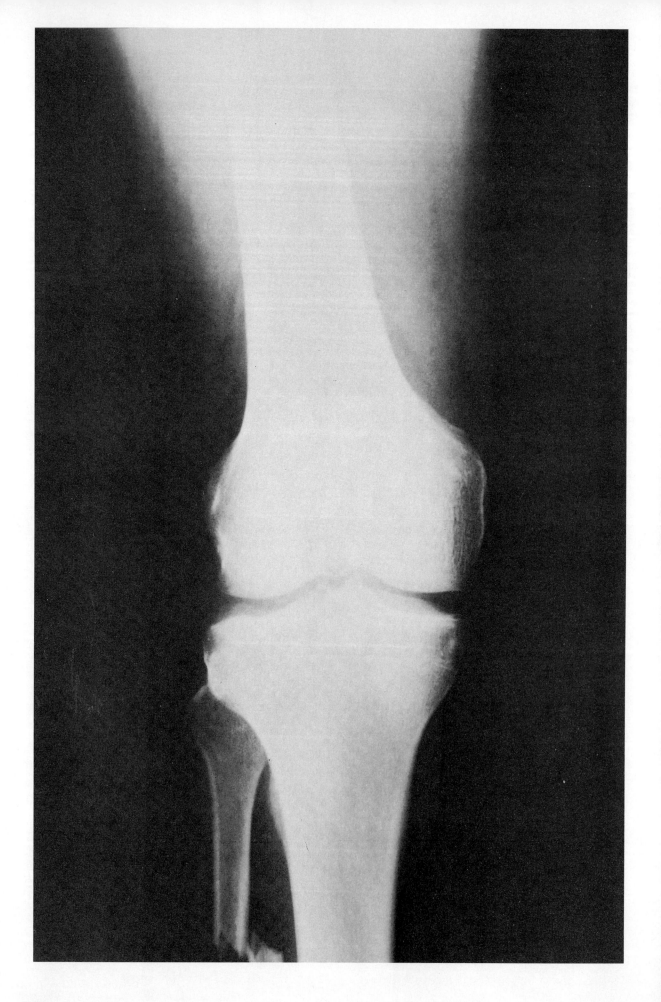

This simple X ray of a leg clearly shows a break in the bone called the fibula. The X ray shows the bone in white because bone stops more of the X rays than the flesh around it.

X rays were first discovered by Wilhelm Roentgen[1] in 1895. Here's how an X-ray camera works. An X-ray camera shoots electrons at a photographic film. A leg, or some other part of the body, is put in the way of the electrons. Those electrons that get through the leg turn the film black. The part of the film that is blocked and receives no electrons stays white.

X-ray electrons pass right through flesh leaving only a vague image on the film. Bones, on the other hand, contain large amounts of minerals which stop the electrons. The crack in the fibula shows up black in the film because that's where there is no bone. An X ray makes it possible for a doctor to quickly find out the extent of an injury to a bone inside the body.

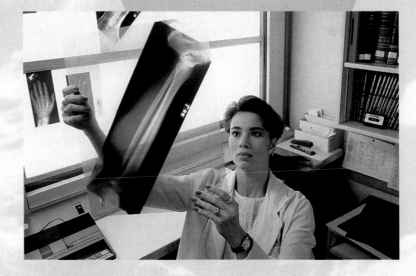

Tough break! A doctor examines an X-ray.

1 **Wilhelm Roentgen** (*VIHL hehlm REHNT guhn*)

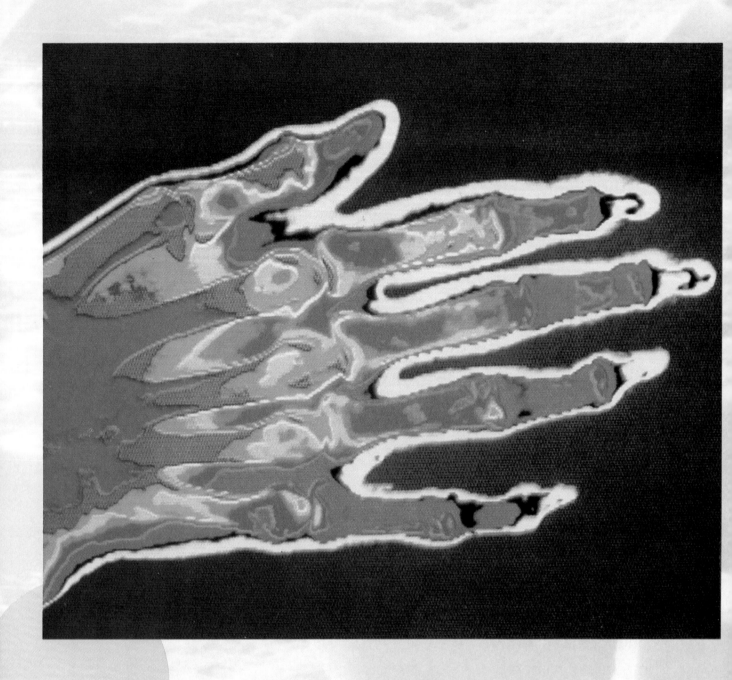

This photo shows a human hand that is crippled with arthritis, a disease of the joints. This is an example of a kind of X-ray technique called tomography which uses focused X rays to photograph a flat cross section of a body organ and get rid of unwanted shadows. The colors were added by a computer to make details easier to see.

This is a cross-sectional X ray of a living person. You are looking at a horizontal "slice" through the middle of the stomach area. The backbone is at the bottom of the picture and the ribs are around the outside. The kidney is at the right and the spleen is at the left.

This technique, called a CAT scan, is an important advance in the medical use of X rays. It involves the use of a flat, thin beam of X rays being sent through a person's body. Dozens of photographs are taken in a circle around the patient. Then computers combine the results. This makes it possible to look at a slice of the body from any angle.

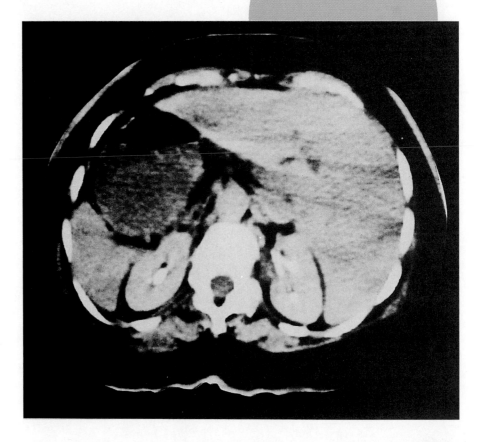

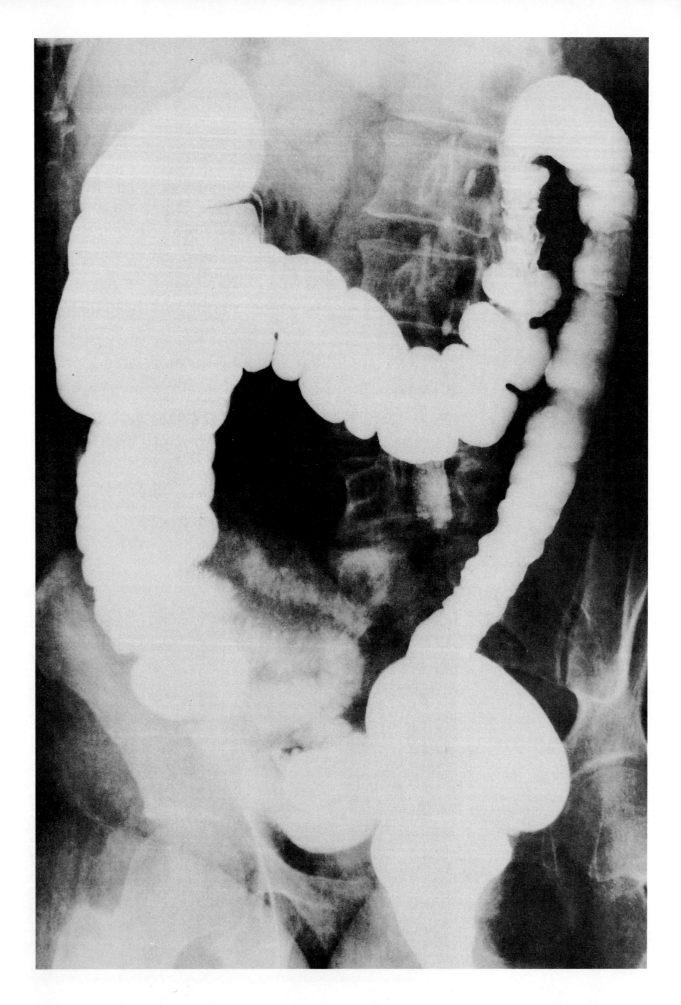

The X ray on the left was made after the patient swallowed a chalky liquid containing barium that coats the intestines so that the rays are blocked from reaching the film. This makes the area appear white in the photo.

It takes guts. A young boy gets his intestines X-rayed.

The X ray below of a person's skull shows the blood vessels in the brain very clearly. A liquid was injected into the blood which made the arteries and veins stand out white in the X-ray photo. This kind of X ray is called an angiograph. It is used to spot internal bleeding or the obstruction of a blood vessel.

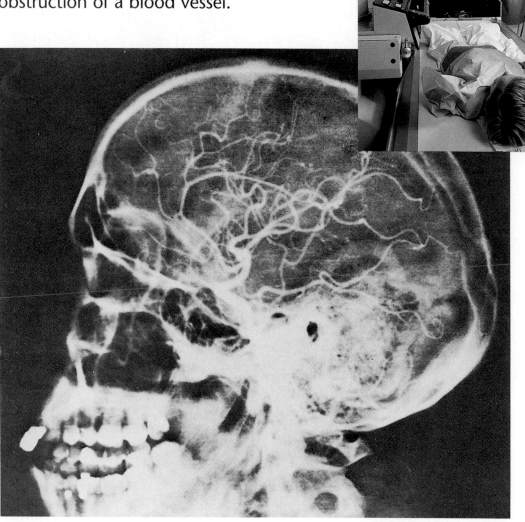

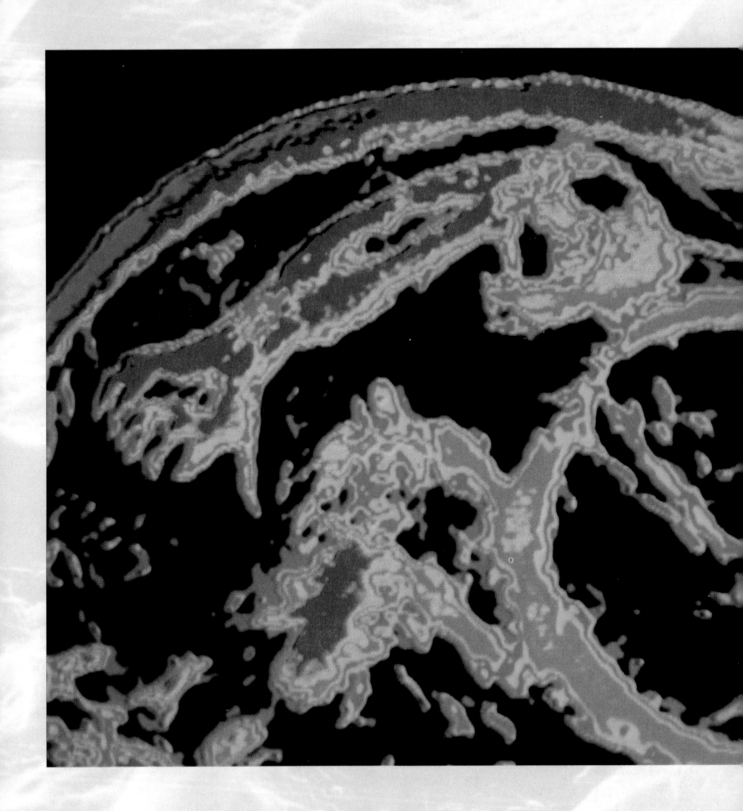

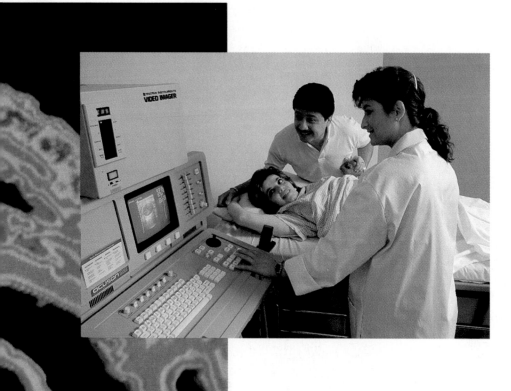

A family catches a glimpse of its newest member before he or she is even born.

This color photo shows a six-month-old human fetus within its mother. Because X rays might damage the living fetus, high-frequency sound waves were used to take the photo. This method of looking within the body is called sonography. The colors were added by computer to make it easier to see. The head of the fetus is at the right with one of its arms (in blue) across the top. Sonography can be used to watch continuous movements within the body such as the heartbeat of an unborn baby.

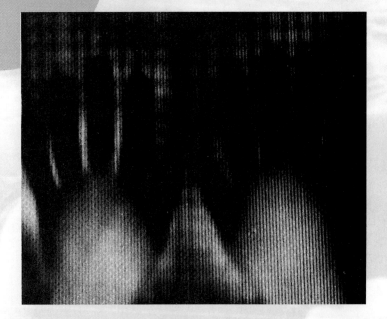

These three photographs are called thermograms. A thermogram is a picture of the heat coming from an object. These thermograms show the hands of a person who smokes a pack of cigarettes a day. The top photo shows normal hands. The middle photo, taken one minute after smoking, shows that the hands have become 6°C cooler. Thirty minutes later (bottom) the fingers are becoming warm again. The change is caused by the effect of tobacco on the tiny blood vessels in the hand.

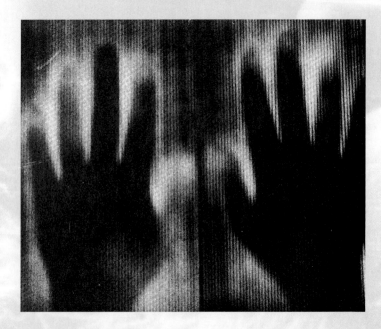

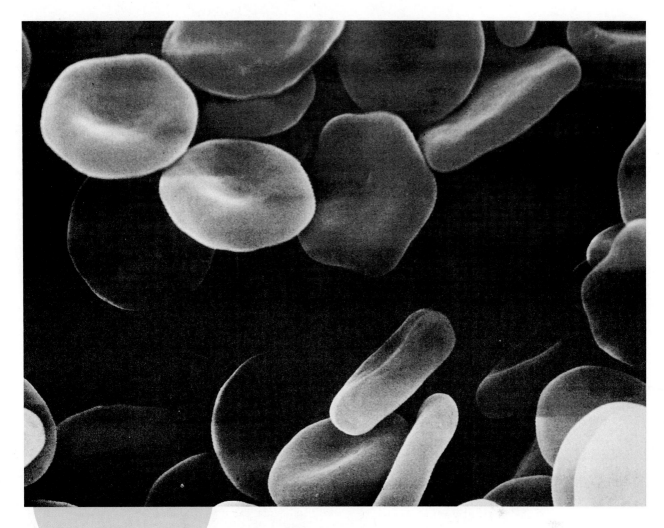

This SEM photograph of red blood cells has a magnification of about 4400X. Red blood cells carry oxygen to other cells of your body. The great number of red blood cells in your blood gives blood its color. This photo shows the doughnutlike shape of the cells.

Take a closer look. To see things so small, an electron microscope must be this big.

The SEM photo above shows two teeth covered with a substance called plaque. The magnification is about 25X. Focusing in closer below, we see what looks like a field strewn with rocks. Actually, it's a 2700X SEM photo of the surface of a tooth.

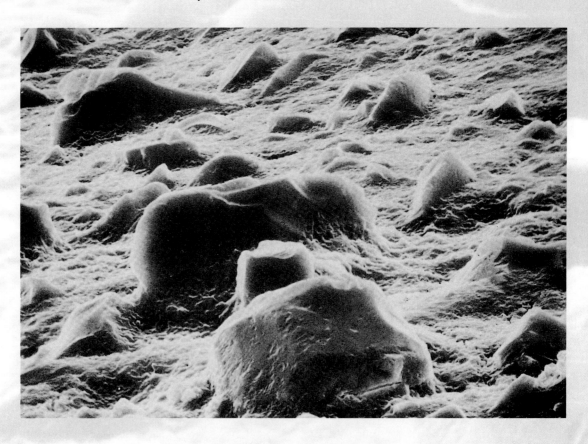

The Inside View

The fiber-optic tube and the X-ray camera are two inventions that allow us to see inside the body. Choose one of these inventions. Then pair up with a classmate who chose the other invention and explain how your invention works.

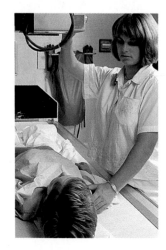

Well Equipped

Special equipment helped people in this theme explore hidden worlds. With a group, choose equipment from each selection and discuss what it helped people discover. Tell the group which equipment you would most like to use and describe the hidden world it would help you explore.

AUTHOR AT WORK

Seymour Simon got the idea for *Hidden Worlds: Pictures of the Invisible* from a *Life* magazine photograph of a drop splashing in milk. He spent many years collecting and researching the photographs for the book. Mr. Simon says he enjoyed writing the book because he loves finding out what is going on inside of something.

★ Award-winning Author

Another Book by . . .

Seymour Simon

Weather by Seymour Simon, Morrow Junior Books, 1993

Library Link "Hidden Worlds Inside Your Body" was taken from *Hidden Worlds: Pictures of the Invisible* by Seymour Simon. You might enjoy reading the entire book to learn about other hidden worlds.

Express Yourself

In Discovering Hidden Worlds, you've taken a peek into some of the hidden worlds around you. Understanding such worlds takes patience, close observation, and sometimes special methods or equipment. Wherever you are, there are hidden worlds like these waiting to be discovered.

World of Stories

"He has watched stories unfold that other people have never dreamed of," writes Kathryn Lasky ("Entering Animal Worlds"). What stories have you watched unfold in this theme? Think about the hidden worlds discussed in this theme. Which world would you most like to explore? Why? Write a plan for exploring this world. What would you need for your exploration? What would you hope to find there?

Illustrating Their Point

Compare the selections in the themes The Stories We Tell and Discovering Hidden Worlds. Start by looking at the pictures in each theme. How are they different from one theme to the other? How do you explain the difference? How does this difference relate to the types of selections in each theme?

Exploring Inventions

In "Hidden Worlds Inside Your Body" and "Entering Animal Worlds," the explorers used special equipment to make their discoveries. Choose one piece of equipment from these selections. Draw what you would see without the invention and what you would see with it. How important are inventions to hidden-world explorations?

Picturing Hidden Worlds

Draw a picture of a scene from "Fire Mountain," "Entering Animal Worlds," or "Dark Depths." In the picture, hide some plants or animals an explorer would find in this world. Ask a classmate to try to find the items you have hidden.

Experiencing Your Surroundings

In "The Desert," Eucario Mendez advises readers to "see things, feel things, and hear things." What do you think he means? How did each of the people who explored the hidden worlds in this theme follow a similar process? Explain your answer, providing examples of animals and plants that the explorers in "Dark Depths" and "Fire Mountain" saw, felt, and heard.

The Silver Bookcase

Down Under, Down Under: Diving Adventures on the Great Barrier Reef

by Ann McGovern, photographs by Jim and Martin Scheiner and the author, Macmillan, 1989

Come aboard the *Coral Princess* for a ten-day diving trip on the Great Barrier Reef. Share scuba-diving adventures with a twelve-year-old girl as she explores a ghost ship and swims among giant sea creatures.

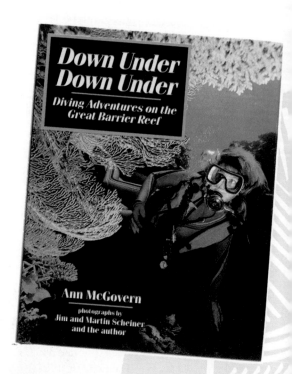

Outside and Inside Spiders

by Sandra Markle, Bradbury Press, 1994

Here's your chance to get a different look at spiders—close up through beautiful photographs. Watch a spider build a web and catch and eat an insect. See baby spiders grow inside an egg right before your eyes. Learn about the clever ways spiders protect themselves.

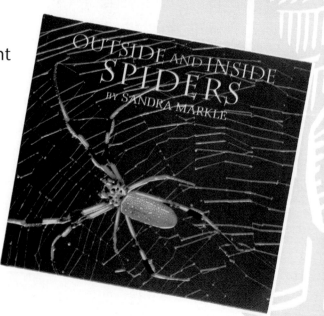

Animal Camouflage: A Closer Look
by Joyce Powzyk, Bradbury Press, 1990

Camouflage helps animals hide from their enemies. This book describes the many ways animals from all over the world go unnoticed because of their color, pattern, or shape.

Antarctica: The Last Unspoiled Continent
by Laurence Pringle, Simon & Schuster, 1992

Antarctica is a beautiful and mysterious frozen desert inhabited by penguins and surrounded by water. This fascinating book tells about its early explorers and describes its climate and wildlife.

The Egyptians and the Valley of the Kings
by Philip Steele, Dillon Press, 1994

The search for treasure led to the discovery of the ancient tombs of Egyptian kings and queens, untouched for thousands of years. Find out why mummies were buried there and the fascinating information archaeologists have uncovered about them.

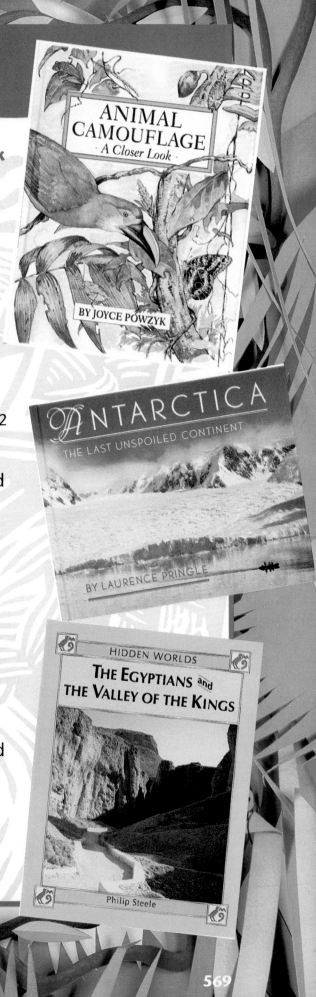

Glossary

The pronunciation of each word is shown just after the word, in this way: **abbreviate** [ə·brē′vē·āt′]. The letters and signs used are pronounced as in the words in the chart at right. The mark ′ is placed after a syllable with a primary, or heavy, accent, as in the example above. The mark ′ after a syllable shows a secondary or lighter accent, as in the following example: **abbreviation** [ə·brē′vē·ā′shən].

Pronunciation Key

Symbol	Key Words	Symbol	Key Words
a	cat	b	bed
ā	ape	d	dog
ä	cot, car	f	fall
e	ten, berry	g	get
ē	me	h	help
i	fit, here	j	jump
ī	ice, fire	k	kiss, call
ō	go	l	leg
ô	fall, for	m	meat
oi	oil	n	nose
oo	look, pull	p	put
o͞o	tool, rule	r	red
ou	out, crowd	s	see
u	up	t	top
ʉ	fur, shirt	v	vat
ə	a in ago	w	wish
	e in agent	y	yard
	i in pencil	z	zebra
	o in atom	ch	chin, arch
	u in circus	ŋ̂	ring, drink
		sh	she, push
		th	thin, truth
		th	then, father
		zh	measure

A

abuelita [ä·bwā·lē′tä] n. Spanish word for beloved grandmother.

accommodate [ə·käm′ə·dāt′] v. to find lodging for.

accomplish [ə·käm′plish] v. to do or complete: Do you plan to accomplish anything in particular on your spring vacation?

ace [ās] n. an expert in a certain activity.

adapt [ə·dapt′] v. to change oneself to fit a new or different environment.

advance [ad·vans′] n. a new development or discovery in a body of knowledge.

afloat [ə·flōt′] adj. floating on the surface of a body of water.

Airedale [er′dāl′] n. a breed of dog with a wiry tan coat and black markings: Nan's parents gave her an Airedale puppy for her tenth birthday.

airs [erz] n. false manners or behavior: The old lady and her daughter were always dressing up and putting on airs.

Alps [alps] n. a mountain range in south central Europe: The Swiss Alps are a favorite vacation spot for skiers.

amiably [ā′mē·ə·blē] adv. in a pleasant, friendly way. syn. cordially.

Airedale

Swiss Alps at Grindelwald

ancestor [an′ses′tər] n. a person from whom one is descended, such as a grandmother or grandfather: People sometimes learn they have a famous ancestor when they study their family tree.

angiograph [an′jē·ə·graf′] n. an X-ray that uses injected dye to find internal bleeding or a blockage of a blood vessel.

applause [ə·plôz′] n. approval or praise, shown especially by clapping or cheering.

The Skydome, an arena in Toronto, Canada

arena [ə·rē′nə] n. an enclosed area for sporting events or other entertainment, surrounded by seats: The children liked to watch the local basketball team play at the sports arena.

artificial respiration [ärt′ə·fish′əl res′pə·rā′shən] n. the process of helping a person breathe either by forcing air into his mouth or by pressing on the chest and releasing at regular intervals: When her baby brother stopped breathing, Shelby saved him with artificial respiration.

ashamed [ə·shāmd´] adj. feeling embarrassed or guilty as a result of something done wrong.

attack [ə·tak´] n. the beginning or return of a disease.

attentive [ə·ten´tiv] adj. observant; paying close attention.

audition [ô·dish´ən] v. to try out for a role in a play or musical event.

avalanche [av´ə·lanch´] n. a huge amount of snow, dirt, or other material that is suddenly loosened and tumbles quickly down a mountain.

awe [ô] n. a feeling of wonder and respect caused by another person or thing.

bait [bāt] v. to use as a lure or temptation for animals.

bank [baṅgk] n. a stretch of land rising on either side of a body of water, such as a stream.

beacon [bē´kən] n. a signal or other thing that offers guidance or encouragement.

bellow [bel´ō] v. to roar loudly.

bend¹ [bend] n. a turn or curve in a path: As I jogged around the bend, I saw the bicyclist in my path.

bend² [bend] v. to force into a curved position.

blind [blīnd] n. a place where people can observe nature without being seen.

boulder [bōl´dər] n. a large rock that has been worn round and smooth by weather and water.

bramble [bram´bəl] n. a prickly type of bush.

brittle starfish [brit´l stär´fish´] n. a kind of sea creature with a central disk and five long, narrow arms that can grow back if broken off.

bull [bool] adj. male (as of a species): The bull moose has antlers but the female does not.

burden [bʉrd´n] n. a heavy load or responsibility that one must put up with. syn. obligation.

burrow [bʉr´ō] n. a hole or tunnel dug by an animal for shelter.

cache [kash] n. a hidden supply: For those days when she missed lunch, Donna kept a cache of granola bars in her locker.

brittle starfish

burrow

a	cat	ô	fall, for	ə = a *in* ago
ā	ape	oi	oil	e *in* agent
ä	cot, car	oo	look, pull	i *in* pencil
e	ten, berry	ōō	tool, rule	o *in* atom
ē	me	ou	out, crowd	u *in* circus
i	fit, here	u	up	
ī	ice, fire	ʉr	fur	
ō	go			

camouflage [kam′ə·fläzh] n. a disguise used to hide something or someone.

canopy [kan′ə·pē] n. in a rain forest, the section formed by the tops of the trees.

canyon [kan′yən] n. a long, narrow valley between steep cliffs, sometimes with a stream flowing through it.

captivity [kap·tiv′i·tē] n. the state of being caged or imprisoned instead of in the wild: If an opossum is born in captivity, it may not be able to survive in the forest.

carcass [kär′kəs] n. the dead body of an animal: We saw the large crow pecking at the carcass of a raccoon on the road.

casting [kas′tiñg] n. the act of choosing and assigning actors for a play.

cathedral [kə·thē′drəl] n. a very large church: Hundreds of people attended the mayor's funeral at St. Patrick's, a Roman Catholic cathedral in New York City.

cease [sēs] v. to stop.

cinch [sinch] n. bands on a horse's saddle or pack: Before they left the stable, Becky tightened the cinches on Starfire's saddle.

clutch [kluch] n. a group of animals or things gathered together: We saw a clutch of chicks following their mother across the road.

Grand Canyon, Arizona

Nôtre Dame Cathedral, Paris

cockle-burr [käk′əl·bur′] n. from the cockle-burr plant, a prickly fruit that sticks to other things: After my dog Pepper explored the prairie, he came home with cockle-burrs stuck in his coat.

cocoon [kə·koon′] n. a protective cover that certain animals can create by spinning.

commercial [kə·mur′shəl] adj. operating as a business, for profit: Although Sara's jewelry making was once a hobby, it is now a commercial project.

commotion [kə·mō′shən] n. a great deal of noise; confusion. syn. uproar.

community [kə·myoo′nə·tē] n. a group of plants or animals living in a particular place and depending on one another for survival.

conceal [kən·sēl′] v. to hide: Ramona concealed the birthday gift behind her back until she stood right in front of her grandmother.

conditions [kən·dish′ənz] n. circumstances or requirements: When it is sunny and warm, conditions are right for a picnic.

confrontation
[kän′frən·tā′shən] n. a face-to-face meeting, often unfriendly.

conscience [kän′shəns] n. one's knowledge of right and wrong, with the urge to do right.

containment crew
[kən·tān′mənt krōō] n. a group whose job is to hold something back or prevent it from spreading.

contaminate [kən·tam′ə·nāt′] v. to spoil or make impure by adding something, especially a harmful substance: If the laboratory equipment is not sterilized, it may contaminate your samples.

continuous [kən·tin′yōō·əs] adj. never stopping: The continuous buzz of the alarm finally woke Jeff.

contrary [kän′trer·ē] adj. tending to disagree or be oppositional.

contribution
[kän′trə·byōō′shən] n. something given: My parents' contribution to the school play was printing the programs.

conversation piece
[kän′vər·sā′shən pēs] n. anything out of the ordinary that causes people to comment, such as an unusual painting or a strange piece of furniture: My cousin's musical necklace is always a conversation piece at parties.

coop [kōōp] n. a small cage or building for animals, especially poultry.

corrode [kə·rōd′] v. to rust or wear away.

council [koun′səl] n. a group called together to discuss matters of importance to them.

crane [krān] n. a machine used for lifting or moving heavy objects : Box by box, the crane loaded cargo onto the ship.

cranky [kraṅg′kē] adj. in an irritable mood. syn. cross.

Meteor Crater, Arizona

crater [krāt′ər] n. a wide, shallow, often bowl-shaped hole in the earth.

crawlspace [krôl′spās] n. an unfinished space in a house, usually beneath the roof or floor and used for storage, and the like: After my little brother outgrew his crib, we stored it in the crawlspace until my sister was born.

creamy [krēm′ē] adj. smooth and yellowish-white, like cream.

corrode

crane

a	cat	ô	fall, for	ə	= a *in* ago
ā	ape	oi	oil		e *in* agent
ä	cot, car	oo	look, pull		i *in* pencil
e	ten, berry	ōō	tool, rule		o *in* atom
ē	me	ou	out, crowd		u *in* circus
i	fit, here	u	up		
ī	ice, fire	ur	fur		
ō	go				

575

Glen Canyon Dam, Arizona

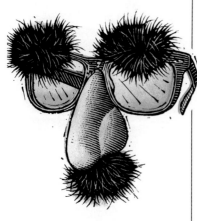

disguise

D

dam [dam] v. to block the flow of water by putting up a barrier.

dappled [dap′əld] adj. spotted.

daybed [dā′bed′] n. a couch that can also be used as a bed: When he stays overnight at our house, Grandpa sleeps on the daybed in our den.

dealer [dēl′ər] n. one who buys and sells.

debris [də·brē′] n. bits and pieces of rubbish, occurring especially after destruction.

deceitful [dē·sēt′fəl] adj. tending to lie or to hide the truth. syn. sneaky.

despair [di·sper′] n. a loss of hope.

desperate [des′pər·it] adj. lacking hope or alternatives.

devour [di·vour′] v. to swallow up or eat hungrily. syn. gobble.

disguise [dis·gīz′] n. clothes, a mask, or other items that help hide one's identity: The private investigator's disguise was so good not even her brother recognized her.

distant [dis′tənt] adj. far off: When we listened carefully, we could hear the distant whirring of a helicopter.

distinct [di·stiñgkt′] adj. clear; unmistakable. syn. definite.

domain [dō·mān′] n. a region where a plant or animal lives.

doomsday [doomz′dā] n. a day of judgment.

dorsal [dôr′səl] adj. on the back.

dreaded [dred′əd] adj. feared intensely.

dreary [drir′ē] adj. gloomy. syn. depressing.

dwell [dwel] v. to live.

dwindle [dwin′dəl] v. to decrease in number or intensity: As Tommy approached his second birthday, his interest in an afternoon nap began to dwindle.

E

ecosystem [ēk′ō·sis′təm] n. a community of living things that rely on each other for survival.

eerie [ir′ē] adj. weird and frightening.

electron
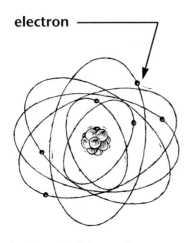

electron [ē·lek´trän] n. a negatively charged particle of an atom.

embed [em·bed´] v. to bury or fix deeply: The splinter embedded itself deeply under the skin.

emerge [ē·murj´] v. to come out.

endangered [en·dān´jərd] adj. facing extinction: The Endangered Species Act, passed in 1973, has saved many of the world's plants and animals from extinction.

engineering [en·jə·nēr´iñg] n. the study of putting scientific knowledge to practical uses: Students who want to build bridges someday should study engineering in college.

engulf [en·gulf´] v. to swallow up or cover completely.

enrage [en·rāj´] v. to make very angry.

environment [en·vī´rən·mənt] n. a plant or animal's complete surroundings.

eruption [ē·rup´shən] n. a breaking forth, an outpouring, as from a volcano or geyser: When they learned of the volcano's eruption, people in Hawaii fled their homes to safety.

extinction [ek·stiñgk´shən] n. being no longer in existence: Although it once faced extinction, the American alligator can now be found throughout Florida.

faint [fānt] adj. weak, almost unable to be heard: Listen carefully and you'll hear the faint honking of Canada geese.

fastener [fas´ən·ər] n. a device that connects two things.

fatal [fāt´əl] adj. leading to or causing death: During the race, one driver was involved in a fatal crash.

fault [fôlt] n. responsibility for something wrong.

fiery [fī´ər·ē] adj. hot or burning like a fire.

finery [fīn´ər·ē] n. beautiful clothes, jewelry, or other things: New Yorkers enjoy displaying their finery in the annual Easter Parade.

flail [flāl] v. to wave around wildly: Toby flailed her arms wildly to get free of the flies.

eruption

finery

a	cat	ô	fall, for	ə	= a in ago
ā	ape	oi	oil		e in agent
ä	cot, car	oo	look, pull		i in pencil
e	ten, berry	ōō	tool, rule		o in atom
ē	me	ou	out, crowd		u in circus
i	fit, here	u	up		
ɪ	ice, fire	ur	fur		
ō	go				

flan

Key Largo, in the Florida Keys

flan [flan] n. a Spanish dessert of custard topped by a burnt-sugar syrup and often decorated with fruit or nuts.

flaw [flô] n. a defect or irregularity.

flexible [flek´sə·bəl] adj. able to be bent back and forth without breaking.

Florida Keys [flôr´ə·də kēz] n. a chain of islands extending from the southern tip of Florida. Because they are islands, you must use a bridge to drive to the Florida Keys.

fluke [flo͞ok] n. part of a sea mammal's tail.

foothill [foot´hil´] n. a low hill at or near the base of a mountain or mountain range.

formaldehyde [fôr·mal´də·hīd´] n. a chemical that is mixed in a liquid and used to clean or preserve something.

foul [foul] adj. stinking; disgusting to the senses. syn. smelly.

frail [frāl] adj. delicate and prone to sickness.

fret [fret] v. to worry or be anxious.

frolic [frä´ik] v. to play or romp about happily.

fungi [fun´jī] n. very simple plants that take their food from other living or once-living things; plural of fungus.

furrow [fûr´ō] n. a deep, narrow groove in the soil.

futon [fo͞o´tän´] n. a thin mattress placed on the floor and used as a bed: Although Ada has a new bunkbed, she still prefers to sleep on her old futon.

gash [gash] n. a long, deep cut.

gawk [gôk] v. to stare stupidly: Motorists caused a traffic jam when they stopped to gawk at the overturned bus.

generation [jen·ər·ā´shən] n. all those born and living at the same time.

glance [glans] v. to look suddenly and briefly.

gore [gôr] v. to pierce with a horn: The matador prayed that the bull wouldn't gore him while his back was turned.

Great Barrier Reef [grāt bar´ē·ər rēf] n. a coral reef off the northeast coast of Australia.

groom [gro͞om] v. to clean or make tidy: We watched the mother pig groom her newborn piglets.

habitat [hab´i·tat´] n. where a living thing naturally grows or lives.

harmony [här´mə·nē] n. a sense of agreement and cooperation: Before the new neighbors arrived, the people in our apartment building had always lived in harmony.

headlong [hed´lông] adv. going headfirst and with uncontrolled speed.

healer [hēl´ər] n. one who helps the sick get well.

hemp [hemp] n. a fiber used to make rope.

heroine [her´ō·in] n. the central female character in a story.

hesitate [hez´i·tāt´] v. to stop or pause, as if undecided.

hoist [hoist] v. raise: After winning the big game, the soccer players joyously hoisted their coach onto their shoulders.

horizontal [hôr´i·zänt´l] adj. in a side-to-side direction (as opposed to up and down).

hover [huv´ər] v. to linger or stay close by.

huff¹ [huf] n. bad temper: After the clerk refused to give us a refund, we left the store in a huff, vowing never to return.

huff² [huf] v. to blow hard.

hummock [hum´ək] n. a low, rounded hill or mound.

husk [husk] v. to remove the outer covering to expose the seeds, as with corn.

iguana [i·gwä´nə] n. a type of lizard found in tropical areas of North and South America that feeds on insects and has a row of spines from its neck to its tail.

image [im´ij] n. a picture of something.

imprint [im·print´] v. to look to someone for care, feeding, and so on: The ducklings imprinted on the man and followed him, thinking he was their mother.

inject [in·jekt´] v. to insert with a needle.

insistent [in·sis´tənt] adj. not giving up: The frazzled parents surrendered to their child's insistent whining for a cookie.

instinctively [in·stiñgk´tiv·lē] adv. in an inborn, natural, and unlearned way.

huff

iguana

a	cat	ô	fall, for	ə = a in ago
ā	ape	oi	oil	e in agent
ä	cot, car	oo	look, pull	i in pencil
e	ten, berry	o͞o	tool, rule	o in atom
ē	me	ou	out, crowd	u in circus
i	fit, here	u	up	
ɪ	ice, fire	ur	fur	
ō	go			

579

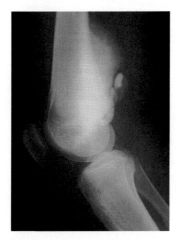

human knee joint

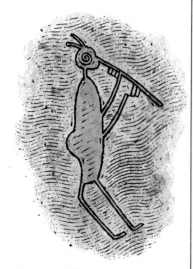

Kokopelli

intently [in·tent′lē] adv. with careful attention; in earnest.

intersection [in·tər·sek′shən] n. where two streets cross.

invertebrate [in·vʉr′tə·brit] n. an animal that does not have a backbone or spinal column.

isolated [ī′·sə·lāt′əd] adj. separated from others, alone: Although James lived on an isolated strip of land, he said he wasn't lonely.

joint [joint] n. a place where two bones meet: How the elbow joint works is the subject of Ellen's report.

kindling [kind′ling] n. wood used to build a fire.

kiva [kē·və] n. a room used for religious purposes.

knife [nīf] v. to move through quickly and decisively.

Kokopelli [kō·kō·pel′ē] n. a mythical figure common among various Native American cultures, often shown playing the flute: Tina's Mexican grandmother told us stories about Kokopelli and his wonderful deeds.

lair [ler] n. a hiding place. syn. den.

landscape [land′skāp] n. any stretch of land as far as the eye can see: From the hilltop, the view of the landscape was beautiful.

lava flowing from a volcano

lava [lä′və] n. melted rock that comes out of an erupting volcano.

lease [lēs] v. to pay a fee in exchange for the right to use property: For a year we saved money so we could lease land for a garden.

lure [lŏor] v. to trick or entice. syn. tempt.

macro [mak′rō] adj. large or showing a wide view.

maestro [mīs′trō] n. a person very skilled in any of the arts, especially music: The audience applauded wildly after the maestro finished a perfect performance.

magical [maj′i·kəl] adj. captivating or done as if by magic: While we watched, Hattie created a magical "zoo" of balloon animals.

magma [mag′mə] n. liquid rock deep in the earth.

magnification [mag′nə·fi·kā′shən] n. the act of enlarging.

majestic [mə·jes′tik] adj. like royalty; grand or stately.

makings [māk′iṅgz] n. the specific ingredients needed to make something: For our picnic, we brought along the makings for sandwiches.

manatee [man′ə·tē′] n. a mammal living in the shallow coastal waters of North and South America and western Africa.

mangy [mān′jē] adj. mean-tempered and messy in appearance. syn. despicable.

manual [man′yoo·əl] n. a book of instructions used as a reference: If the washing machine stops working, check the owner's manual to find out how to fix it.

marine [mə·rēn′] adj. having to do with the sea or ocean.

masterwork [mas′tər·wurk′] n. an artist's greatest work.

matador [mat′ə·dôr′] n. a bullfighter.

measure [mezh′ər] n. a step or action.

mesa [mā′sə] n. a high, flat land with steep sides.

mesquite [mes·kēt′] n. a thorny tree or shrub found in the southwestern United States.

migration [mī·grā′shən] n. the act of moving from one region to another, often with the change of seasons: Warblers stopped for water at our fountain during their spring migration from South America.

mime [mīm] n. an actor who performs with gestures and actions rather than with words.

minute [mi·noot′] adj. very small.

monastery [män′ə·ster′ē] n. a place to which monks, priests, or others have withdrawn to live and work for religious reasons.

moral [môr′əl] n. a lesson taught by a story, fable, or event.

mortar [môrt′ər] n. a small, hard bowl in which softer materials are pounded or ground into powder with a small, clublike tool.

mount [mount] v. to climb onto the back of a horse or other animal: Before we go riding, we must learn how to mount the horse.

mug [mug] v. to attack a person, usually with the desire to rob: On his way to school, Mike was mugged by a group of bullies.

manatee

mesa

a cat	ô fall, for	ə = a *in* ago
ā ape	oi oil	e *in* agent
ä cot, car	oo look, pull	i *in* pencil
e ten, berry	oo tool, rule	o *in* atom
ē me	ou out, crowd	u *in* circus
i fit, here	u up	
ī ice, fire	ur fur	
ō go		

Niagara Falls

outcropping

multitude [mul′tə·tood′] n. a large group. syn. crowd.

muster [mus′tər] v. to collect or gather up. syn. summon.

mutter [mut′ər] v. to talk in a low, hard-to-hear way without moving the lips.

netsuke [net′soo·ke′] n. an ornamental figure carved out of ivory once used as a button for attaching a purse or other item to a kimono sash.

Niagara Falls [nī·ag′ə·rə fôlz] a large waterfall on the Niagara River, between New York and Canada.

nocturnal [näk·tur′nəl] adj. active during the night: The raccoons slept all morning because they are chiefly nocturnal animals.

nourishment [nur′ish·mənt] n. food.

obstacle [äb′stə·kəl] n. anything that stands in the way.

obstruction [əb·struk′shən] n. a blockage.

olé [ō·lā′] interj. in Spanish, a shout of approval or joy.

omelette [äm′ə·lət] n. a dish made of beaten eggs that are fried and then folded over a filling of some kind: For breakfast, Seth ordered a cheese omelette and toast.

organ [ôr′gən] n. in a living thing, a group of tissues that perform a specific function: Jed argued that the heart is the most important organ in the human body.

outcropping [out′kräp′ing] n. a jutting out, as of rock or stone: The hawk sat high above us on an outcropping, looking into the distance.

owlet [oul′it] n. a baby owl.

oxygen [äks′i·jən] n. a gas that occurs naturally in the earth's air: Without oxygen to breathe, human beings could not live.

pace [pās] n. speed: Once on the trail, Leslie's horse settled into a comfortable pace.

pallet [pal′it] n. a thin pad placed on the floor and used for sleeping: The prison cell contained only a pallet and a light bulb hanging from the ceiling.

parasite [par′ə·sīt′] n. a plant or an animal that lives on or in another living thing from which it feeds.

pathologist [pə·thäl´ə·jist´] n. a medical doctor who studies the nature of disease and how living things get sick.

peer [pir] v. to squint and look closely.

persimmon [pər·sim´ən] n. a sweet yellow or orange-red fruit.

pestle [pes´əl] n. a hard, small, clublike tool used to pound or grind materials into powder.

petition [pə·tish´ən] n. a written request, often made by a group of people: Everyone in our class signed the petition for a new park, and we sent it to City Hall.

Pilgrim [pil´grəm] n. one of the group of English settlers who founded Plymouth Colony in 1620.

plague [plāg] n. widespread trouble or sickness: People who survived the plague told stories of suffering and loss.

plain [plān] n. an area of level land.

plentiful [plen´ti·fəl] adj. more than is needed.

plod [pläd] v. to move or walk heavily, as with effort. syn. trudge.

poisonous [poi´zə·nəs] adj. able to cause death. syn. toxic.

pollen [päl´ən] n. in seed plants, the fine grains of material that contain male cells.

pollinate [päl´ə·nāt´] v. in seed plants, to transfer pollen from the male to the female parts of the flower: Bees pollinate flowers by moving from blossom to blossom.

poncho [pän´chō] n. a cloth with a hole in the middle, slipped over the head and worn as a coat.

pontoon [pän·tōōn´] n. a floating object used as a support.

pottery [pät´ər·ē] n. bowls, dishes, and so on, made of clay and hardened by heat: Kay proudly displayed her collection of Inca pottery to our class.

predator [pred´ə·tər] n. an animal that hunts other animals for food.

prejudice [prej´ōō·dis] n. a deeply held suspicion, fear, or hatred of others based on race, religion, or other factor.

prey [prā] n. an animal that is hunted for food by another animal: Cautiously, the lions circled their prey, a jackal.

pilgrim

pottery

a	cat	ô	fall, for	ə	= a *in* ago
ā	ape	oi	oil		e *in* agent
ä	cot, car	oo	look, pull		i *in* pencil
e	ten, berry	ōō	tool, rule		o *in* atom
ē	me	ou	out, crowd		u *in* circus
i	fit, here	u	up		
ī	ice, fire	ur	fur		
ō	go				

priest

pumice rock in Crater Lake, Oregon

priest [prēst] n. a person whose job is to perform certain religious functions.

professional [prō·fesh´ə·nəl] adj. involved in a certain job for a living.

property [präp´ər·tē] n. anything that belongs to someone, especially land.

protégée [prōt´ə·zhā´] n. a female who is being taught or guided by someone more experienced: As the protégée of a famous violinist, Lila would soon perform in Orchestra Hall.

protrude [prō·trōōd´] v. to stick out.

pucker up [puk´ər up] v. to draw together the lips as when getting ready to kiss.

pueblo [pweb´lō] n. a village, especially in the southwestern United States or Latin America: For Alejandro, everyday life in the pueblo was quite a change from spending the summer with his uncle in Chicago.

pumice [pum´is] n. a light, spongy rock found in a volcano.

purposefully [pur´pəs·fəl·ē] adv. headed toward a definite goal: The speaker strode purposefully to the microphone with a copy of her speech in hand.

puzzle [puz´əl] v. to think about carefully. syn. wonder.

quaver [kwā´vər] v. to shake or tremble.

radiating [rā´dē·āt´iñg] adj. spreading out from a central point.

rain forest [rān´ fôr·ist] n. a thick forest that receives plenty of rainfall throughout the year.

ransack [ran´sak´] v. to search through as if to rob.

rare [rer] adj. unusual and special: We could tell the jewels in the museum exhibit were of rare beauty.

raspy [ras´pē] adj. scraping or grating.

recite [ri·sīt´] v. to repeat or say aloud from memory: Our assignment on Friday was to memorize our favorite poem and recite it in class on Monday.

recovery [ri·kuv´ər·ē] n. returning to good health after sickness or an accident: After breaking its wing in a storm, our parakeet made a complete recovery.

reef [rēf] n. a line or ridge of rock or coral lying at or near the surface of a body of water.

refuge [ref´yo͞oj] n. shelter or protection: The lost cat found refuge from the storm in the garage.

regulator [reg´yə·lāt´ər] n. equipment used by divers to help them breathe underwater.

rehabilitation [rē´hə·bil´ə·tā´shən] n. the process of putting something back in good condition: After her skating accident, Paula needed rehabilitation to help her walk again.

rein [rān] n. a strip of leather attached to each end of a bit inside a horse's mouth, used by the rider or driver to control a horse: It wasn't until Adam learned to use the reins that he enjoyed riding Comet.

reservoir [rez´ər·vwär´] n. a place where something is collected or stored: To collect rainwater, Dad built a reservoir out of a steel drum.

retired [ri·tīrd´] adj. having stopped working. My retired uncle uses his free time to fish.

rhythmic [rith´mik] adj. following a certain pattern of sound or movement.

ridge [rij] n. a long, narrow rise of land.

Rocky Mountains [räk´ē mount´nz] n. a group of mountains in western North America, extending from central New Mexico to northern Alaska.

Roentgen, Wilhelm [rent´gən vil´helm´] n. a German physicist who discovered X-rays.

rotten [rät´n] adj. decayed or spoiled: When Dad stepped on the rotten wood, his foot went right through the floorboard.

ruin [ro͞o´ən] n. an area that has been spoiled or destroyed: After the fire, the forest lay in ruins.

rustling [rus´ling] n. a soft sound, as if moving through leaves or grass: When the wind picked up, Juan heard a rustling outside his window.

sage [sāj] n. a plant with a strong aroma, used in cooking and for decoration: We dined on roast turkey with sage dressing.

sanctuary [sāngk´cho͞o·er·ē] n. a shelter or place of protection: We gently carried the injured squirrel to a wildlife sanctuary near our house.

savannah [sə·van´ə] n. a tropical grassland having few or no trees.

Rocky Mountains

a	cat	ô	fall, for	ə =	a in ago
ā	ape	oi	oil		e in agent
ä	cot, car	oo	look, pull		i in pencil
e	ten, berry	o͞o	tool, rule		o in atom
ē	me	ou	out, crowd		u in circus
i	fit, here	u	up		
ī	ice, fire	ur	fur		
ō	go				

scroll

sea urchin

scour [skour] v. to pass over quickly and completely.

script [skript] n. the copy of the text of a play: Having memorized their lines, the actors could rehearse without the script.

scroll [skrōl] n. a rolled strip of paper, usually with writing or pictures on it.

sea urchin [sē´ur·chin] n. a water animal that has a round body and sharp, movable spines.

seek [sēk] v. to look for.

semaphore [sem´ə·fôr´] n. a signal used to control traffic.

Serengeti [ser·ən·get´ē] n. grasslands in the African nation of Tanzania.

sewer [soo´ər] n. a large underground pipe used to carry off water and waste.

shapeless [shāp´lis] adj. without a distinct form.

shard [shärd] n. a broken piece, usually sharp: Although we thought we'd cleaned up all the broken glass, Bob stepped on a shard this morning.

shortening [shôrt´n·iŋg] n. edible fat used in making many types of food: To make her famous pie crust, Aunt Vi preferred a certain brand of shortening.

shriveled [shriv´əld] v. shrunken and wrinkled.

silhouette [sil´oo·et´] n. a dark outline or shape against a lighter background.

sliver [sliv´ər] n. a small, thin piece.

snout of a wild boar

snout [snout] n. an animal's nose and jaws.

socket [säk´it] n. a hollow part of something where another piece is held.

sonography [sə·näg´rə·fē] n. the process of using sound waves to look inside a human body.

Spaniard [span´yərd] n. a native of Spain.

specialty [spesh´əl·tē] n. what one spends time on, does the best, or likes best to do: Uncle Don is a great cook, but candy making is his specialty.

species [spē´shēz] n. a particular kind of living thing.

spectacle [spek´tə·kəl] n. a public show on a grand scale.

spell[1] [spel] n. a trance or magical state that keeps one from acting normally: The old woman cast a spell that put the princess to sleep.

spell² [spel] n. an attack of an illness or poor health.

spell³ [spel] v. to name the letters that make up a word.

spiny [spī´nē] adj. covered with sharp, often long, thornlike objects.

stagger [stag´ər] v. to walk unsteadily, as if about to fall.

stake [stāk] v. to claim or choose.

stall [stôl] n. a small section of a stable for one animal.

steamy [stē´mē] adj. filled with water vapor: On that steamy August day, we were too uncomfortable to play basketball.

stench [stench] n. a terrible smell or disgusting odor: No one could ignore the stench of rotting garbage in the house.

stoop [sto͞op] n. a small porch or platform with one or more steps at the door of a house.

storyteller doll [stôr´ē·tel´ər däl] n. a clay figure of a storyteller made by some Pueblo groups.

stream [strēm] n. a small river: Jackie led the cattle to a nearby stream for a drink.

stumpy [stump´ē] adj. short and stubby: When our terrier, Percy, wagged his stumpy tail, it looked more like a wiggle than a wag.

stun [stun] v. to daze or make senseless. syn. astonish.

submerge [sub·murj´] v. to go underwater.

suffocation [suf´ə·kā´shən] n. the inability to breathe freely.

summons [sum´ənz] n. a command to come or to do something.

superheated [so͞o´pər·hēt·id] adj. heated beyond the boiling point.

surge [surj] n. a great increase or wave. syn. swell.

survey [sur·vā´] v. to examine or review closely.

swarm [swôrm] n. a moving group: When Gary accidentally disturbed a hornets' nest, he was attacked by an angry swarm.

swerve [swurv] v. to turn aside suddenly from a straight path.

T

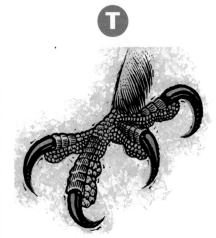

talon [tal´ən] n. claw of a bird of prey.

taut [tôt] adj. tightly stretched: The lake was dotted with boats of all sizes, each one with its own taut sail.

stream

swarm

a	cat	ô	fall, for	ə	= a in ago
a	ape	oi	oil		e in agent
ä	cot, car	oo	look, pull		i in pencil
e	ten, berry	o͞o	tool, rule		o in atom
ē	me	ou	out, crowd		u in circus
i	fit, here	u	up		
ī	ice, fire	ur	fur		
ō	go				

a famous threesome

tipi

technique [tek·nēk´] n. method of doing something.

telegram [tel´ə·gram´] n. a message sent by telegraph: Because we couldn't attend my cousin's wedding in Kansas, my family sent a telegram congratulating the bridal couple.

thermogram [thur´mō·gram´] n. a picture of an object, taken by detecting the heat coming from it.

threesome [thrē´səm] n. a group of three, usually persons.

threshold [thresh´ōld] n. a doorsill.

tipi [tē´pē] n. a cone-shaped tent used for shelter in some Native American communities.

toxic [täks´ik] adj. poisonous: Firefighters wore gas masks to protect them from the toxic fumes at the waste dump.

toxicologist [täks´i·käl´ə·jist] n. a scientist who studies poisons and their effect on living things.

trade [trād] n. a job or skill.

trance [trans] n. a dreamlike condition or state of great mental concentration.

transparent [trans·per´ənt] adj. clear; able to be seen through.

trigger [trig´ər] v. to cause: An explosion on the mountain may trigger a rockslide.

understory [un´dər·stôr´ē] n. in a rain forest, the section at ground level.

unsuspecting [un´sə·spek´ting] adj. not imagining or expecting. syn. innocent.

uproot [up·rōot´] v. to forcibly tear out: A tornado can flatten homes, uproot huge trees, and toss a moving automobile into the air like a toy.

upturned [up·turnd´] adj. pointed or turned upward.

utensil [yōo·ten´səl] n. a tool used in the kitchen or at the table, such as a knife or a spoon. syn. implement.

vagabond [vag´ə·bänd´] n. a person who wanders from place to place without having a real home.

vague [vāg] adj. unclear, not defined.

variety [və·rī´ə·tē] n. a number of different things in a group.

vast [vast] adj. very large.

venture [ven´chər] n. a business undertaking.

Virginia reel [vər·jin´yə·rēl´] n. a lively country dance with couples facing each other in two parallel lines.

volunteer [väl´ən·tir´] n. a person who chooses to do something without being asked, usually for free: During his free time, Bruce is a volunteer at a local hospital.

wary [wer´ē] adj. cautious or watchful.

wasteland [wāst´land] n. an area where nothing grows or lives.

waver [wā´vər] v. to sway to and fro: It was halfway through her balance-beam routine that Sue began to waver and finally fell.

whine [hwīn] v. to make a high-pitched, piercing sound of complaint or distress.

widow [wid´ō] n. a woman whose husband has died: After Mr. Lo's death, his widow carried on the family business while raising the Lo children.

winch [winch] n. a machine, consisting of a drum and a crank, used for lifting, lowering, or hauling.

windmill [wind´mil] n. a machine with propellerlike arms powered by the wind; used for pumping water, grinding grain, and so on.

wound¹ [wo͞ond] n. an injury in which the skin is cut or punctured.

wound² [wound] v. turned around or coiled (past tense of *wind*).

wrecking ball [rek´ing·bôl] n. a heavy weight attached to a crane and used to demolish buildings, homes, and other structures: With a loud bang, the wrecking ball crashed against the deserted building.

yam [yam] n. a moist, orange variety of sweet potato.

yearling [yir´ling] n. a two-year old animal.

winch

windmill

a	cat	ô	fall, for	ə = a *in* ago
a	ape	oi	oil	e *in* agent
ä	cot, car	oo	look, pull	i *in* pencil
e	ten, berry	o͞o	tool, rule	o *in* atom
ē	me	ou	out, crowd	u *in* circus
i	fit, here	u	up	
ī	ice, fire	ur	fur	
ō	go			

A C K N O W L E D G M E N T S

Grateful acknowledgment is made to the following publishers, authors, and agents for their permission to reprint copyrighted material. Every effort has been made to locate all copyright proprietors; any errors or omissions in copyright notice are inadvertent and will be corrected in future printings as they are discovered.

"AND NOW THE GOOD NEWS" from *And Then There Was One: The Mysteries of Extinction* by Margery Facklam, illustrated by Pamela Johnson. Text copyright ©1990 by Margery Facklam. By permission of the American publisher, Little, Brown and Company and of the author's agent, Lucas-Evans Books, Inc.

"HAIKU BY BASHO" by Basho from *Haiku Harvest*, translated by Peter Beilenson and Harry Behn. Copyright ©1962 by The Peter Pauper Press. Reprinted by permission of the publisher.

"BETWEEN FRIENDS" from *Felita* by Nicholasa Mohr. Text copyright ©1979 by Nicholasa Mohr. Used by permission of Dial Books for Young Readers, a division of Penguin Books USA Inc. and of the author.

"BIRDFOOT'S GRAMPA" by Joseph Bruchac from *Entering Onondaga*. Copyright ©1978 by Joseph Bruchac. Reprinted by permission of the author's agent, Barbara S. Kouts.

THE BOY WHO DREW CATS by Arthur A. Levine, illustrated by Frederic Clement. Copyright ©1993 by l'ecole des loisirs, *Paris on Paintings*. Used by permission of Dial Books for Young Readers, a division of Penguin Books USA Inc.

BUFFALO WOMAN by Paul Goble. Text and illustrations copyright ©1984 by Paul Goble. Reprinted with permission of Macmillan Books for Young Readers, Simon & Schuster Children's Publishing Division.

"BY MYSELF" from *Honey, I Love* by Eloise Greenfield. Text copyright ©1978 by Eloise Greenfield. Reprinted by permission of HarperCollins Publishers and the author.

"CHANGES" from *A Moon in Your Lunch Box* by Michael Spooner. Copyright ©1993 by Michael Spooner. Reprinted by permission of Henry Holt & Co., Inc.

"THE CHICKEN-COOP MONSTER" from *The Dark Thirty: Southern Tales of the Supernatural* by Patricia C. McKissack. Text copyright ©1992 by Patricia C. McKissack. Used by permission of Alfred A. Knopf, Inc.

CITY GREEN by DyAnne DiSalvo-Ryan. Copyright ©1994 by DyAnne DiSalvo-Ryan. By permission of Morrow Junior, a division of William Morrow & Company, Inc.

"DANCING BEES" from *Bees Dance and Whales Sing: The Mysteries of Animal Communication* by Margery Facklam. Text copyright ©1992 by Margery Facklam. Reprinted by arrangement with Sierra Club Books for Children and the author's agent, Lucas-Evans Books, Inc.

"DARK DEPTHS" from *Night Dive* by Ann McGovern. Photographs by Martin Scheiner and James B. Scheiner. Copyright ©1984 by Ann McGovern. Copyright ©1984 by Martin Scheiner. Copyright ©1983 by James B. Scheiner. Reprinted with permission of Atheneum Books for Young Readers, an imprint of Simon & Schuster Children's Division.

"THE DESERT" by Eucario Mendez from *A Tree Full of Leaves Which Are Stars: An Anthology of Native American Student Poetry* edited by Mick Fedullo.

EL CHINO by Allen Say. Copyright ©1990 by Allen Say. Reprinted by permission of Houghton Mifflin Co. All rights reserved.

"ENTERING ANIMAL WORLDS" from *Think Like an Eagle* by Kathryn Lasky. Text copyright ©1992 by Kathryn Lasky; photographs by Christopher G. Knight copyright ©1992 by Christopher G. Knight. By permission of Little, Brown and Company and of the author.

"THE FABULOUS FORK" from *The Invention of Ordinary Things* by Don L. Wulffson. Text copyright ©1981 by Don L. Wulffson. By permission of Lothrop, Lee & Shepard Books, a division of William Morrow & Company, Inc.

"FIRE MOUNTAIN" from *Volcano: The Eruption and Healing of Mount St. Helens* by Patricia Lauber. Copyright ©1986 by Patricia Lauber. Reprinted with permission of Macmillan Books for Young Readers, an imprint of Simon & Schuster Children's Publishing Division.

"GARRETT MORGAN" from *Take a Walk in Their Shoes* by Glennette Tilley Turner. Copyright ©1989 by Glennette Tilley Turner. Used by permission of Cobblehill Books, an affiliate of Dutton Children's Books, a division of Penguin USA Inc.

THE GOLD COIN by Alma Flor Ada, illustrated by Neil Waldman. Translated from the Spanish by Bernice Randall. Text copyright ©1991 by Alma Flor Ada. Illustrations copyright ©1991 by Neil Waldman. Reprinted with permission of Atheneum Books for Young Readers, an imprint of Simon & Schuster Children's Division.

THE GREAT KAPOK TREE: A TALE OF THE AMAZON RAIN FOREST by Lynne Cherry. Copyright ©1990 by Lynne Cherry. Reprinted by permission of Harcourt Brace & Company.

"HIDDEN WORLDS INSIDE YOUR BODY" from *Hidden Worlds: Pictures of the Invisible* by Seymour Simon. Copyright ©1983 by Seymour Simon. By permission of William Morrow & Company, Inc.

"I CAN" from *Singing Black* by Mari Evans. Copyright ©1976 by Mari Evans. Reprinted by permission of the author.

IF YOU SAY SO, CLAUDE by Joan Lowery Nixon, pictures by Lorinda Bryan Cauley. Copyright ©1980 by Joan Lowery Nixon. Copyright ©1980 by Lorinda Bryan Cauley for illustrations. Used by permission of the American publisher, Viking Penguin, a division of Penguin Books USA Inc., the British publisher, Writer's House Inc., and the artist.

"JUSTIN AT THE RANCH" from *Justin and the Best Biscuits in the World* by Mildred Pitts Walter. Text copyright ©1986 by Mildred Pitts Walter. By permission of Lothrop, Lee & Shepard Books, a division of William Morrow & Company, Inc.

"THE LION AND THE MOUSE" adapted by June Barr from *Thirty Plays for Classroom Reading* by Donald D. Durrell and B. Alice Crossley. Copyright ©1957, 1968 by Plays, Inc., Publishers. Reprinted by permission of the publisher.

MIRETTE ON THE HIGH WIRE by Emily Arnold McCully. Copyright ©1992 by Emily Arnold McCully. Reprinted by permission of G.P. Putnam's Sons.

"OTTER EMERGENCY" from *Sea Otter Rescue* by Roland Smith. Photographs by Roland Smith. Copyright ©1990 by Roland Smith. Used by permission of Cobblehill Books, an affiliate of Dutton Children's Books, a division of Penguin USA Inc.

ACKNOWLEDGMENTS

"THE PHASE I'M GOING THROUGH" from *A Moon in Your Lunch Box* by Michael Spooner. Copyright ©1993 by Michael Spooner. Reprinted by permission of Henry Holt & Co., Inc.

SATO AND THE ELEPHANTS by Juanita Havill, illustrated by Jean and Mou-sien Tseng. Text copyright ©1993 by Juanita Havill. Illustrations copyright ©1993 by Jean and Mou-sien Tseng. By permission of Lothrop, Lee & Shepard Books, a division of William Morrow & Company, Inc.

SLEEPING UGLY by Jane Yolen. Text copyright ©1981 by Jane Yolen. Reprinted by permission of Curtis Brown, Ltd.

"SONG" from *Sing to the Sun* by Ashley Bryan. Copyright ©1992 by Ashley Bryan. Reprinted by permission of HarperCollins Publishers.

"SPEECH AT EARTH SUMMIT" from *Tell the World* by Severn Cullis-Suzuki. Copyright ©1993 by Severn Cullis-Suzuki. Reprinted by permission of Doubleday Canada Limited.

THE STORYTELLER by Joan Weisman, illustrated by David P. Bradley. Text copyright ©1993 by Joan Weisman. Illustrations copyright ©1993 by David P. Bradley. Reprinted by permission of the publisher, Rizzoli International Publications, Inc.

THE TALKING EGGS by Robert D. San Souci, pictures by Jerry Pinkney. Copyright ©1989 by Robert D. San Souci, text. Copyright ©1989 by Jerry Pinkney, pictures. Used by permission of the American publisher, Dial Books for Young Readers, a division of Penguin Books USA Inc. and of the British publisher, Random House UK Ltd.

"TALL-TALE MAN" from *Plays from African Tales* by Barbara Winther. Copyright ©1992 by Barbara Winther. Reprinted by permission of the publisher, Plays, Inc.

"THINGS" from *Honey, I Love* by Eloise Greenfield. Text copyright ©1978 by Eloise Greenfield. Reprinted by permission of HarperCollins Publishers and the author.

"THE TIGER, THE PERSIMMON AND THE RABBIT'S TAIL" from *Korean Folk & Fairy Tales* retold by Suzanne Crowder Han. Copyright ©1991 by Suzanne Crowder Han. Reprinted by permission of Hollym International Corp.

"TODAY IS VERY BORING" from *The New Kid on the Block* by Jack Prelutsky. Text copyright ©1984 by Jack Prelutsky. By permission of Greenwillow Books, a division of William Morrow & Company, Inc.

"UNDERWATER RESCUE" from *Dolphin Adventure: A True Story* by Wayne Grover. Text copyright ©1990 by Wayne Grover. By permission of Greenwillow Books, a division of William Morrow & Company, Inc.

WHY MOSQUITOES BUZZ IN PEOPLE'S EARS by Verna Aardema, illustrated by Leo and Diane Dillon. Text copyright ©1975 by Verna Aardema. Illustrations copyright ©1975 by Leo and Diane Dillon. Used by permission of the American publisher, Dial Books for Young Readers, a division of Penguin Books USA Inc. and of the British publisher, Curtis Brown, Ltd.

"YOU—TU" from *The Tamarindo Puppy and Other Poems* by Charlotte Pomerantz, illustrated by Byron Barton. Text copyright ©1980 by Charlotte Pomerantz. Illustrations copyright ©1980 by Byron Barton. By permission of Greenwillow Book, a division of William Morrow & Company, Inc.

ILLUSTRATION: 4 Sterling Brown (r.); 4–5 Higgins Bond (t.); 5 Ruben Ramos (l.); Mercedes McDonald (r.); 6–7 Robert Sagerman (t.); 8–9 Kathi Ember (t.); Susan Guevara (t.c.); Steven Guarnaccia (c.); 10–11 Stacy Schuett (t.); 11 Tony Griff (b.); 12–13 Andrea Barrett (t.); 14–15 Susan Swan (t.); 16–19 Higgins Bond; 20–21 Yoshi Miyake; 40–41 Tony Caldwell; 42–58 Larry Johnson; 59 Sterling Brown (b.l.); 60–82 Ruben Ramos; 84–91 Mercedes McDonald; 108–111 Higgins Bond; 112–115 Robert Sagerman; 115 Terry Widener (b.); 184–185 Yoshi Miyake; 198–201 Robert Sagerman; 202–205 Kathi Ember; 226–227 Eliza Schulte; 226–241 Susan Guevara; 244–259 Yoshi Miyake (t.); 260–265 Steve Guarnaccia; 282–291 Jean and Mon-Sien Tseng; 292–295 Kathi Ember; 296–299 Stacey Schuett; 299 Travis Foster (b.); 300–319 Michael Bryant; 322–323 David Slonim; 344–359 Paul Dolan; 360–361 Tony Griff; 364–381 Paul Mirocha; 382–385 Stacey Schuett; 386–389 Andrea Barrett; 478–481 Andrea Barrett; 482–501 Susan Swan; 522–523 Shonto Begay; 546–551 Tony Morse; 573–589 Greg King.

PHOTOGRAPHY: 4 Courtesy Nicole Gallery, photo by Sharon Hoogstraten (i.); 5 Sharon Hoogstraten (b.); 6 Courtesy Edward Thorp Gallery (b.); Courtesy the Museum for African Art, Collection of Mr. and Mrs. Robert Billion Richardson, Africa Explores: 20th Century African Art exhibition (r.); 7 Roland Smith (t.); © Zig Leszczynski/Animals Animals (c.); © Ralph A. Reinhold/Animals Animals (b.); Sharon Hoogstraten; 10 Photo by Paul Rocheleau; courtesy Charlie Lucas (b.); 14 Neg. Trans. No. 4481(5) (Photo by Lynton Gardiner) Courtesy Department Library Services American Museum of Natural History (l.); Austin Post (r.); 15 Dr. Jack Farman, Downstate Medical Center, New York (t.); Dr. A. John Gwinnett, Department of Oral Biology, Sate University of New York at Stony Brook (b.l.); © John E. Swedberg (b.r.); 19 Michael Ulsaker Studio (t., c.); © SBG, photo by Allen Penn (b.); 20 © SBG, photo by Sharon Hoogstraten; 37 Courtesy Emily McCully (t.l.); Ambrosi and Associates (c.r., b.r.); 38 Courtesy Nicole Gallery (© SBG, photo by Sharon Hoogstraten) (b.); 38–39 © SBG, Sharon Hoogstraten; 39 Photo © Cradot Bagshaw, courtesy Inee Yang Slaughter (c.); 43 Ambrosi and Associates (t.r.); 58 Macmillan Books for Young Readers. An Imprint of Simon and Schuster Children's Publishing Division (l.); Ambrosi and Associates (c., r.); 59 Reproduced from the Collections of the Library of Congress (t.r.); Courtesy Buffalo Bill Historical Center, Cody, WY (b.r.); 83 Courtesy Penguin USA (t.); Ambrosi and Associates (c., b.); 92 © SBG, photo by Sharon Hoogstraten; 104–105 © SBG, photo by Sharon Hoogstraten; 106–107 © SBG, photo by Sharon Hoogstraten; 107 Courtesy Houghton Mifflin (t.); Ambrosi and Associates (c., b.); 110 Michael Ulsaker Studio (t., b.); 111 Michael Ulsaker Studio (t., c., b.); 115 Michael Ulsaker Studio (t., c.); 116 © SBG, photo by Sharon Hoogstraten; 132 Courtesy Harcourt Brace (t.); 132–133 © SBG, photo by Sharon Hoogstraten (b.); 133 © Katie P. McManus (t.l.); Ambrosi and Associates (t.r., c.r., b.r.); 134 Courtesy Salander–O'Reilly Galleries, Inc. (b.c.); 134–135 © SBG, photo by Sharon Hoogstraten; 135 Courtesy Phillips Collection (c.); 136 Courtesy Edward Thorp Gallery (b.); 136–137 © SBG, photo by Sharon Hoogstraten; 137 Milwaukee Art Museum, Gift of Mr. and Mrs. Harry Lynde Bradley (t.); Courtesy the Museum for African Art, Collection of Mr. and Mrs. Robert Billion Richardson, Africa Explores: 20th Century African Art exhibition (b.); 138–141 © SBG, photo by Sharon Hoogstraten; 153 Ambrosi and Associates (r.); Courtesy Dyanne DiSalvo-Ryan (l.); © SBG, photo by Sharon Hoogstraten (b.r.); 154 Courtesy of Ashley Bryan; 156 Barbara Woodley/Doubleday Canada (l.); © Charles Mauzy/Tony Stone Images (t.); © Frans Lanting/Tony Stone Images (b.); © Robert Frerck/Tony Stone Images (r.); © SBG, photo by Sharon Hoogstraten; 157 © Ron Sanford/Tony Stone Images (l.); © Charles Mauzy/Tony Stone Images (r.); 158 © Robert Frerck/Tony Stone Images (l.); © Antonio Ribeiro/Gamma Liaison (c.); © Tom Walker/Tony Stone Images (b.); 158–159 © Ricardo Funari/Imagens Da Terra/Impact Visuals; 159 © Kevin Morris/Tony Stone Images (t.l.); © Kevin Schafer/Tony Stone Images (b.r.); © Robert Frerck/Tony Stone Images (r.); © Antonio Ribeiro/Gamma Liaison (c.l.); 160 © Frans Lanting/Tony Stone Images (l.); © Art Wolfe/Tony Stone Images (t.c.); Severn Cullis–Suzuki (b.); 161 Severn Cullis–Suzuki (t., c.); © Norbert Wu/Tony Stone Images (b.); © Frans Lanting/Tony Stone Images (r.); 162 © SBG, photo by Sharon Hoogstraten; 163 © Roland Smith (.); 164 © Stephen J. Krasemann/DRK Photo (c.); 164–166 © SBG, photo by Sharon Hoogstraten; 165 © Francois Gohier (b.); 166 © 1989 Alissa Crandall (b.); 167 © Roland Smith (t.); © SBG, photo by Sharon Hoogstraten (b.); 168 © Roland Smith (b.); 168–169 © SBG, photo by Sharon Hoogstraten; 169 © Roland Smith (t.); 170 © Roland Smith (b.); 170–171 © SBG, photo by Sharon Hoogstraten; 171 © Roland Smith (t.); 172 © Roland Smith (t.r.); © SBG, photo by Sharon Hoogstraten (l.); 173 © Roland Smith (b.); Courtesy U.S. Fish and Wildlife Service, Alaska Region (© SBG, photo by Sharon Hoogstraten) (r.); 174 © Roland Smith (b.); 174–175 © SBG, photo by Sharon Hoogstraten; 175 © Roland Smith; 176 © Roland Smith (t.); 176–177 © SBG, photo by Sharon Hoogstraten; 177 © Jeff Foott Productions; 178 © Roland Smith (c.); 178–179 © SBG, photo by Sharon Hoogstaten; 179 © Roland Smith (t.l., b.r.); 180 © Roland Smith (t.l., b.r.); 181 © Roland Smith (t.l., b.r.); 181–182 © SBG, photo by Sharon Hoogstraten; 182 © Roland Smith (b.r.);

183 Courtesy Roland Smith (t.l.); Ambrosi and Associates (c.); © SBG, photo by Sharon Hoogstraten (b.); **184–185** © SBG, photo by Sharon Hoogstraten; **186** © Paul Berger/Tony Stone Images (b.); Ambrosi and Associates (t.l) © Kim Westerkov/Tony Stone Images (t.r.); **187** © Kim Westerkov/Tony Stone Images; **188** © Lee Kuhn/FPG International Corp.; **189** © Michael Dick/Animals Animals (t.); © Ralph A. Reinhold/Animals Animals (b.); **190** © Gerard Lacz/Animals Animals; **191** © Joel Bennett/Tony Stone Images; **192** © E.R. Degginger/Animals Animals (t.); © Peter Lamberti/Tony Stone Images (b.); **193** © Zig Leszczynski/Animals Animals; **194** © Henry Ausloos/Animals Animals; **195** © Patti Murray/Animals Animals; **196** © Ralph A. Reinhold/Animals Animals; **197** Margery Facklam (t.); Ambrosi and Associates (b.); **200** Michael Ulsaker Studio (t., b.); **201** Michael Ulsaker Studio (t., c., b.); **205** Michael Ulsaker Studio (t.,c.); © SBG, photo by Allan Penn; **207** Ambrosi and Associates (r.); **207–219** © SBG, photo by Sharon Hoogstraten; **219** Courtesy Joan Weisman (l.); Ambrosi and Associates (c.); Ambrosi and Associates (b.); **220** Courtesy Harper Collins (c.); **220–221** Tim Seed; **222** Courtesy Estate of Romare Bearden (c.); **222–223** © SBG, photo by Sharon Hoogstraten; **223** Vicki Ragan (c.); **224** Neg. Trans. No. 2493 (2), Photo by Lee Boltin Courtesy Department Library Services American Museum of Natural History (t.); Scala/Art Resource, NY (b.); **224–225** © SBG, photo by Sharon Hoogstraten; **225** © 1986 Carmen Lomas Garza. Photo by Wolfgang Dietze. Collection of Dudley D. Brooks and Tomas Ybarra–Frausto, Seattle, WA (c.); **242** Jason Stemple, from *A Letter from Phoenix Farm* by Jane Yolen published by Richard C. Owen Publishers, Katonah, NY (t.); **242–243** © SBG, photo by Sharon Hoogstraten; **243** Jason Stemple, from *A Letter from Phoenix Farm* by Jane Yolen published by Richard C. Owen Publishers, Katonah, NY (t.l.); Ambrosi and Associates (c.r., t.r.); **259** Courtesy Penguin USA (t.l.); Ambrosi and Associates (c., c.r.); **266** © SBG, photo by Sharon Hoogstraten; **267–280** Leo and Diane Dillon; **281** Leo and Diane Dillon/Penguin U.S.A. (b.r.); Courtesy Penguin USA (t.l.); Lee Dillon/Penguin USA (b.l.); Ambrosi and Associates (t.r.); **291** Courtesy Susan Crowder Han (l.); Ambrosi and Associates (r.); **294** Michael Ulsaker Studio (t., b.); **295** Michael Ulsaker Studio (t., c., b.); **299** Michael Ulsaker Studio (t., c.); **320** © SBG, photo by Sharon Hoogstraten; **321** Courtesy of Patricia McKissick (t.l.); Ambrosi and Associates (t.r., c.r.); **324** © SBG, photo by Sharon Hoogstraten; **340** Courtesy of Arthur Levine (l.); Ambrosi and Associates (c., r.); **342** Photo by Paul Rocheleau, courtesy Helen and Vernon Raaen (c.); **342–343** © SBG, photo by Sharon Hoogstraten; **343** Photo by Paul Rocheleau, courtesy Charlie Lucas (c.); **345** Ambrosi and Associates; **354** Ambrosi and Associates (c.l.); Courtesy of Glennette Tiley (c.r.); **356** © SBG, photo by Allan Landau; **358** © SBG, photo by Allan Landau; **360–363** © SBG, photo by Sharon Hoogstraten; **381** Courtesy of Wayne Grover (b.l.); Ambrosi and Associates (b.r.); **384** Michael Ulsaker Studio (t., b.); **385** Michael Ulsaker Studio (t., c., b.); **389** Michael Ulsaker Studio (t., c.); © SBG, photo by Allan Penn (b.); **406** Courtesy of Paul Goble (t.); **406–407** © Craig Blacklock; **407** Ambrosi and Associates (t., c.); **411** Ambrosi and Associates (t.r.); **429** Alan S. Orling, courtesy Penguin USA (c.); Ambrosi and Associates (b.); **430** Phil 1969 acrylic on canvas, 108" X 84" Photo courtesy PaceWildenstein, collection The Whitney Museum of American Art (c.); **430–431** © SBG, photo by Sharon Hoogstraten; **431** *April*, 1990–91, oil on canvas, 100" X 84" Photo courtesy PaceWildenstein, private collection (c.); **432** Ambrosi and Associates; **453** © David Maung (t.); Ambrosi and Associates (c., b.); **457** Ambrosi and Associates (b.); **477** © Gustav Masuke (c.); Ambrosi and Associates (b.); **480** Michael Ulsaker Studio (t., b.); **481** Michael Ulsaker Studio (t., c., b.); **485** Michael Ulsaker Studio (t., c.); © David Scharf/Photo Researchers (b.); **486** Ambrosi and Associates (c.); **486** © Tom Stack; **501** Courtesy Ann McGovern (t.); Ambrosi and Associates (c.r., b.r.); **502** Ambrosi and Associates (c.); **502–503** Austin Post; **504** Austin Post (t.); **504–505** Steven Muir/Earth Images; **505** John V. Christiansen/Earth Images (b.); **506** Lyn Topinka (c.); **506–507** Steven Muir/Earth Images; **507** Lyn Topinka (t.); **508** Lyn Topinka (t.); **508–509** Steven Muir/Earth Images; **509** Philip J. Carpenter (b.); **510–511** Steven Muir/Earth Images; **511** Harry Glicken (t., b.); **512** Johnson Cascades Volcano Observatory, Vancouver, WA (b.); **512–513** Steven Muir/Earth Images; **513** USDA Forest Service (c.); **514** USDA Forest Service (t.); James M. Gale (b.); **514–515** Steven Muir/Earth Images; **515** Jim Quiring (t.); **516** Jim Quiring (t.); **516–517** Steven Muir/Earth Images; **516–517** Stephen Nofield (b.); **518** Jim Hughes (c.); **518–519** Steven

Muir/Earth Images; **519** Jim Quiring (t.); **520** Steven Muir/Earth Images (b.l.); USDA Forest Service (b.r.); **520–521** © SBG, photo by Sharon Hoogstraten; **521** Courtesy of Patricia Lauber (t.l.); Ambrosi and Associates (t.c., t.r.); **524** Scala/Art Resource, NY (c.); **524–525** © SBG, photo by Sharon Hoogstraten; **525** Claude Monet, French, 1840–1926, *Water Lily Pool*, oil on canvas, 1900, 89.9 x 101 cm, Mr. and Mrs. Lewis Learned Coburn Memorial Collection, 1933.441; photograph © 1994, The Art Institute of Chicago, All Rights Reserved (c.); **526** Pola Lopez de Jaramillo (b.l.); **526–527** © SBG, photo by Sharon Hoogstraten; Neg. Trans. No. 4481(5) (Photo by Lynton Gardiner) Courtesy Department Library Services American Museum of Natural History (c.); **527** Neg. Trans. No. 4480(2); (Photo by Lynton Gardiner) Courtesy Department Library Services American Museum of Natural History (b.); **528** © Christopher G. Knight; **529** Ambrosi and Associates (t.r.); © Bryan Peterson/West Stock (r.); **529–530** © SBG, photo by John Morrison; **531** © Christopher G. Knight (t.); © Jeff Gnass/West Stock (r.); **532** ©John E. Swedburg (t.); © SBG, photo by John Morrison; **533** © Bryan Peterson/West Stock; **534** © SBG, photo by John Morrison; **535** © Christopher G. Knight (t.); © Bryan Peterson/West Stock (r.); **536** John E. Swedburg; **537** © Bryan Peterson/West Stock (r.); **538** © John E. Swedburg (t.); © SBG, photo by John Morrison; **539** © Matt Brown/West Stock; **540** © Christopher G. Knight (t., c., b.); **541** © Christopher G. Knight (l.); © Matt Brown/West Stock (r.); **541–542** © SBG, photo by John Morrison; **542** © Christopher G. Knight (t.); © John E. Swedburg (b.); **543** © Matt Brown/West Stock; **544** © SBG, photo by John Morrison; Christopher G. Knight (b.); **545** © Matt Brown/West Stock (t.); © Christopher G. Knight (l.); Ambrosi and Associates (t.r., c.r., b.r.); **552** Dr. Sam Iwer, Downstate Medical Center, New York; **552–553** © Robert Becker, Ph.D./Custom Medical Stock Photo All rights reserved; **554** Dr. Jack Farman, Downstate Medical Center, New York; **555** © Warren Morgan/Westlight; **556** Howard Sochurek; **557–558** Dr. Jack Farman, Downstate Medical Center, New York; **559** © Bachmann (t.); American Cancer Society (b.); **560–561** Howard Sochurek; **561** © David Joel/Tony Stone Images; **562** American Cancer Society (t., c., b.); **563** Dr. David M. Phillips, Center for Biomedical Research, Rockefeller University; © Lawrence Migdale/Science Source/Photo Researchers (b.); **564** Dr. A. John Gwinett, Department of Oral Biology, State University of New York at StonyBrook (t., b.); **565** © Robert Becker, Ph. D./Custom Medical Stock Photo All rights reserved; © Bachmann (t.); Seymour Simon (b.l.); Ambrosi and Associates (b.r.); **568** Michael Ulsaker Studio (t., b.); **569** Michael Ulsaker Studio (t., c., b.); **572** © Trevor Wood Picture Library/The Image Bank (t.); © David R. Frazier/Tony Stone Images (b.); © Stephen Studd/Tony Stone Images (r.); **573** © Chris Huss/The Wildlife Collection; **574** © Tony Craddock/Tony Stone Images (t.l.); © Peter Scholey/Tony Stone Images (b.); **575** © Tom Till/Tony Stone Images (t.); © David Woodfall/Tony Stone Images (t.); **576** © Manfred Gottschalk/Westlight; **577** © Greg Vaughn/Tony Stone Images (t.r.); © Jim Cornfield/Westlight (b.r.); **578** © Michael Skott/The Image Bank (t.); © Wendell Metzen/Southern Stock Photos (b.l.); © Hilarie Kavanagh/Tony Stone Images (b.r.); **580** Simon Fraser/RVI, Newcastle–upon–Tyne/Science Photo Library (t.l.); © G. Brad Lewis/Tony Stone Images (t.r.); **581** © C.C. Lockwood/Animals Animals (t.); **582** © Sam Zarember/The Image Bank (t.l.); © Larry Dale Gordon/The Image Bank (b.); © Maresa Pryor/Animals Animals (r.); **583** © Timothy O'Keefe/Bruce Coleman. Inc. (b.r.); **584** © Breck P. Kent/Animals Animals (b.); © Doug Wechsler/Earth Scenes (r.); **585** © Chuck Kuhn/The Image Bank (t.); © Norman O. Tomalin/Bruce Coleman, Inc. (l.); The Bettmann Archive (b.); **586** © R.F. Head/Animals Animals (b.); **587** © Danny Daniels/AlaskaStock Images (t.); **588** Everett Collection (t.); © Antonio M. Rosario/The Image Bank (r.); **589** © Bill Hickey/The Image Bank (l.); © Steve Dunwell/The Image Bank (b.).**590** Neg. Trans. No. 2493 (2), photo by Lee Bottin, Courtesy Department Library Services, American Museum of Natural History.